Manichaeism

Manichaeism

An Ancient Faith Rediscovered

Nicholas J. Baker-Brian

t&t clark

Published by T&T Clark International
A Continuum Imprint
The Tower Building, 11 York Road, London SE1 7NX
80 Maiden Lane, Suite 704, New York, NY 10038

www.continuumbooks.com

British Library Cataloguing-in-Publication Data
A catalogue record for this book is available from the British Library

ISBN: 978-0-567-03166-2 (Hardback)
         978-0-567-03167-9 (Paperback)

Typeset by Fakenham Photosetting Ltd
Printed and bound in Great Britain

Contents

Introduction

My own modest area of expertise makes me rather unqualified to take on a phenomenon as vast as Manichaeism, and expert readers of this book will notice that I have largely stayed away from many of the linguistic and historical complexities of a religion which, during its lifetime, had a presence in the worlds of the Roman Mediterranean, Sasanian Persia, and imperial-era and early modern China. Whilst my interest in Manichaeism ranges across all periods of its prolific existence, this book emerges from a number of years of teaching Manichaeism in its late-antique guise to undergraduate students. In the process of turning a series of lectures into an introductory work, I wish to thank the students who first took my module on Gnostic Religions in the autumn of 2007 at Cardiff University. Any ambitions I may have harboured to go beyond what I could confidently discuss were quickly tempered by the students' entirely reasonable demand for clarity on the part of their teacher. This book aims to provide an introduction to Manichaeism, employing a religious studies-based approach to this ancient religion across four chapters.

In Chapter 1, the creation and manipulation of religious identities are examined: the various taxonomies which prior traditions and their commentators have used to talk about Manichaeism's 'essence' are discussed, followed by a survey of recently discovered writings composed by Manichaeans themselves, which have enabled scholars to overturn many established ideas about the religion by bringing to light Manichaeism's complex religious character. Chapter 2 considers the role of religious biography in Manichaeism: the way in which Manichaeans reflected on the achievements of Mani (d. AD 276), the visionary whose teachings supplied the foundations for the practices and beliefs of Manichaeism, played a crucial part in shaping perceptions of their own community in relational terms, as a church of exceptional significance, in comparison with other 'competitor' religions in Late Antiquity and beyond. The opponents of Manichaeism also took advantage of the fact that the religion was indeed 'personality-centred' in terms of its devotional focus on Mani, by creating their own biographical portraits of Mani, which in turn assisted in the formation of their own ideas about orthodox religious identity. Chapter 3 investigates the influence of texts in the development of Mani's ideas about God and the world: the importance placed by Mani himself on the role of writing as an extension of memory became a central feature of Mani's own sense of prophetic identity. Developing the idea of the nineteenth-century philologist Max Müller, Guy Stroumsa has recently noted that Manichaeism is the most likely immediate influence on the emphasis placed by Islam on a revealed book, as a formative influence in the notion of 'Religions of the Book':[1] Mani's emphasis on text as the most suitable medium

---

[1] See Stroumsa 2009, 34–8.

for the communication of religious truth was developed by his later followers into a canon of his writings, which was an additional influence on the way in which other religions since Manichaeism have fixed the teachings of their founders in an authoritative body of scripture. Chapter 4 considers the relationship between the myth of Manichaeism and the ritual practices of the Manichaean church, an association that has traditionally received little attention in Manichaean studies, where the emphasis continues to fall on analyses of the infamous myth alone, the very thing which has influenced the popular characterisation of Manichaeism as a dualistic religion which taught an account of the universe where Good battled Evil. However, whilst it certainly qualifies as a 'gnostic' religion, Manichaeism was also once a living faith with its own detailed liturgical traditions and rituals; both aspects informed the distinctive identity and ethics of the Manichaean church throughout its long history.

The history of Manichaeism and the history of the study of Manichaeism involve the study of texts, i.e., the sacred writings of Manichaean communities stretching all the way back to the literary endeavours of Mani himself during the third century AD. The task of modern readers approaching this bewildering array of writings has been made immeasurably easier by the availability of English translations of key primary sources for Manichaeism, of which two source collections in particular are accessible to general, undergraduate and postgraduate readers. The impressive achievement of Hans Joachim Klimkeit's *Gnosis on the Silk Road: Gnostic Texts from Central Asia* from 1993, has supplied English-language students of Manichaeism with a vast quantity of translated Iranian and Turkic texts from Turfan and Dunhuang, which have helped throw light on the so-called 'Sogdian face' of the religion. Nearly all of these texts survive in badly damaged states of repair, and the patience and expertise of scholars from the 1900s onwards have ensured their continued survival. Klimkeit's source-volume brings very many of them together for the first time, along with a useful series of critical notes. Alongside the discoveries of Manichaean writings from central Asia at the beginning of the last century, the emergence of Manichaean psalms, homilies, treatises, histories and letters from Roman Egypt represents the other remarkable development that has contributed to the meteoric rise of Manichaean studies of recent times. The source-collection of Iain Gardner and Samuel Lieu, *Manichaean Texts from the Roman Empire* from 2004, is a judicious selection of those Manichaean writings which illuminate Manichaeism's origins in the late-antique Mesopotamian and Roman worlds, including a complete translation of the famous 'Mani Biography', otherwise known as the *Cologne Mani Codex* (CMC), one of the smallest parchment codices surviving from antiquity. Where appropriate I have employed both Klimkeit's and Gardner and Lieu's collections, for the ease which they offer in consulting some of Manichaeism's most sacred writings.

For readers with training in languages other than English, additional important collections of sources for Manichaeism include: Alfred Adam's *Texte zum Manichäismus* and Alexander Böhlig's *Der Manichäismus* (see bibliography for full details).

As a result of the constraints of time and space, I have not devoted a great deal of attention to the historical study of Manichaeism. Besides, this has been done before, and in much greater detail than I could possibly hope to offer in a book of this kind. Whilst I make reference to historical treatments of the religion throughout the work, I would like at this point to highlight a number of studies that will be indispensible to readers seeking detailed narrative treatments of Manichaeism's history. Noteworthy among the more detailed works is the 'trilogy' of historical studies of Manichaeism by Samuel Lieu, *Manichaeism in the Later Roman Empire and Medieval China* (1992), *Manichaeism in Mesopotamia and the Roman East* (1994), and *Manichaeism in Central Asia and China* (1998), all of which are 'treasure-troves' of dates, facts, texts and personalities in Manichaeism's long history, and should be consulted as a matter of routine by any serious student. For those students who have come to the study of Mani via work on Patristics, Church History and Augustine in particular, François Decret's two-volume French-language work *L'Afrique manichéenne (IVe–Ve siècles)* from 1978 will provide an excellent starting point for appreciating the deep associations which existed between ancient Catholic Christianity and Manichaean Christianity in Late Antiquity. Valuable shorter studies include the historical and thematic work *sans pareil* by Michel Tardieu, *Manichaeism*, available in English translation from 2008. The recent consolidation of an on-line version of the incomparable *Encyclopaedia Iranica* – available at www.iranica.com – edited by Ehsan Yarshater has meant that numerous indispensible articles pertaining to the history, theology and literary traditions of Manichaeism can now be accessed free of charge.

With these recommendations, I am of course barely touching the tip of a vast iceberg, for which reason I would also suggest that readers consult a bibliographical resource such as Gunner Mikkelsen's *Bibliographia Manichaica: A Comprehensive Bibliography of Manichaeism through 1996*, which will ensure that readers 'catch' many of the most important scholarly monuments in Manichaean studies. Many important works have appeared since the publication of Mikkelsen's *Bibliographia*, and I have endeavoured to include some of them in this book, full details for all of which can be found in the bibliography. Some studies, however, have come too late for this work – indeed are still due – including John C. Reeves's long-awaited treatment of Manichaeism as seen from the perspective of Islamic writers from antiquity,[2] which my own discussion of the Islamic sources of Manichaeism would undoubtedly have profited from consulting.

The arrival of Luke at the beginning of last year has made the writing of this book an unexpected pleasure, and it is to him and Sarah that I dedicate this work.

N.J. Baker-Brian, Cardiff, Wales, August 2010

[2] J.C. Reeves, Prolegomena to a History of Islamic Manichaeism (London: Equinox, 2010).

The Sasanian Empire

Chapter 1

The Rediscovery of Manichaeism: Controversies and Sources

1. Introduction: Controversies Old and New

What is Manichaeism? Traditionally characterised as having taught an elaborate myth describing a cosmic war between two co-eternal powers of Light and Darkness, the name of this ancient religion is presently more likely to be invoked in order to describe a seemingly transparent, 'simplistic' state of affairs, in which two opposing agendas are set against one another. Indeed, it seems that in recent times the term 'Manichaean' has been making something of a comeback, not least in the media coverage of political events during the period when both the Republican party in the United States and New Labour in the United Kingdom were in power, during the first years of the present century. The 'political dualism' widely regarded as characteristic of both George W. Bush and Tony Blair's approach to foreign policy was often described as being 'Manichaean': as one commentator for the *Wall Street Journal* wrote in 2002: 'President Bush is serious about his Manichaean formulation of the war on terror – "either you are with us, or you are with the terrorists".'[1]

The assured use of the term 'Manichaean' in modern political commentary corresponds neatly with the appearance of the same term in ancient religious dialogue whenever discussions arose of the dualist religion whose origins lay in the world of late-antique Persian Mesopotamia at its southernmost end bordering Babylonia. In this context, 'Manichaean' denoted the followers of the Mesopotamian prophet Mani (AD 216–76), the 'founder' of a religion characterised by its opponents as an aberrant form of Christianity. These opponents portrayed Mani as a heresiarch, and Manichaeans were regarded as heretical Christians of a particularly opportunistic kind. Yet 'Manichaean' was an identity imposed on a type of Christian belief, the origins of which lay in a culture that was significantly different from the one which shaped the attitudes of its late-antique opponents.

With these preliminary considerations in mind, this chapter will prioritise two concerns. In the first place, it will consider the taxonomic presentation of Manichaeism in both ancient and modern treatments of the religion. Whilst

---

[1] Cited by G. Leupp in his article 'The Revival of Mani', published in *Counter-Punch*, 21 August 2002: available on-line at www.counterpunch.org/leupp0821.html

1

the polemical intentions of Mani's ancient Catholic Christian opponents[2] are absent in the context of modern studies of Manichaeism, it will be evident that the tenacity of the ancient challenge to Manichaeism has continued to influence the conceptual language used by modern commentators to discuss the origins, beliefs and ambitions of Mani and his followers, the result of which is a distortion in the way that modern commentators think about the religion in their treatments of Manichaeism. The chapter will then move on to introduce a handful of recently discovered Manichaean writings – literary works written by late-antique and central Asian Manichaeans (including Mani himself), composed in the service of the theological and liturgical life of the Manichaean church – in order to expose to a little more daylight the religious identity of the Manichaeans.

2. Manichaeism as 'The Other'

The visionary prophet Mani, whose teachings formed the basis of the Manichaean religion, lived nearly all his life within the territory of the last great Persian empire of antiquity. Growing to maturity under Ardashir I (ruling 224–40), the founder of the Sasanian dynasty and the architect of a revived Iranian imperialism, and operating for a lengthy period of his life under the patronage of his son and successor Shapur I (ruling 240–72), Mani lived during a time of considerable change in Iranian society, a transformation driven by an imperial ideology which sought to reclaim the ascendant status of a united Persian Empire among the world's powers, founded on the notion of the Sasanian monarchy as the successors of the ancient Achaemenids.[3] One of the apparent hallmarks of Mani's religious teachings was his striving to achieve a universalism for his message,[4] an ambition that mirrored the territorial expansionism of the kings Ardashir and Shapur. Aspirations of cultural conquest are, by and large, only possible in a society which has already made its presence known militarily and politically to other nations, and has relayed details of its contacts with them to its own population. Mani was certainly aware of Persia's rediscovered ascendancy in the world, and undoubtedly demonstrated a degree of worldly acumen in this regard by placing himself in a position to take advantage of it, not least in terms of the initial organisation of his church.[5] However, in the case of Mani's universalism, it was the cultural as much as the physical frontier separating this newly resurgent Persian Empire from the territory of the Roman world – the other great ancient superpower of the time – which tempered the nature of those ambitions and influenced their ultimate form.

The physical limit of both Persian and Roman military power ran along the natural boundary of the Euphrates river, with eastern Syria and northern

---

[2] Catholic in the late-antique sense of a universal 'orthodox' church, which defined itself in contradistinction to the 'Other', 'heretical' churches of the time.
[3] For an analysis of this controversial theme, see Dignas and Winter 2007, 56–62.
[4] See Puech 1949, 61–3.
[5] See Tardieu 2008, 25–30.

Mesopotamia becoming 'a repeated battleground'[6] between the two empires for the best part of the third century and beyond.[7] However, natural boundaries are one thing, whilst imperially-imposed frontiers that influence the reception of cultures are another.[8] The early history of Mani's religion and its historical legacy can only be properly discussed in relation to the influence which the imperial-cultural divide between Rome and Persia brought to bear on the teachings of the prophet from southern Mesopotamia. However, this divide is opaque, and reduction of the divide's significance to the concerns raised by imperial and national agendas alone is misleading, despite the fact that the rhetoric of many late-antique sources against Manichaeism often drew upon such crude lines of demarcation. Fear, ignorance, entrenched tradition and open hostility greeted the arrival of Mani's followers in the Roman Empire from the late third century onwards, not least in the Christian communities of the West. These reactions were in part inspired by the assumed 'Persian' origins of Mani and his message,[9] which thereby helped shape the memorialisation of Manichaeism in the historical memory of the occidental world by imposing a particular stamp on the identity of the Manichaean church, turning it into something far removed from the original intentions of its supposed 'founder', Mani.

This is the Manichaeism of patristic culture. Writing in their role as heresiologists, patristic authors forged a normative Christian identity during Late Antiquity through the creation and refinement of a boundary that introduced a form of theological absolutism in the guise of a religious orthodoxy. This strategic process simultaneously defined and subsequently isolated those 'other' Christian parties who chose – for a wide spectrum of reasons influenced by a range of geo-political and intellectual influences – a different way of formulating and expressing their Christian beliefs. Under these conditions, Mani's teachings fell on the 'wrong side' of the divide, and the heresiologists – largely on the Western side of the frontier – sought to emphasise Manichaeism's fundamental distinctiveness by exploiting the perceived *foreignness* and inherent *wrongness* of Mani's beliefs, which shadowed a standard of Christian belief that itself was still struggling to achieve an orthodox definition of faith. In the processes of labelling and categorising Mani's ideas and the activities of his church, patristic authors called upon a series of longstanding typologies according to which normative Christian identity could be defined and measured, but which also in turn created a number of new typologies that appeared especially applicable to Manichaeism. In this way, the follower of Mani became 'the Other' – the theological and societal outcast – an identity based on a series of misleading, perverted and often contradictory labels: for example, the Manichaean as the Christian heretic, the deviant, sex-crazed, pale ascetic who consumed semen during ritualised orgies,[10] and who followed a theology based on a determinism that ruled out any possibility of hope or liberation from suffering for the majority of humankind (see Chapter 4).

---

[6] Millar 1994, 149.
[7] See Dodgeon and Lieu 1991.
[8] See esp. Whittaker 1997, 10–30.
[9] See van der Lof 1974.
[10] Augustine, *On Heresies* 46.9–10, trans. I. Gardner and S.N.C. Lieu 2004, 144–5.

However, by far the most enduring contribution made by Roman heresiological discourse to the reputation of Manichaeism was its challenge to the Christian identity which Mani and his followers claimed for themselves in the exposition of their faith. The presence of the orthodox counter-claim challenging this identity amounted to a concerted strategy on the part of the heresiologists who wrote against Mani's religion, and played a fundamental role in widening the gap between orthodox Christians and Manichaean Christians during the fourth and fifth centuries. In this regard, the orthodox strike against Manichaeism utilised the full conceptual and linguistic range of tools employed in the process of early Christian identity formation, a process which had been in development since the transformation of the meaning of the Greek word 'heresy' (*hairesis*) from 'sect' or 'school' by Christian writers into a word denoting a pejorative separation between 'true' and 'false' Christians, i.e., between orthodoxy and heresy.[11]

The heart of the orthodox challenge to Manichaeism's Christian roots lay in the success which patristic authors achieved in convincing their audiences that Manichaeism was a simulacrum of Christianity as the 'true religion'. Although variations existed in the way that this was achieved, nearly all anti-Manichaean works from Late Antiquity adopted a near-identical strategy in their presentation of Manichaeism's Christian persona. Reducible to four main points, heresiologists sought to portray Manichaeism as:

1. determined by a worldly expediency, manifest in a desire to attract followers, *simply for the sake of winning converts*; or, influenced by the Devil, to lead souls into error (e.g., *Acts of Archelaus* 65.2 (see Chapter 2); *Life of Porphyry* 85 (see below));
2. a strategy attained principally by the appropriation of the cultural apparatus of normative (orthodox) Christianity, specifically the name 'Christian' (*Life of Porphyry* 85), and the Christian scriptures (*Acts of Archelaus* 65.2–6); the reason for the focus by Manichaeans on all things Christian explained by Christianity's evident success in winning respect and followers (cf. *Acts of Archelaus* 65.2). The 'poisonous' teachings of Mani and his followers are therefore commonly said to have been sweetened by the addition of 'Christ's name': e.g., Augustine, *Against Faustus* 13.17.
3. However, that which had been appropriated is also commonly portrayed as having been corrupted through the desire of Manichaeans to take on other influences, mainly the ideas and terminology of Greek philosophy, for proselytising purposes or for the sake of intellectual credibility.
4. Thus, a central preoccupation of patristic authors was to highlight Manichaeism's corruption of Christian traditions by its drawing on a wide range of religious and philosophical sources (with Christianity at the forefront), with the effect that heresiologists judged Manichaeism to be a composite religion (i.e. a *syncretism*; cf. *Life of Porphyry* 86), which itself was presented as having been conceived in order to draw into its ranks those believers who belonged to the traditions from which Mani had appropriated certain ideas and teachings: e.g., Mani's assumed pantheon of deities was

---

[11] On this process see King 2005, 22–3, who in turn follows Le Boulluec 1985, 36–7.

taken to be a lure for pagans as a result of their polytheistic tendencies (see Epiphanius, *Medicine Chest*, 66.88.3; Augustine, *Against Adimantus* 11; Augustine, *Against Faustus* 20.5; *Life of Porphyry* 85).

These four heresiological characterisations of Manichaeism in Late Antiquity can be contextualised and cast in greater relief by examining one of the more remarkable anti-Manichaean episodes from the late Roman world. Forming an important section in the Greek biography (a literary form customarily referred to as a *vita*, Lt. for 'life-writing') of Porphyry, bishop of Gaza (395–420) by Mark the Deacon, is a public exchange between Porphyry and a female Manichaean Elect – a high-ranking member of the faith – named Julia.[12] The work presents Julia, recently arrived in the Palestinian city from Antioch, as seeking to win the newly converted Christians of the city to Manichaeism. The account follows the well-trodden polemical characterisation of Manichaean thought and practice as outlined above, and, whilst it very possibly reflects an encounter of some sort between Catholic and Manichaean Christians, its debt to the anti-Manichaean tradition of literary polemicising is clearly apparent: for this reason, positivist interpretations of the encounter are best avoided.

Concerning the corrupt missionary strategies of the Manichaeans (compare point 1 above), Mark the Deacon writes about Julia that,

... discovering that among the Christians there were some neophytes who were not yet confirmed in the holy faith, this woman infiltrated herself among them, and surreptitiously corrupted them with her impostor's doctrine, and still further by giving them money. For the inventor of the said atheist heresy was unable to attract followers except by bribing them (*Life of Porphyry* 85; trans. I. Gardner and S.N.C. Lieu 2004, 126).

And in relation to the composite, syncretic character of the religion (linking points 1 and 3 together), the author notes that ...

[t]his false doctrine of different heresies and pagan beliefs was created with the treacherous and fraudulent intention of enticing all kinds of people. In fact the Manichaeans worship many gods, thus wishing to please the pagans (*Life of Porphyry* 85; trans. I. Gardner and S.N.C. Lieu 2004, 126–7).

And finally, Mark the Deacon's presentation of the 'Christian face' of Manichaeism neatly illustrates point 2, whilst tying together its expedient and syncretic qualities at the same time. References to the Greek authors Philistion and Hesiod, the former a composer of mimes and the latter the famous poet, provided a way of highlighting that Mani's teachings about the operation and

---

[12] For a discussion concerning the doubts expressed about the 'historical reliability' of Mark the Deacon's work, see, Trombley 2001, 246–82.

governance of the universe – his cosmogony and cosmology – were *even more* ridiculous and scandalous than that which could be found in pagan literature:[13]

> They also confess Christ, but claim that he was only apparently incarnate [a 'docetic Christianity'; see Chapter 4]. As well as that, they who claim to be Christians themselves only appear to be so. I leave aside that which is ridiculous and offensive in order to avoid filling my audience's ears with the sound of scandalous words and monstrous suggestions. For they constructed their heresy by mixing the fables of the comic Philistion, Hesiod and other so-called philosophers with Christian beliefs. Just as a painter obtains the semblance of a man, an animal or some other object by mixing colours to delude the viewers, so that fools and madmen believe these images are real, whereas sensible people will only see in them shadows, portent and human invention. In the same way, the Manichaeans have created their doctrine by drawing on many beliefs; or, in other words, they have mixed the venom from various reptiles to make a deadly poison capable of destroying human souls (*Life of Porphyry* 86; trans. I. Gardner and S.N.C. Lieu 2004, 127).

The allegation concerning the superficial yet opportunistic nature of the Manichaean claim to a Christian identity was also given an elegant voice by Augustine (354–430), Catholic Bishop of Hippo – himself a Manichaean for the best part of a decade – in his *Confessions*.[14] Speaking about his involvement with the North African followers of Mani during his youth, Augustine noted:

> … I fell in with men proud of their slick talk, very earthly-minded and loquacious. In their mouths were the Devil's traps and a birdlime compounded of a mixture of the syllables of [God's] name, and that of the Lord Jesus Christ, and that of the Paraclete, the Comforter, the Holy Spirit. These names were never absent from their lips; but it was no more than sound and noise with their tongue (*Confessions* 3.6.10; trans. H. Chadwick 1998, 40).[15]

According to Augustine, the Christian credentials of the Manichaean religion – in the case of the passage from the *Confessions* cited above its allusion to a Trinitarian theology – were hollow truths ('sound and noise'), intentional corruptions of the authentic message of Christianity, designed to lure in those seeking more substantive truths. Speaking broadly, therefore, patristic authors were preoccupied with portraying Mani's religion as a fraudulent form of Christianity: a plastic religion with derivative components which, by way of an inversion of the Catholic doctrine of apostolic succession, derived its heretical

---

[13] See Scopello 2005, 265–7.
[14] On the relationship between the *Confessions* and Augustine's Manichaean background, see Kotzé 2004.
[15] On this passage, see esp. van Oort 1997.

credentials from the Devil himself.[16] The characterisation of Manichaeism as a heretical sect of Christianity stuck fast for well over a millennium, and the charge that the religion was of a syncretistic character formed an important part of the language of heresiology: the author of the influential anti-Manichaean *Acts of Archelaus*, Augustine of Hippo, and countless other late-antique Christian writers, all promulgated the characterisation of Mani's religion as a composite system which borrowed heavily from existing traditions and produced nothing original or germane from within the boundaries of its own culture. The implication of this polemically-imposed identity was entirely negative: Manichaeism was judged derivative and artificial, fundamentally a dishonest and impure version of Christianity.[17]

3. Gnosis, Gnosticism and Syncretism

In this regard a bridge can be made between the legacy of patristic rhetoric directed towards the Manichaeans and the modern academic study of Manichaeism. Bubbling away beneath the surface of Manichaean studies lies the continuation of some of these heresiological characterisations of Mani and his religion, although forced out into the open under very different historical and cultural conditions than those prevalent during Late Antiquity. In her valuable revisionist study on ancient Gnosticism, Karen King has noted the parallels between the patristic preoccupation with positing the derivative nature of ancient heresy and the way in which modern scholars – principally those within the intellectual school of thought known as the History of Religions School – constructed frameworks for the analysis of Gnosticism (Manichaeism often being placed within this category) by defining 'cultural interaction basically in terms of syncretism, by which [these commentators] meant the borrowing of a discrete element ('motif') from one culture by another. The goal of motif history was to identify the original location in some primitive nature religion, and then trace its path through various stages of syncretic borrowing.'[18]

Similarly, modern studies of Manichaeism have also sought the historical origins of the religion by dissolving Manichaean teachings into discrete parts (for instance, its dualistic theology; its saviour figure(s); its ideas concerning the metempsychosis of the soul) and pursuing the foundations of these 'motifs' into an assumed and often arbitrarily constructed historical and cultural 'past' for Mani and his church, and then by projecting the genesis of the parts backwards in order to provide an explanation for the origin of the whole. Thus, cultural interaction in Manichaeism has not only tended to be discussed in terms of syncretism, but Mani and his followers have in addition been portrayed as conscious syncretists, in the sense that they are believed to have intentionally appropriated terminological and doctrinal features from other traditions, and displayed a tendency to activate particular 'borrowed elements' as the need

---

[16] See Spät 2004.

[17] Cf. King 2005, 222–4.

[18] King 2005, 79.

arose within the environment from which they were taken, i.e., from within the context of missionary activity: a process viewed as being undertaken in order to increase the share of converts during those periods when the religion was engaged in proselytising activities.

Assessments of Manichaeism in this vein are now slowly being re-evaluated by many commentators, not least because of the problems surrounding the notion of syncretism in relation to the historical application of the term. As Charles Stewart and Rosalind Shaw have highlighted, syncretism tends towards being 'an "othering" term applied to historically distant as well as geographically distant societies',[19] and as King has demonstrated in her study of Gnosticism,[20] it replaces that more ancient 'othering' term, heresy, by reduplicating its prejudicial assumptions about competitor traditions, most notably in its conveying of the sense of contamination and distance from 'authentic' faiths (as illustrated by the juxtaposition between *syncretism* [= contaminated tradition] vs. *anti-syncretism* [= pure tradition]).

Nevertheless, attempts to characterise Manichaeism in this manner continue to arise in the study of the religion. The inevitability of such an assessment in the context of Manichaean studies should, however, be noted: the evidence for Manichaeism is comprised, in part, of primary textual sources composed by Manichaeans themselves. These sources, whilst relatively abundant, nevertheless present countless challenges for the persons studying them, not least in relation to the linguistic variations and chronological range presented by the material. As a religious faith which endured for approximately thirteen centuries,[21] ranging from the post-classical West to medieval China – the distinction between what Michel Tardieu refers to as Babylonian Manichaeism and Sogdian Manichaeism[22] – and with a literary tradition which employed arguably the widest variety of languages and dialects for a single religion in the pre-modern world, tendencies among followers of Mani towards syncretic practice are to be expected, not least in the way that core doctrinal ideas were communicated during the process of linguistic and cultural translation to nascent converts.[23] However, whilst 'syncretism is a feature of all religions',[24] it is the peculiar fate of Manichaeism to be singled out among late-antique religions as being 'self-consciously absorbent'.[25]

However, in the context of historical inquiry, modern judgements positing the syncretistic character of early Manichaeism are especially problematic, considering that much of the religious and cultural background of Mani and his early followers remains underworked and therefore undefined.[26] Indeed, it can be argued that the assessment that Mani 'looked here and there' for ideas

---

[19] Stewart and Shaw 1994, 4–5.
[20] King 2005, 223.
[21] See S.N.C. Lieu 1992, 303–4.
[22] Tardieu 2008, 100–1.
[23] Cf. BeDuhn 2002, 6–7.
[24] Steward and Shaw 1994, 5.
[25] BeDuhn 2002, 6.
[26] See, for example, Widengren 1965, 72–3.

from existing religions – or, as Hans Jonas put it, Mani's 'many-sided affinities'[27] – impedes investigations into determining with any greater clarity the specific set of social, religious and cultural influences that shaped Mani and formed his religious beliefs. However, upon looking at the issue from the other side, explanations can be found to account for the perpetuation of these syncretistic assumptions. At least four powerful concerns reside at the heart of this matter:

1. The enduring legacy of patristic polemics against Mani's teachings from Late Antiquity – i.e., as heretical, derivative and pseudo-Christian – most notably in the perpetuation of such characterisations in the controversial language employed by both Catholic and Protestant Christians against one another during the European Reformation, and the subsequent fossilisation of this language in the historiographical traditions of early modern Europe.[28]
2. The apologetical agendas present in early 'critical' histories of Mani and Manichaeism, which piggybacked the claims and counterclaims made in Reformation discourse: for instance, in the (still none the less) pioneering work of Isaac de Beausobre from 1734 to 1739 in two volumes, *A Critical History of Mani and Manichaeism*.[29]
3. The absence of source material at crucial points in the history of Manichaean studies, particularly during the late eighteenth and nineteenth centuries, challenging the ancient Catholic judgement of expediency in the Manichaean use of the *Christian name* (*nomen Christianum*).
4. The reception of newly emergent Manichaean sources from the late nineteenth century onwards, which appeared to privilege perhaps only one or two religious influences acting on Mani, over and above any normative Christian influence – which was, nevertheless, not seriously entertained on the basis of the intellectual trend noted in point three.

In reserving judgement on the language of syncretism to describe the historical formation and character of Manichaeism, we find ourselves in good company. Henri-Charles Puech, the late Professor of Religions at the Collège de France, and author of a pioneering study of Manichaeism from 1949 that employed many newly discovered Manichaean texts to develop a grand narrative of Mani's origins and his teachings, noted that certain Manichaean writings do indeed create the impression of the religion as being actively inclusive – i.e., syncretistic. Such an impression is evident in the important early (fourth-century) Manichaean work, *The Chapters* (Gk *Kephalaia*), a theological commentary on Mani's teachings by his early disciples, which came to light among a collection of Manichaean writings discovered in Egypt in 1929 (see below).[30] Puech draws attention to the following passage from *The Chapters* in which Mani is expounding the merits of his own church over and above all previous ('first') churches:

[27] Jonas 1992, 207.
[28] See Ries 1988, 17–57; also Baker-Brian forthcoming.
[29] See Stroumsa 2000.
[30] See Pettipiece 2009, 7–13.

The writings and the wisdom and the revelations and the parables and the psalms of all the first churches have been collected in every place. They have come down to my church. They have added to the wisdom that I have revealed, the way water might add to water and become many waters. Again, this also is the way that the ancient books have added to my writings, and have become great wisdom; its like was not uttered in all the ancient generations (*The Chapters* 151. 372; trans. I. Gardner and S.N.C. Lieu 2004, 266).[31]

As Puech notes, Mani's upbringing in southern Mesopotamia would have exposed him to a range of religious influences, and Mani's assimilation of this diversity is in some way reflected in the cumulative mindset evidenced in the passage from *The Chapters*. However, as Puech adds, Mani's religion should not be reduced to a simple assemblage of borrowed elements. Indeed,

... the principal [scholarly] instinct is to search for an answer beyond this [concern with syncretism]. The truth that Mani had conceived, was pliable with regard to its abstract and general character, and it was capable of being translated equally under diverse forms according to the character of the different environments in which it found itself during its dissemination. However, at its foundation the religion comprised a fixed collection of ideas which guaranteed the identity of its assigned revelation, although it was capable of casting itself into multiple moulds.[32]

Whether intended by Puech to be understood in this way or not, the passage is indeed suggestive of the need to distinguish between, on the one hand, the body of Mani's teachings which, taken as a coherent and unified whole, convey a specific revelatory message to his followers; and on the other hand, the cultural translation of these teachings during Manichaean missionary endeavours throughout the course of the religion's history. What is interesting is the extent to which very many commentators often conflate the two distinctions, resulting in the misguided assumption that it is possible to be able to isolate and discuss in a meaningful manner those specific elements, as immediate influences, acting on Mani and giving shape to his teachings. Thus, eschewing the genealogical approach to Manichaeism as the search for the historical origins of Mani's ideas, Puech chose instead to talk about 'the essence of Manichaeism', which he regarded as being reducible to the idea of the religion as primarily concerned with imparting to its followers a salvific knowledge, referred to in shorthand via the Greek word *gnosis* (= knowledge).

The characterisation of particular religious traditions from Late Antiquity, which, through an apparent participation in a commonly shared body of dogma reducible to a concern with gnosis, has permitted scholars to identify and discuss a seemingly separate tradition called Gnosticism, remains one of the most controversial definitional areas of study in the history of ancient religions.

---

[31] Cf. Puech 1949, 150, nt. 264.
[32] Puech 1949, 69.

The nub of the controversy concerns the provenance of this body of dogma and its objectification by modern academic research, in spite of the fact that much of it has been drawn from a patristic culture which actively campaigned against 'gnostic' ideas and writings; and, the extent to which the patristic representation of gnostic teachings and groups has been employed – sometimes wholly uncritically – by academic commentators to posit the existence of a tradition independent of normative Christianity in that period.[33] In his study, *Rethinking Gnosticism: An Argument for Dismantling a Dubious Category*, Michael Williams offers a nuanced summary of these concerns:

> Initially, the category 'gnosis' or 'gnosticism' in modern scholarship was constructed on the basis of what was perceived to be the self-definition of early Christian 'heretics' such as the followers of Valentinian or Ptolemy ... or figures such as the early-second-century Egyptian Christian teacher named Basilides, and others ... The category 'gnosis' or 'gnosticism' was eventually made to accommodate all groups that were perceived to have certain doctrinal similarities to Valentinian and the others, whether or not there was evidence that the actual self-designation 'gnostics' was used. Finally, comparative research led many scholars to conclude that 'gnosticism' was not necessarily merely a subordinate element in the religious identity of 'gnostics.' According to this view, a pattern of religion we should call 'gnosis' or 'gnosticism' existed even apart from and probably even prior to Christianity, and 'gnostic' religious phenomena as a whole are sufficiently coherent and distinctive to be treated as 'the Gnostic religion.'[34]

Received ideas about Gnosticism have been challenged during the previous century – and indeed continue to be revised – with new findings emerging from analyses of texts composed, so it seems, by the very 'gnostic' groups and personalities challenged by patristic writers, the most famous of which are the apocryphal gospels and apocalypses – i.e., inauthentic writings, rejected during the formation of the New Testament – unearthed in the town of Nag Hammadi in Upper Egypt during 1945–6.[35] The contents of many of these texts – which perhaps formed part of a fourth-century monastic library – reinforce some of the general impressions of gnostic belief conveyed polemically by heresiologists, but by no means all of them: however, the possibility for generalising about Gnostic-*ism* looks more and more remote, and recent research has been concerned with documenting detail through studies of individual works rather than creating grand theories of Gnosticism's origins.[36]

---

[33] This is but a very short summary of a problem much more complex in its historical depth than can be dealt with here. The most stimulating revisionist accounts of the relevant issues are by Williams 1999 and King 2005.

[34] Williams 1999, 30–1.

[35] For an account of the discoveries at Nag Hammadi and the first academic studies of the collection, see Pagels 1990, 13–32.

[36] See Logan 2004, *passim*.

However, Puech's quest for the intrinsic element of Manichaeism, and his claim that this essence is gnostic, is an indication of his partiality for one of the two dominant approaches to gnostic studies in the twentieth century. As Karen King has indicated, modern studies of Gnosticism have demonstrated a preoccupation with the search for the essentials of the gnostic tradition, realised either according to the historical-genealogical model as manifest in the approach of 'motif history' (see above), or according to the typological model, whereby Gnosticism's essence is regarded as capable of being distilled into 'a typological (phenomenological) delimitation of the essential characteristics of Gnosticism as a way both to define Gnosticism and to explain its existential meaning'.[37] The latter approach indeed emerged as a reaction against the former, judged as 'the bewildering harvest of the genetic method',[38] which more often than not relied on dubious ethnic judgements (Orientalism), and questionable analytical frameworks (Historicism) for the formation and deployment of its findings.[39] Taking his lead from three important twentieth-century studies on Gnosticism,[40] and principally from the influential *Gnosis and the late antique Mind* (*Gnosis und spätantiker Geist*) by Hans Jonas, Puech discusses Manichaean doctrine from the perspective of the phenomenology of Gnosticism: 'What is Manichaeism other than a religion which claims to supply or arouse in humankind this saving knowledge?'[41]

Puech's delineation of the *essence* of the religion according to the phenomenological approach that emerged during the study of Gnosticism in the previous century – his categorical assessment of Mani's religion as another example of a gnostic religion explainable by the fact that he was one of the earliest scholars to work on the Nag Hammadi writings – follows the 'classical' model of gnostic phenomenology, with its emphasis on a radical, dualistic cosmogony – the loss of the absolute good to the absolute evil – the subsequent recovery of this good, and the internalisation of this process in the 'existential dilemma' facing the individual human being.

> As is the case with all Gnosticisms, Manichaeism is born from the inherent agony of the human condition. The situation into which man is cast is experienced by him as alien, unbearable and extremely nasty. He feels bound to the body, to time and to the world, and having been mixed with evil, it constantly menaces and tarnishes him. From this experience arises the desire for liberation. But if I am able to experience this need, if I have the desire to discover or indeed to rediscover it (since it is the recollection of a lost condition), a state where I apprehend myself, in liberty and in complete purity which is my very being, my true essence, then I am truly superior to my condition and a foreigner to this body, to this time, and to this world. From that point on, my

---

[37] King 2005, 115.
[38] Jonas 1992, preface, xvii.
[39] Reservations raised throughout King 2005.
[40] Puech 1949, 151, nt. 270.
[41] Puech 1949, 70.

present position will appear as one of utter decay. I must seek answers for myself: how and why I came to be, and in particular with regard to my present situation here.[42]

Puech's description thus brings to light a further important stage in the study of Manichaeism, namely the near-universal acceptance among modern commentators that the religion of Mani is gnostic in very many facets of its character. Hans Jonas referred to Manichaeism as 'the most important product of Gnosticism',[43] and more recent treatments of the religion regard it as the 'culmination' of gnosis: 'the conclusion of the development of the great ancient systems of gnosis'.[44] Indeed, it is arguable that research into Manichaeism has not only assisted in the development of thinking about Gnosticism, but in many respects has also made the very idea of Gnosticism – as a categorical phenomenon of ancient religion – possible.

The discovery of primary sources for the Manichaean religion – curiously always lagging behind the glamour that accompanies the finds at Nag Hammadi in the popular imagination – from the long-forgotten rooms and rubbish-tips of the extinct empires of antiquity, has been instrumental in the development of the approach which Puech prioritised in his study, namely the phenomenology of Gnostic-Manichaeism. The data plundered from Manichaean texts has assisted in building up a broad narrative of gnostic beliefs and habits of thought, not least in the way that commentators have conceptualised gnostic mythology, gnostic ideas about salvation and gnostic rituals and ascetic practices. The end point of this conceptualisation has been the production of something like a 'check list' of the distinguishing features of Gnosticism, favoured by those scholars such as Jonas and Puech, who have chosen to discuss Mani's religion in phenomenological terms.

Furthermore, in the quest for the historical origins of Gnosticism, the Iranian Manichaean sources which came to light in the early years of the previous century have been read as indicating Mani's role as one of the principal cultural channels for an Iranian strand of Gnosticism. This argument rests on the interpretation of specific texts that appear to portray Mani and his teachings as intermediaries for Mazdean (i.e., the worship of Ahura Mazda, the principal deity of Zoroastrianism) dualism and ideas about salvation[45] – primarily in the apparent similarity between the Manichaean cosmic saviour called the 'First Man' and the gnostic soteriological motif of the 'Redeemed Redeemer'[46] – a theory which has looked especially credible considering the little that was known about Mani's Babylonian background and his contacts with Sasanian Persia, beyond his familial roots as described by the tenth-century Islamic author al-Nadim (see Chapter 2), together with the use of the names of certain Zoroastrian deities and demons (e.g., Zurvan, Ahriman, Ohrmezd, Mithras

---

[42] Puech 1949, 70.
[43] Jonas 1992, 208.
[44] Markschies 2003, 101.
[45] Widengren 1983, 973f.
[46] King 2005, 85.

[Mihr]) in Manichaean writings from Central Asia, including in one of Mani's own writings, the *Šābuhragān*.[47] The 'pan-Iranianism' of Manichaeism[48] and its gnostic character have, therefore, formed the dominant strands of research into the religion for a significant proportion of the twentieth century.

Incidentally, the emphasis placed by Puech on Manichaeism's gnostic qualities has been read as a reaction against the pan-Iranian tendencies in twentieth-century Manichaean studies,[49] and is but one example of the attempt by scholars to represent Manichaeism as a religion which, from its earliest days, not only held ambitions of universality, but indeed had been fabricated as such by Mani: in other words, where local influences were actively overcome by Mani in a move towards a trans-cultural religious system.

However, the tendency towards generalising and anachronistic judgements upon which the category of Gnosticism rests have been challenged in recent times: the concern of gnostic studies with the historical-genealogical model of inquiry for identifying either the 'Greek', 'Jewish' or 'Iranian' origins of certain gnostic theologies and sensibilities has been criticised for being too loosely-defined, together with displaying a tendency to reproduce prejudicial assumptions about particular cultural and ethnic forms. Similarly, the phenomenological position has been called into question for positing too broad a series of correspondences across hugely diverse traditions and cultures, and therefore running the risk of de-contextualising local details through a constructivist approach to category formation. The combined results of these investigative approaches, which have suggested that Gnosticism had either an origin independent of other religions, or that it emerged into independence from existing religious forms, are now also judged to be misapprehensions of the complex and dynamic operation of religions and cultures in the ancient world.[50]

Indeed, many scholars of Manichaeism have long been aware in particular of the essential differences between the religion of Mani and the standard, typological definitions of Gnosticism. However, this has not stopped some commentators from 'carelessly conflat[ing] Manichaeism with Gnosticism'.[51] Phenomenological descriptions of gnostic mythology, cosmogony and anthropology, e.g., that the universe is the product of an evil creator god (Gk *demiurgos* = a workman), that the soul falls into the world as a result of the confusion brought about through the process of creation, and that the ethical inclinations of both matter and the soul are pre-determined, which taken all together add up to a 'cosmic pessimism' (cf. Puech's assessment, above),[52] contrast significantly with the way in these concerns are formulated in Manichaean myth and theology (see Chapter 4 for more on these issues). However, it should also be borne in mind that these very same descriptions are themselves clichés about Gnosticism which do not stand up to closer scrutiny: indeed, many of them are now being

---

[47] Cf. Colpe 1983, 836-840.
[48] Nyberg 1977, 17.
[49] Spotted by Reeves 1992, 5 nt. 5.
[50] See King 2005, 218–36, for a complete summary of the problems.
[51] BeDuhn 2005, 12.
[52] See King 2005, 123–4.

reconsidered by commentators engaged in the process of picking apart the construction of modern categorical assumptions about gnostic beliefs.[53]

However, in historical terms, the most serious reservation about placing the Manichaean religion into the category of Gnosticism concerns the effect which this continues to have on the definition and the appreciation of the Christian foundations of Manichaeism's origins, i.e., during Mani's lifetime and the early history of the religion during the formation of its institutional structures. In this regard, numerous features that have arisen in the study of Gnosticism come into play, most especially the dominant trends in gnostic research that have emphasised the seeming oriental origins and the apparent syncretistic tendencies of ancient gnostic traditions, which have been taken as being suggestive of its independence from Christian faith and practice. As we have seen, however, these features are especially problematic, as judgements about the non-Christian nature of Gnosticism (and Manichaeism when it is brought within the category of Gnosticism) ultimately derive from and thereby perpetuate the archetypal patristic complaint of heretical, 'gnostic' religions as being derivative and pseudo in character. Assessments therefore which piggyback the findings drawn from the study of Gnosticism, that Manichaeism is 'an independent religion ... [and] an attempt at a deliberate synthesis of previous tradition',[54] even though such claims may now posit a Christian origin for Gnosticism, should at the very least be challenged in spite of the fact that an argument for a 'gnosis-oriented' element within Manichaeism remains a valuable way of understanding the soteriological character of Manichaean theology: in other words, knowledge of one's real self did indeed play a crucial part in the strategies for salvation offered by the religion.

4. Manichaean Identities

However, can we be so certain that a Christian dimension was central to Manichaeism in Late Antiquity, to the point where we are able to prioritise the Christian components of the religion above any other categorical option available to us? In the light of this, a pertinent question to address would be: what would 'Christian' have meant to Mani and his followers? Furthermore, would a declaration of Manichaeism's Christian character be compatible with the highly visible label 'Manichaean' as a badge of identity for Mani's followers? Indeed, where does the categorical term 'Manichaean' or 'Manichaeism' come from? Does it appear to be self-designated on the part of Mani's followers, or was it imposed on them by their opponents?[55]

We have good reason to be suspicious of 'Manichaean', emerging as it does from the heresiological practice of naming heterodox Christians after a real or alleged founder or current leader of their group:[56] for instance, a prominent heresiologist from the fourth century, Epiphanius, relates in his work the

---

[53] For instance, see M.A. Williams 1999, 98–100; 189–212

[54] Markschies 2003, 101; also, Böhlig 1983.

[55] See Lim 2008; also S.N.C. Lieu 1998b.

[56] Bauer 1972, 22.

Medicine Chest the information that the Manichaeans in the region of Palestine were known as Acuanites, after Acuas, a veteran soldier who returned from Mesopotamia to disseminate Mani's teachings in the West.[57] The historical value of Epiphanius' observation is beyond our consideration; instead it is the decision we reach in judging whether or not this act of naming emerged from practitioners of Manichaeism, or from its opponents, which is central to our line of inquiry. The role played by evidence supplied by practitioners, comprising the 'self-definition' of believers, is frequently privileged by commentators seeking to determine a religion's categorical identity, since it enables them '[to attend] to how those whom we are studying seem to group *themselves* [and] how *they* seem to construct *their* own communal or traditional identity'.[58] However, understanding the construction of a community's religious identity is not as straightforward as simply following the labels of self-designation which appear in the sources for a tradition.

As Judith Lieu has emphasised, identity should be viewed as being both contextualised and contingent, considerations which loom large when discussing the Manichaeans.[59] The geographical, linguistic and chronological contexts for the diffusion of religions are of great significance in the study of identity in Manichaeism, since the extent of Manichaeism's 'universal reach' consequently meant that Manichaean identities were affected, consolidated or transformed in their interactions with other religions and cultural forms, which suggests that Manichaean self-identity did not remain completely stable through the sixteen or so centuries of its existence. Furthermore, when dealing with the Manichaeans, we are left almost solely with identities which are constructed in literary texts: thus, in considering the range of sources, the variety of literary forms and genres, together with the breadth of source languages which Manichaeans used to compose their writings, we would expect to find expressed a variety of religious self-designations.

Even when turning to those texts which are closest in time to the earliest foundation of the religion within its Mesopotamian context and during the early periods of its missionary expansion, understanding the nature of Manichaean religious identity is a challenging task. There are no unambiguous declamations by either Mani or his followers to either a Christian or a Manichaean identity:[60] we do see, following other confessional patterns of declamation (such as in ancient martyr *Acts*), followers of Mani proclaiming their identity in seemingly unambiguous terms ('I Felix, a Christian, a worshipper of the law of Mani'[61]), although clearly such instances appear only in exceptional circumstances, notably during episcopally-sponsored legal trials

---

[57] Epiphanius, *Medicine Chest* 66.1.1; trans. Amidon 1990; see Stroumsa 1985; also S.N.C. Lieu 1992, 96.

[58] Williams 1996, 29, emphasis added.

[59] J.M. Lieu 2004, 18.

[60] Prominent in this regard is the claim ascribed to Mani in the *Kephalaia* (105.259.13) that 'people who love me are called of my name' (trans. Gardner 1995, 264), the ambiguity of which is discussed in Pedersen 2004, 8–10.

[61] Felix in Augustine, *Answer to Felix* I.20; trans. Teske 2006, 297.

where the entire proceedings have been working towards the eliciting of a confessional identity.[62]

Nevertheless, glimpses of how certain Manichaeans saw themselves can be caught from the ancient sources. As editors for the collection of fourth-century Manichaean writings discovered on the site of the Roman village of Kellis in the Upper Egyptian area of the Dakhleh Oasis during the 1990s (see below), Iain Gardner, Anthony Alcock and Wolf-Peter Funk have noted the Manichaeans' partiality for 'terminology that implies sectarianism or some especial status'.[63] Within the collection of personal correspondence in Coptic, exchanged between followers of Mani, that forms part of the Kellis find, the Greek word *ecclesia* meaning *church*, denoting an assembly of religious practitioners, features on a number of occasions in the letters (e.g., P.Kell.Copt. 31.2–3; P.Kell.Copt. 32.1–2), although it tends to be qualified by additional terms implying a sense of special election. In what was probably a 'circular letter' requesting alms, authored by a church elder and sent to Manichaean communities in the region (P.Kell. Copt. 31; trans. I. Gardner, A. Alcock and W.-P. Funk (1999), 209–13), the author opens his missive in the following manner:

> My loved daughters, who are greatly revered by me: The members of the holy church, [the daughters] of the Light-Mind, they who [also are numbered] with the children of God; the favoured, blessed, God-loving souls; my *shona* children. It is I, your father who is in Egypt, who writes to you; in the Lord, – greetings! (P.Kell.Copt. 31.1–9; trans. I. Gardner, A. Alcock and W.-P. Funk 1999, 211).

The terms 'holy church' and the 'children of God' are likely Manichaean 'community designations', referring to the Manichaean church as a corporate body, whilst the expression 'daughters of the Light-Mind', which invokes the name of the guiding divine force (the Light-Mind, or Light-Nous) in the church, is probably a hierarchical designation denoting the class of female catechumens – Hearers – who formed the logistical backbone of the church (see Chapter 4). Indeed, the editors of the letters regard the use of 'holy church' as itself a designation of Christian distinctiveness, in contrast to attestations in other texts from Kellis which referred to the 'catholic church', denoting non-Manichaean (i.e., orthodox) Christians.[64] There is a clear sense, therefore, that late-antique followers of Mani, at least, regarded themselves as forming a distinctive *ecclesia*, in which term were reconciled multiple commitments of the corporate body to Jesus, Mani, its own beliefs, its own rituals, and its own internal hierarchies. As is the case, however, with most identities, relational complexities characterise Manichaean self-identity: indeed, when individual and communal allegiances are announced by Manichaeans, they stand somewhere within what is the equivalent of a religiously-styled Venn diagram, where claims to an identity – such as those made by Mani himself as an 'Apostle of Jesus Christ' – overlap other claims

---

[62] See Humfress 2007, 243–68.
[63] Gardner, Alcock and Funk 1999, 74.
[64] Gardner, Alcock and Funk 1999, 74.

and are dependent upon being read within the context of a specific theological setting.

However, as Michael Williams has also pointed out, 'one can in principle explore aspects of an individual's religious self-definition by looking at things other than specific labels she gives to herself.'[65] Thus, for the moment, one way of gaining a clearer impression of the religious identity of Manichaeans, especially during Late Antiquity, is to examine some of the reasons for their conflict with rival Christians in the period. Individuals and groups fall out over shared ground, so to speak, and common interests, and they imbue the contested objects with a significance which means they are worth defending against competing claims to authority and ownership. In other words, disputes emerge when identities are held in common. Therefore, some obvious clues to the Christian content and orientation of Mani's teachings can be found in the literary polemics of patristic culture, in relation to the fact that the principal points of discussion in nearly all anti-Manichaean works deal with certain themes and issues which are intrinsic components for someone professing a self-identity as 'Christian': their indispensable role being in evidence even when there is an absence of a specific Christian self-designation.

Therefore, a number of distinct concerns can be identified which may be said to form an inherent part of the essence of ancient Christian identity which, in spite of the cultural and linguistic diversity of the Christianities of Late Antiquity that necessarily meant differences in the way that Christian groups formulated their thoughts on these matters, nevertheless reappear with such frequency in the literature of the period that they may be said to be central to the shared constituents of a Christian identity. These may be reduced to the following: (i) the role and status of Jesus in religious thought and action; (ii) the exegetical use and interpretation of the Bible (comprising the Old and New Testaments) and its place as a cultural determinant for the Christianities of Late Antiquity; (iii) a concern with apostolic tradition in determining religious authority.

These three issues are dominant concerns in both Manichaean and Christian texts, and constitute the main areas of disagreement in the literary exchanges between the two faiths. With this in mind, it is clear that an almost complete polarisation of attitudes existed between Catholic Christians and Manichaeans with regard to these three areas. The gulf between these two ancient models of Christianity is seemingly most evident in the way that Manichaeans formulated their Christology. Central to normative Christian experiences of Jesus Christ was the figure of the *logos* incarnate, the historical person from Nazareth who taught a gospel of forgiveness, and, whilst the formulation of the relationship between the divine and human heritage of Jesus marked the christological controversies of the early Christian period, attentions remained fixed on only one figure. By contrast, Manichaeans not only contested the idea of the incarnation, but expressed their understanding of Jesus' significance to their tradition by splitting the historical Jesus into a variety of roles, e.g., as an apostle ('Jesus the Apostle'), as a cosmic revealer ('Jesus the Splendour'), and as a symbol of universal suffering ('Jesus *patibilis*'). However, the Manichaean desire to understand Jesus as a figure

[65] Williams 1999, 31–32.

of transcendent power yet immanent endurance likely underpinned these formulations, and in this sense they were little different from normative expressions of Jesus' significance for Christians.[66]

However, as Augustine's vitriolic reaction to the Manichaean teaching on Jesus *patibilis* illustrates,[67] the broad strategy of patristic writers in their handling of any one or all of these areas was to undermine the claims which Mani and his followers made for an authoritative stance on the issues, leaving a 'credibility void' which they then filled with the characterisation of Manichaeans as aberrant (heretical) Christians: the classical approach to branding 'the Other'. However, in the destabilisation of Manichaean claims, even more subtle strategies can be discerned in the patristic sources, one of which was to suggest that Mani and not Jesus was the principal authority for Manichaeans,[68] which may indeed have been accurate, although Mani's self-identity, as we shall see, derived from his ability to locate his own teachings within a Jesus-centric concept of religious apostolicity (see Chapter 2). As we have seen, modern scholarship has to a certain extent perpetuated the decisions of these long-dead heresiologists.

It was only, however, during the twentieth century that the intrinsic role for Mani and his church of the principal elements of a Christian identity became apparent. The interpretation of the discoveries of primary Manichaean sources, including a limited number of fragments from works written by Mani himself, indicate the importance of these elements for Mani and his followers. The identification and decoding of the context and composition of Manichaeism's Christian character, whilst ongoing, has nevertheless made slower progress than one would perhaps hope, arguably for at least two main reasons. To begin with, commentators have been reluctant or simply unwilling to assign a 'Christian' label to very many elements within Manichaeism, since the concerns which they encounter in the source material, although Christian in appearance, nevertheless appear unfamiliar when set against normative models of early Christianity (principally in its Mediterranean guise). Whilst scholars of Manichaeism are, in the main, sophisticated commentators of the texts they are working with, highly sensitive to their own predilections in their efforts to understand material, along with being fully aware of the ubiquity of the normative model of early Christianity in clouding definitions about what is and is not Christian, the basic fact remains that scholarly judgements continue to be influenced by the seemingly unfamiliar nature of Manichaean Christianity. Indeed, the lack of appreciation of what might actually be 'Christian' within the context of Manichaean sources, for instance as a possible explanation for the dualism of its theology which academic consensus had assumed to be Zoroastrian, is an ongoing concern:[69] a deficiency which is nevertheless also tied to a relative dearth of information about the religious profile of the regions where early Manichaean writers and writings had their origin, primarily in Sasanian-controlled Mesopotamia.

---

[66] See Franzmann 2003, 141–5.

[67] See Augustine, *Answer to Faustus* 2.5; trans. Teske 2007, 73–4.

[68] For instance, Augustine, *Answer to Secundinus* 25; trans. Teske 2006, 387–8.

[69] De Blois 2000, esp. 13–14.

And so we return to a consideration of the imperially-defined cultural frontier that separated the Persian and the Roman empires with which we began this chapter. During the third century, over on the western side of this divide, Christian identity had begun to develop a more uniform skin: the proliferation of the diverse Christian groups which marked the Christian landscape in the Roman world of the previous century began slowly to diminish, and a gradual consolidation of certain aspects of Christian identity and dogma emerged, which over time and with the requisite patronage developed into the orthodoxy that characterised the imperially-sponsored Christianity of the fourth century and beyond. By far the most influential factor responsible for hardening Christian identity in the Roman world at this time was the round of persecutions initiated by the emperors Decius (ruling 249–51) and Valerian (253–60), and which characterised the relationship between Christians and the ruling Roman elite during the later part of the third century.[70]

By contrast, on the eastern side of the frontier, religious diversity was very much the order of the day during the early period of Sasanian rule, fostered by a climate of toleration encouraged by their royal predecessors, the Arsacids. Whilst the origins of many religions in Late-Antique Persia are shrouded in legend and mystery, not least with regard to the spread and forms which Christianity took there,[71] we can nevertheless catch a glimpse of an ancient religious pluralism, ironically at the very stage when eirenic attitudes were hardening. Indeed, so pronounced was the presence of other faiths in this period that the Zoroastrian high priest Karder, feeling suitably threatened by competitor traditions,[72] took action under the rule of Vahram II (ruling 276–93) 'to assail in the land [of Iran]' Jews, Buddhists, Hindus, Nazarenes, Christians, Baptisers and 'heretics'.[73] Alongside the Nazarenes, presumably Aramaic-speaking Christians, and the Greek-speaking Christians memorialised in Karder's inscription on the cube-like tower structure at Naqsh-i Rustam near Persepolis, an argument can also be made for the inclusion of two other groups with Christian orientations. The 'Baptisers' may refer to either Elchasaite (see Chapter 2) or Mandaean parties,[74] or perhaps to both, the two being fundamentally distinct from one other in countless areas of belief and practice, although both sharing a ritual concern with the purificatory properties of water. The identification of the 'heretics' is less clear-cut, although the majority of commentators assume that this is a reference to the followers of Mani.[75] The association with the Manichaeans is made on the

---

[70] Lane-Fox 1988, 450; esp. 450–92.

[71] Asmussen 1983, 924–48.

[72] Pourshariati 2008, 328.

[73] From Karder's inscription on the Ka'ba of Zoroaster (*Ka'ba-yi Zardusht*), dated to between 276 and 293; trans. Boyce 1984, 112, taken from the principal edition of the inscription by M. Back, *Die sassanidischen Staatsinschriften. Acta Iranica* 18 (Leiden, 1978). See also Dignas and Winter 2007, 215–16; and the comments by BeDuhn and Mirecki 2007b, 3. An alternative identification for the Heretics in the inscription with 'Mazdean Heretics' is made by Duchesne-Guillemin 1983, 882, and in the appendix of the chapter by Bailey, 907–8.

[74] Buckley 2002, 4–5.

[75] As in Dignas and Winter 2007, 215–16.

basis of what is known about Karder's attempts to effect a Mazdean restoration in Iranian society, and his presence during the condemnation of Mani by the ruling king, Vahram I (ruling 273–6), which led to Mani's imprisonment and eventual death.[76] The term employed to denote heretics (*zndyky*) in Karder's Middle Persian inscription[77] derived from the word used to describe those who propagated an interpretation (*zand* = gloss) of the sacred scriptures of Zoroastrianism (known collectively as the Avesta) which went beyond the revealed word.[78] Thus, the word 'interpreter' was synonymous with 'heretic', and a heretic in the mind of Karder would be one who produced his own exegesis of a canonical passage (i.e., against an 'established' interpretation), although the possible extension of its meaning to designate the Iranian followers of Mani is perhaps an indication that Mani's teachings had stirred the interests, and aroused the chagrin, of the Sasanian religious elite.[79] This, however, begs the question that if indeed the 'Heretics' are Manichaeans, how much of Mani's 'Christian face' was actually shown to Karder, since his assessment of Manichaeans as heretics could not have been based on any perceived deviation from a religion which he did not personally subscribe to. Instead we are left to make the assumption that Mani and/or his followers were perceived by Karder as having caused offence by corrupting some aspect of Zoroastrian teaching. However, as we shall see below in the final section of this chapter dealing with Manichaean sources, Mani did present a work written in Middle Persian (the *Šābuhragān*) for the edification of Shapur I, in which Mani framed his ideas using names and terms drawn from Zoroastrian thought – although the ideas were of an overwhelmingly Christian orientation.[80] Thus, considering the fact that Karder was initiating a revival of ancient Iranian nationalism, in part through a hardening of religious attitudes towards 'outsider' faiths, Mani's attempts to present Christian ideas using the language and religious terminology held in regard by the Sasanian elites very likely led to Mani and his followers being branded as 'heretics'.

What the inscription highlights, aside from the lack of more detailed descriptions of the parties concerned, is the conceptual inadequacy that exists in the application of labels employed by modern commentators to reduce and categorise the different religions and religious identities, especially 'Christian', that existed in Babylonia and Mesopotamia at this time. As the inscription from the Ka'ba indicates, Semitic-speaking groups and peoples evidently had a considerable presence in Sasanian-controlled Mesopotamia, comprising most notably a historically entrenched Jewish population, along with Aramaic-speaking Christians.[81] That Greek-speaking Christians are also likely attested in the inscription is to be expected, given the historical presence of Hellenistic influences in the region – evidenced in the foundation of the city of Seleucia (on the Tigris) – a presence which had most recently been consolidated by

---

[76] See Gardner and Lieu 2004, 79–85.
[77] See Daryaee 2009, 100.
[78] Pourshariati 2008, 341–2.
[79] See Skjærvø 1997.
[80] See Hutter 1992, 139.
[81] See S.N.C. Lieu 1992, 33–5.

Shapur's settling of prisoners from eastern Roman cities, including Antioch, in Mesopotamia and other Sasanian-controlled provinces during his successful period of military campaigning in the middle of the third century.[82] That the term used by Karder to describe such Christians (*klstyd'n*, from Syriac *krystyn*[83]) had also been used to designate followers of the second-century Christian from Sinope named Marcion is significant, but cannot lead us to conclude categorically that the settled Romans were Marcionite Christians. The relatively late date for the inscription also means that it is not possible to offer any more precise an image of the status and character of those Christian-oriented groups who may have been active in Mesopotamia during the formative period of Mani's teachings, including his initial success in attracting followers, at least half a century earlier.[84]

Whilst we are certainly better informed about the religious context for Mani's formative years than we were before the publication in the 1970s and 1980s of a Greek Manichaean biography of Mani (the so-called *Cologne Mani Codex* [*CMC*]: see Chapter 2), what is still lacking is detailed evidence for the historical context of Christianity in Mesopotamia and Babylonia during the third century. Furthermore, what is also little understood is the interaction of these Semitic, Greek and Iranian cultural forms (as evidenced in Karder's inscription), in particular within a religious context; and the extent to which the interaction between them assisted in the emergence of forms of religious expression that both ancient and modern commentators – rather clumsily, but out of habit and necessity – refer to in exclusive, monocultural terms as being, for instance, either 'Jewish', 'Christian' or 'Zoroastrian'. The importance of the evidence pertaining to Mani and his teachings is therefore crucial in this regard, since it is in a range of Manichaean writings that we witness the 'cultural triangulation' of Semitic, Greek and Iranian influences.[85] Mani's ideas appear to be the outcome of the diverse religious and cultural forms existing in the region of Mesopotamia during the third century, and in one sense Manichaeism occupies the historical void associated with Late-Antique west Asia by allowing us to see what one type of Christianity looked like in the region at this time.

However, it is our subsequent lack of knowledge of these separate religions and the way in which they interacted with each other, principally the nature and status of Christianity in Mesopotamia, which has encouraged the dependency in Manichaean studies on terms such as 'gnostic' or 'syncretic' to describe not only Mani's religious ambitions and activities, but also the religious environment from which Mani and his followers emerged. Whilst the thesis published by the historian and theologian Walter Bauer in 1934 has opened the eyes of many commentators to the diverse forms which Christianity took in west Asia ('the oriental danger zone': Bauer, p. 230) during the first three centuries, Mani's teachings continue to be regarded as something more than, or indeed other than, Christian. Nevertheless, as Jason BeDuhn and Paul Mirecki have so perceptively

---

[82] Dignas and Winter 2007, 254–9.
[83] Following BeDuhn and Mirecki 2007b, 3.
[84] See Tardieu 2008, 9.
[85] BeDuhn and Mirecki 2007b, 6.

declared: 'Mani worked within the modes of expression available to him in [a Mesopotamian] environment; he knew no others. The limits of what he could think and say and do were set by those conditions.'[86] These 'modes of expression' were partly consolidated in the Mesopotamian Christianity encountered by Mani as revealed by the *CMC*, which he sought to practise in a committed manner. Indeed, rather than the labels of 'Gnosticism' or 'Syncretism' being used to characterise the endeavours of Mani, the evidence would seem to suggest that Mani be most appropriately thought of as a reforming Christian, who sought to reclaim a more ancient and more authentic form of religious belief than the one that he had encountered during the formative years of his life.

And yet arguably the most problematical label in Manichaean studies continues to be the term 'Manichaean' itself, in the sense that it obscures the original cultural nexus from which Mani's ideas emerged, together with impeding a fuller appreciation of what those ideas were all about. The essence of this problem is that a descriptor developed by Mani's ancient Christian opponents has been and continues to be retrospectively applied to describe Mani's teachings, and the systematisation of those teachings by his church during the late-antique period. The connotation of 'Manichaean' with the naming strategies of ancient heresiology, and in particular the avowed aim of patristic authors to impugn the Manichaean interpretation of the elements regarded as so essential to their own 'Christian' identity – e.g., christological definition, scriptural exegesis and apostolicity – should make us stand up and take notice every time it is used. The alignment of 'Manichaean' with legal definitions which sought to crimi-nalise theological error – i.e., heresy – towards the end of the fourth century, in relation to the legal codification of Christian belief under the Roman emperor Theodosius I and his successors, should make us doubly aware.[87] Indeed, it is not that the 'othering' significance of 'Manichaean', the ultimate purpose of which was 'to accuse someone of being a Manichaean [which] served as a well-known smear tactic',[88] is the sole difficulty raised by the term; rather, the perpetuation of 'Manichaean' or 'Manichaeism' has furthermore suggested to both ancient and modern commentators the absolute novelty of Mani's teachings which has not only freed him from being viewed within a historical paradigm where formative influences remained to anchor his teachings within a continuous tradition, but has also encouraged the related assumption that Mani's teachings appeared fully formed, systematised and institutionally-implemented from the very earliest days when Mani began to disseminate his ideas in Mesopotamia and beyond. None of these rather crude and misguided assumptions would be tolerated in modern research into any other ancient Christian tradition, but they continue to be so whenever Manichaeism is discussed in general introductions to the religions of Late Antiquity, and also occasionally in supposed specialist treatments of the subject. That we have been able to demonstrate the ancient polemical roots of very many of these concerns illustrates the longevity of the patristic defamation of Manichaeism.

---

[86] BeDuhn and Mirecki 2007b, 6.
[87] See Lim 2008, 150f.
[88] Lim 2008, 164.

And so, as we shall see in the final section of this chapter on Manichaean writings, clearly distinguishable lines of continuity proceed from the Christian influences acting on Mani into the formulation and systematisation of his thought. Whilst this study, therefore, does not propose an alternative to either 'Manichaean' or 'Manichaeism' as descriptors for the historical progression of the teachings of Mani through the centuries, it should be evident that a case can be made for regarding Manichaeism as one example of an ancient Mesopotamian form of Christianity.

5. The Re-emergence of Manichaean Writings

The foregoing discussion has focused on the situation in third-century Mesopotamia as a way of introducing some of the considerations involved in studying the teachings of Mani. However, one of the main considerations involved in studying Manichaeism is the awareness that these teachings were systematised – i.e., transformed into a religion with an institutional structure – over time, and in historical circumstances different from those encountered by Mani during the initial formulation of his own theology. This observation is particularly important when considering the literary sources for Manichaeism, both those which emerge from within the Manichaean church, and those which relate valuable information about Manichaean thought and practice although contained in the replies of Christian heresiologists.

The claim that the study of Manichaeism has been transformed by the discovery of texts written by Manichaeans is now a commonplace of the discipline. There are four main literary discoveries generally highlighted in modern Manichaean studies, all of which constitute textual encounters with long-forgotten Manichaean writings which, because of their impact on shaping perceptions of the religion, take precedence over other discoveries which are nevertheless remarkable (for instance, the Late-Antique Latin Manichaean ecclesiological treatise found in 1918 at Tebessa in Algeria[89]). These textual encounters have slowly revealed the dynamism of the religion, by illustrating the linguistic and geographical diffusion of Mani's teachings, from Narmouthis (Medinet Madi) and Kellis – and possibly also Lycopolis – in Roman Egypt, to the cities of Turfan and Dunhuang in the heartland of central Asia. Furthermore, developments in textual and philological sciences have also led to other significant intellectual contributions in the recovery of Manichaean writings from the midst of the polemical literature of the religion's opponents. What follows, then, is a brief survey of these contributions, and their impact on the shaping of the discipline of Manichaean studies in this and the previous century. In line with the theme of this chapter, and mindful of the three areas identified above as revealing of the Christian orientation of the religion in its late-antique context, the discussion here will seek to highlight the preoccupations of Mani and his followers with the concerns of a 'Christian culture'.

---

[89] See Stein 2004; portions of the text may be found in English translation by Gardner and Lieu 2004, 268–72.

Building on the important contributions of scholars to the burgeoning study of Manichaeism in the nineteenth century – foremost among them being the edition by Gustav Flügel of the entry on Mani and his teachings in the tenth-century work the *Fihrist* by the Muslim encyclopaedist al-Nadim (see Chapter 2) – a series of excavations in central Asia at the turn of the twentieth century brought to light a diverse range of Manichaean writings – found in highly fragmented states – along with examples of Manichaean artwork. Recovered from the cities of Turfan and Dunhuang, which lie on the so-called 'Silk Road', a network of trading routes linking China with the West, the texts cover a range of theological, liturgical, didactic and historical concerns of the religion.[90] The writings represent a literary treasure-trove which had been collected and consolidated by the ruling Uighur Turks who, as prominent converts to the religion in the eighth century, had settled in the region during the ninth century and sponsored a network of Manichaean monastic foundations that were responsible for the production of the texts.

The Manichaean literature from Turfan is written in a range of Iranian (Parthian, Middle Persian, Sogdian), Turkic and Chinese languages, and research on the writings has spawned its own academic discipline, something akin to a 'Turfanology'.[91] Taken collectively, the texts illuminate the Iranian and central Asian manifestations of Manichaeism which, over a prolonged period of time, experienced a somewhat chequered history.[92] However, the difficulties involved in creating a grand narrative of Manichaean history and thought from such a thematically and linguistically diverse range of texts is roundly acknowledged, as demonstrated in the judgements of Werner Sundermann across three major articles ('Studies of the Church-Historical Literature of the Iranian Manichaeans') in the German-language journal *Altorientalische Forschungen* (1986–7), with reference to the Manichaeans' own historical accounts of their origins. Although appearing to provide invaluable evidence for the earliest personalities of the late-antique Manichaean church and their activities in service of Mani – including important depictions of Mani's own personality and activities – the historical fragments in the Turfan collection are, as with most other accounts of the significant past, constructed by later writers in order to present a particular impression of Manichaean origins relevant to their own specific circumstances: thus, *reader beware.*[93]

Painstaking reconstructive work on the fragments from Turfan has produced incredible results, an instance of which is the re-emergence of one of Mani's own most controversial writings. Both the ancient and modern historiographies of Manichaeism stress Mani's self-conscious literality, his marked desire to leave behind written accounts of his teachings in order to avoid the fate of other prophets and visionaries, who, having failed to write down their concerns,

---

[90] An excellent introduction to the discovery of the central Asian texts can be found in the preface to Klimkeit 1993, in which is also to be found a collection of Turfan texts in English translation.

[91] Tremblay 2001, 9.

[92] See S.N.C. Lieu 1992, 219–42.

[93] References to the articles by Sundermann can be found in this book's bibliography.

condemned their teachings to oblivion.[94] Mani is traditionally credited with seven writings – regarded as his canon – all composed in his native eastern Aramaic dialect, better known as Syriac (see Chapter 3): however, not one of these writings survive intact, existing now only in various fragmentary states, often only recoverable as quotations from the writings of his opponents. However, one work not included in this seven-fold canon has since resurfaced, certainly not in its entirety but in a sufficiently complete state to enable one to appreciate some of Mani's ideas and to witness the interplay of various cultural influences at work in the communication of those ideas. The genesis of the work in question, entitled the *Šābuhragān*, emerged out of Mani's contacts with the Sasanian royal court, likely sometime during the years between 240 and 250.[95] Beyond the contents of the work, its significance lies in the fact that Mani wrote the work in Middle Persian as opposed to his apparently preferred literary language of Syriac, which has led to its characterisation as a work intended to appeal to the inquisitive sensibilities of the ruling monarch, Shapur I, an intention also evident in the title given to the work (i.e., dedicated to Shapur). The *Šābuhragān* appears not to have been known beyond Iran and central Asia: it is unattested in the majority of Manichaean canonical formulations of his writings, evidence for which is drawn predominantly from western Manichaean sources.[96]

For these and other reasons the *Šābuhragān* is seen as the anomaly of Mani's writings, although the real nub of the matter relates to its contents. In the presentation of his understanding of the world, and with an especial focus on the divine judgement preceding its end – for this reason it is frequently, although incorrectly, referred to as Mani's 'eschatological work' (Gk *eschaton* = 'the last time') – Mani conveyed his ideas using the names of the gods and demons of the Zoroastrian pantheon, including for example Mithras (Mihr), Ohrmazd and Ahriman. These 'iranising tendencies' in the *Šābuhragān*, explainable in part by the work's intended audience, have understandably added to the perceived Iranian origin for Mani's theology. Furthermore, it has provided seemingly incontrovertible evidence for the judgement that Mani was the 'arch-syncretist', tailoring his teachings to whichever audience he was appealing to at any given time: and so, concerning the *Šābuhragān*, it is said that,

> Mani was able to present Iranian concepts and traditions, including the dualistic ones, in a totally new form, which enabled him to implant the belief that what he was proclaiming was the Zoroastrian faith of the fathers, perhaps modified on Zurvanitic lines. This was basically the same as what he propounded in other works, written in an Aramaic dialect, where he adapted his doctrine to syncretistic religions including Syriac Christianity.[97]

Here again, the language (and politics) of syncretism is in evidence, in the observation concerning Mani's intentional borrowing from other religions and cultures

---

[94] See Stroumsa 2009, 36–8.
[95] See Reck 2010.
[96] See the comments by Reeves 1992, 10–13.
[97] Colpe 1983, 857.

in the service of propagating his teachings. However, it is surely the case that any religion which has ambitions to range across cultural frontiers – be they large in scale, i.e., 'transnational', or small, i.e., 'sectarian' – necessarily borrows from and adapts the linguistic and cultural apparatus of its target groups: this is the act of translation writ large. The prevalence of this manner of interpretation in the study of Manichaeism, especially in relation to the 'anomalous' *Šābuhragān*, has prevented commentators from appreciating the most striking features of the text.

The *Šābuhragān* reveals Mani as first and foremost a religious thinker and biblical exegete, steeped in Jewish-Christian theological and scriptural traditions. In the opening chapter of the *Šābuhragān*, preserved in a later Arabic work by al-Biruni (see Chapter 2), Mani located himself and his teachings at the final point in a line of divinely-commissioned apostles: a tradition that formed part of the theology of the community in which Mani was raised, the so-called Elchasaites, who looked to a cast of biblical forefathers as the divine revealers of teachings to their ancestors, which in turn formed the basis of their own traditions and beliefs (see Chapter 2). In the *Šābuhragān*, Mani, possibly as a reaction against his Elchasaite upbringing, extended the range of this succession to include figures who were unlikely to have been acknowledged by his former Jewish-Christian coreligionists as apostles or prophets:[98]

> Wisdom and deeds have always from time to time been brought to mankind by the messengers of God. So in one age they have been brought by the messenger, called Buddha, to India, in another by [Zoroaster] to Persia, in another by Jesus to the West. Thereupon this revelation has come down, this prophecy in this last age through me, Mani, the messenger of the God of truth to Babylonia (*The Chronology of Ancient Nations* 207; trans. C.E. Sachau 1879, 190).

Whilst Mani appears to have set his teachings within a Babylonian context, it is apparent from other preserved fragments (M5794 I and M5761), which 'probably derived from'[99] the *Šābuhragān*, that he also expressed ambitions of universalism for his revelations.[100] The 'improvements' that Mani was claiming to make to existing religions outlined in these other fragments – including more robust ecclesiastical structures, and the completion of existing teachings and revelations that had remained unfulfilled until his arrival – formed a section from the *Šābuhragān*'s opening chapter, in addition to the portion cited above from al-Biruni. The delineation of Mani's improvements, the things which would be 'above and better than the other religions of the ancients' (trans. I. Gardner and S.N.C. Lieu 2004, 109) – all of which had been established by Mani's apostolic predecessors – formed an important tradition in later Manichaean writings, for instance in a later section of the Coptic work *The Chapters*,[101] and constituted an intrinsic part of Manichaean identity as the culminant religious tradition.

---

[98] Tardieu 2008, 13–19.
[99] Gardner and Lieu 2004, 109.
[100] Fragments collected and translated in Gardner and Lieu 2004, 109.
[101] English translation in Gardner and Lieu 2004, 265–8.

However, arguably too much has been made of these claims, with many commentators seeing in them Mani's blueprint for a 'ready-made' religion. The imperial audience for the *Šābuhragān* almost certainly encouraged Mani to make the boldest claims possible for himself and his teachings, in anticipation of deepening the manner of patronage extended to him and his followers by Shapur: thus the theological imperialism of the *Šābuhragān* should be seen as complementing the imperial authority of Shapur. The work itself is an eloquent vehicle for Mani's ideas, focusing on the mechanics of the universe's creation – as related in fragments M98/99 I and M7980–M7984 identified by Manfred Hutter as belonging to the work – and its eventual decline and collapse, preceded by a final judgement. As Hutter has shown, correspondences exist between themes in Mani's cosmogony and cosmology, and those found in Jewish apocryphal writings, from the so-called Enochic tradition, which has reinforced the view that Mani used Jewish literature in a fairly extensive fashion, as an inspiration and guide for many aspects of his theology.[102]

The eschatological portions of the *Šābuhragān* further reveal Mani's talents as a biblical exegete.[103] The focus for the final section of the work was the nature of the eschaton in Manichaean thought and the role of the divine figure, the Xradesahryazd (Pahlavi: 'The God of the World of Wisdom', i.e., Jesus 'the Splendour'[104]) in judging souls, an elaborate scene laid out by Mani on the basis of his adaptation of Jesus' teachings on the Last Judgement from chapters 25 and 26 of Matthew's gospel. At a basic level, the role of the gospel passages and allusions in the work was to provide support for the ecclesiastical structures of Mani's religion, and in particular the lives of the highest ranking adherents, the Elect, whose ascetic way of life was only made possible because of the alms provided by the Hearers (see Chapter 4). Therefore, those who will be saved are 'the religious ones', namely the Elect, and their 'helpers', namely the Hearers. Thus, by citing and then adapting the gospel text, the foundational, communal structure of the Manichaean church *looked as if* it derived from the gospel. However, with the opening chapter of the work in mind, 'On the Coming of the Apostle', Mani as the final apostle was also providing a clear demonstration of the way in which his teachings brought to fruition the teachings of his predecessor Jesus, as related for instance in the gospel. As Mani noted in this fragmentary portion from the work's early chapters, the ways in which his apostolate completed previous revelations – 'all writings, all wisdom and all parables of the previous religion when they to this (religion of mine came …)'[105] – meant that Mani felt justified in placing himself at the centre of the Christian gospel, and that rather than seeing himself as adapting those writings, he was instead completing their true religious meaning: in this sense, therefore, the final apostle is regarded as offering the definitive interpretation of all scripture.[106]

---

[102] Hutter 1992, 135–9; the cosmogonic fragments from the work are collected and translated in Klimkeit 1993, 225–35.

[103] English translation in Klimkeit 1993, 242–7.

[104] Franzmann 2003, 103–4.

[105] Trans. S. Lieu, in Gardner and Lieu 2004, 109.

[106] See Baker-Brian 2009, 103–6.

Whilst the *Šābuhragān* presents evidence of Mani's own teachings at a relatively early stage of their development, the next major discovery of Manichaean texts in the twentieth century from Medinet Madi in the Fayuum in Egypt revealed writings (in total seven *codices*) from a religious tradition that was at a reasonably advanced stage of its cultural and institutional development. Discovered initially in 1929, the codices from Medinet Madi (also occasionally referred to by its ancient name, Narmouthis) are works written in Coptic, the language of non-Greek-speaking Christians in Late-Antique Egypt.[107] The collection represents in the main an astonishing body of Manichaean material in translation, with many individual texts having originally been composed in Syriac.[108] That the collection contained works of a devotional and liturgical nature, for instance a codex of Homilies[109] and a codex of Psalms,[110] has been construed as providing evidence of a living and well-organised faith. Many of the writings represented in the Coptic collection likely emerged in the post-Mani era, during the late third century in a Mesopotamian environment, at a time when the nascent Manichaean communities there were experiencing persecution at the hands of the Sasanian authorities.[111] A number of homilies and psalms in the collection make reference to the repeated sufferings of Manichaeans at this time, experiences that contributed to the development of a strong sense of Late-Antique Manichaeans as forming a 'church of martyrs', and that also influenced meditation on the identity of Mani as the religion's prototypical martyr, who died in the dungeons of Vahram I for the Manichaean cause.[112]

That literature of this type found favour in Roman Egypt of the fourth century may in part be explained by the intermittent persecutions experienced by Egyptian Manichaeans during that century, this time at the hands of both pagan and Christian emperors.[113] Manichaean communities in Egypt also held great store by their translations of Mani's own letters, a collection of which was unearthed in the Medinet Madi cache, although the great majority of leaves have subsequently been lost – a fate also experienced by another Coptic codex which apparently told the story of the early history of the religion, a sort of Manichaean Acts of the Apostles (the so-called *Acts codex*).[114]

Arguably the best known, and certainly most frequently cited, codex from the Medinet Madi collection remains *The Chapters* (*Kephalaia*). The work survives in two separate codices, one entitled 'The Kephalaia of the Teacher' (housed in Berlin), the other 'The Kephalaia of the Wisdom of my Lord Mani' (housed

---

[107] See the introductory comments by Gardner and Lieu 1996, 148–54.

[108] See Lieu 1994, 65–78.

[109] The definitive English translation of the Coptic Manichaean homilies is by Pedersen 2006. A selection of homilies in translation is also available in Gardner and Lieu 2004.

[110] Whilst improved editions and German translations of the Manichaean Psalm book have emerged by Wurst 1996 and Richter 1998, the English translation by Allberry 1938 remains valuable. Again, translations of Coptic Psalms are available in Gardner and Lieu 2004.

[111] See S.N.C. Lieu 1992, 106–15.

[112] See the English translations by Sarah Clackson of select Coptic homilies that make reference to the persecutions of Vahram II, in Gardner and Lieu 2004, 79–108.

[113] See Brown 1969, and S.N.C. Lieu 1992, 192–218.

[114] For further discussion, see Robinson 1992.

in Dublin). The 'Berlin' *Kephalaia* has been edited by a number of scholars over the years,[115] and a sizeable proportion of it has also been translated into English by Iain Gardner (1995), with a recent additional English translation of pages not handled by Gardner in 1995 appearing in the source volume edited by Gardner and Samuel Lieu from 2004 (154; 226–9; 265–8). The 'Dublin' *Kephalaia* remains its poor relation, the poor condition of the manuscript making editorial work on the text a great challenge; however, a recent notification in the Newsletter of the *International Association of Manichaean Studies* (no. 23. 2008–9) has indicated that an international project is underway to begin the editing of the Dublin codex. Reference and citations to *The Chapters* in this book are taken exclusively from the 'Berlin' *Kephalaia*.

The Chapters is a work which in the past has been ascribed to Mani himself, although the Coptic codex belongs to a later stage in Manichaeism's history: '... the product of later theological developments and elaborations that seek to respond to a wide array of specific questions, many of which appear to be in rooted in ambiguities found in the [Manichaean] canon.'[116] The work resolves by systematising certain ambiguities in Manichaean theology, in such a way that Mani himself is portrayed as providing solutions to questions raised by his disciples – which may perhaps have been the case in the transmission of early versions of individual *chapters* originating from Mani and his immediate circle – that were then gathered together and edited to form an authoritative work sometime during the early part of the fourth century.[117] As the incorporation of *The Chapters* into the Medinet Madi collection demonstrates, Mani remained very much the central figure of authority for Egyptian Manichaeans, held in high regard because of his own sense of self-identity as an apostle of Jesus Christ.[118]

The determination of valid lines of apostolic succession is also a major concern of a 'biography' of Mani written in Greek – although originally a work composed in Syriac – that dates from sometime during the fourth or possibly the fifth century. The work, which appeared in Cologne towards the end of the 1960s, likely derived from ancient Lycopolis in Upper Egypt, an acknowledged centre of Manichaeism in Late Antiquity. Devoured by modern commentators for its disclosure of precious information about Mani's early life and upbringing among Christians with Jewish leanings in third-century southern Mesopotamia (the Elchasaites), the *Cologne Mani Codex* (henceforth abbreviated to *CMC*) is an example of one of the smallest codices from antiquity (measuring 38mm × 45mm, being roughly the same size as a passport photograph), intended by its creator(s) to be worn upon the body as an amulet.[119] The codex

---

[115] Polotsky and Böhlig 1940; Böhlig 1966; Funk 1999; 2000.

[116] Pettipiece 2009, 9.

[117] See Pettipiece 2009, 12–13.

[118] For an English translation of *The Chapters* (*The Kephalaia of the Teacher*), see Gardner 1995; selections are also available in Gardner and Lieu 2004.

[119] An English translation of the *CMC* by J.M. Lieu and S.N.C. Lieu is included in Gardner and Lieu 2004, 47–73. The *editio princeps* of the *CMC* is edited by Henrichs and Koenen across a number of articles from 1975 to 1982. The critical edition of the work is edited by Koenen and Römer 1988.

carries the title 'On the Birth of His Body' as a running heading throughout the work: the title's significance has thus far eluded modern commentators on the work, although the relationship between Mani and his spiritual persona, his Twin, in the narrative of the *CMC* may be suggestive of the belief that Mani the apostle enjoyed a prenatal divine existence, which was then brought to an end by his 'incarnation' in bodily form, in order that he could accomplish his appointed task as the final apostle of humankind. Thus 'the birth of (Mani's) body' appears to refer to the beginning of his teachings (i.e., with his birth), and the beginnings of the institution of his church.

A detailed examination of the *CMC* will be provided in Chapter 2 of this book, although it is worth noting at this stage the extent to which Mani is portrayed in the work as the rightful successor to the apostolic legacy of Jesus, who is referred to repeatedly in the *Codex* as 'the Saviour'. Whilst the *CMC* was discovered in a very poor state of repair, with the final sections of the work largely illegible,[120] its readers nevertheless catch glimpses of a religious teacher whose life was styled in imitation of the principal figures of the Christian tradition: thus, Mani is seen imitating the confrontational zeal and ascetical ambitions of Jesus as portrayed in the Christian gospels; and Mani's desire to devote the remainder of his life to propagating his teachings, as related in the *Codex*'s later sections, is evidently patterned on representations of Paul of Tarsus's travels during the first century AD.

Furthermore, the *CMC* portrays Mani as establishing a theological association between himself and his apostolic predecessors Jesus and Paul, through an awareness (a 'knowing about'; cf. *gnosis*) that there is only one authentic religious tradition which demands from its followers not simply an exclusive adherence to ritual practices, but a purity of thought and action; teachings which the *CMC* credits Jesus as having made known during the time of his apostolate. And so Mani, confronting the practices of the Elchasaites, gives voice to a statement relating the contents of his revelations to his co-religionists: 'the purity [of which Jesus spoke] ... is the purity through knowledge; it is the separation of light from darkness, of death from life, and living waters from turbid ones; so (you) may know (that) each ... from the others, and you (will keep) the commands of the saviour (so that) he may redeem (your) soul from destruction and from perdition'.[121]

Whilst the basis for much of what is narrated by the *CMC* takes place in the setting of a Jewish-Christian baptist community in Mesopotamia, the representation of which was partially imagined in order to accommodate the image of Mani that the *Codex* wanted to create, the final discovery of significance for Manichaean studies provides us with a view of an actual historic community of Manichaean believers from Late-Antique Egypt. A collection of various ancient texts came to light in the 1990s during excavations in the Dakhleh Oasis at the

Remarkable images of leaves from the *CMC* may be viewed online at the website of the Cologne papyri collection: www.uni-koeln.de/phil-fak/ifa/NRWakademie/papyrologie/Manikodex/mani.html

[120] See Römer 1994.

[121] *CMC* 84.12–85.1; trans. J.M. Lieu and S.N.C. Lieu in Gardner and Lieu 2004, 61.

site of the modern village of Ismant el-Kharab. In Late Antiquity, the village was known as Kellis, and one specific site within the archaeological complex – referred to as House 3 – contained a sizeable cache of papyri and wooden boards which, when restored and translated, turned out to be of Manichaean provenance, dating from sometime between the mid and late fourth century.[122] The texts, in Coptic, Greek and bilingual fragments of Syriac and Coptic, have been gathered by their editors into two main divisions: literary texts, comprising psalms and prayers;[123] and documentary texts, comprising in the main letters exchanged across Egypt between members of a Manichaean community with its roots in Kellis.[124] The emergence of the Kellis material is a landmark in the history of Late-Antique Manichaeism, as the discovery of the texts at an ancient site provides for the first time a situational context for the activities of Manichaeans in the Roman world. Whilst work on the Kellis material is ongoing, the edited texts have revealed that the Manichaeans of the Dakhleh Oasis subscribed to a complex range of religious attitudes and identities (see above), which were nevertheless reconciled in the teachings and claims of Mani.[125]

Manichaeism remains one of the most controversial religions from antiquity, with modern investigations commonly seeking to apprehend the 'essence' of the religion. Whilst regarding Manichaeism according to a range of terminological labels assists in our ability to comment on and categorise the teachings of Mani and the history of his church, the fact of the matter is that whatever term we choose to apply generally falls short of offering a complete explanation for the origins and history of Manichaeism in Late Antiquity. The historical evidence from which commentators build their interpretations of Manichaeism is diverse, emerging from different periods in the history of the religion and composed by a host of different writers in a range of different languages. For this reason, a uniform impression of Manichaeism is difficult to achieve. However, certain aspects of Manichaeism appear to have remained constant throughout its long history: some commentators prioritise states of stability as being most evident in the ritual practices performed by Manichaeans,[126] others in the core of Manichaean ecclesiastical identity that was linked to the original sense of self posited by Mani in the translation of his teachings to his immediate followers. However, even in this regard, what we think we know about Mani as a historical figure should also be scrutinised, since his own sense of identity was communicated by him and by his early followers in literary texts that were not intended to be received as if presenting either a dispassionate or an accurate portrayal of his personality or his immediate environment. Chapter 2 will discuss these concerns.

---

[122] See the comments in Gardner and Lieu 1996, 161–8.

[123] For editions and English translations of the literary texts, see Gardner 1996 and 2007a.

[124] For editions and English translations of the documentary texts, see Gardner, Alcock and Funk 1999; see also Gardner 1997, 77–94.

[125] A selection of translated material from the Kellis archive may be found in Gardner and Lieu 2004, 259–81.

[126] BeDuhn 2002, *passim*.

Chapter 2

Lives of Mani

1. Introduction: Religious Biography in the Formation of Manichaean Identity

This chapter discusses the life of Mani not only in terms of the fundamental components of his biography – e.g., his family background, his early life in a Mesopotamian religious community and his later achievements as an apostle – but it also raises some issues surrounding the role of biography as a literary genre in the religious landscape of Late Antiquity. With regard to knowing about Mani 'the man' we are especially well informed, with sources that imparted details of his life appearing at almost every stage of Manichaeism's re-emergence into the modern age, via the discovery of writings from the long-abandoned towns, dwellings and caves of the ancient world. Arabic sources supplying details of his life have been available to modern European scholars since the nineteenth century. A number of the fragments and texts unearthed in Turfan are 'biographical', supplying important evidence, for instance, about Mani's 'networking abilities' in gaining support for himself and his followers from powerful patrons during their early exploratory journeys (trans. H.-J. Klimkeit 1993, 201–21). The Greek life of Mani, the *Cologne Mani Codex* (*CMC*) introduced in Chapter 1, provides what is arguably the fullest picture of Mani's formative years – his emergence as an apostle of light – known to date. There is no shortage of information illuminating the life and times of this late-antique Mesopotamian teacher, since the writing of biography represented one way in which Manichaeans honoured the memory of Mani.

However, accounts of Mani's life were also written by his opponents. Biography was therefore not only used to discredit Mani himself, but by challenging his achievements his opponents also sought to undermine the credibility of the religion based on his teachings. The biography of Mani in the *Acts of Archelaus*, an early fourth-century anti-Manichaean work, was enormously influential in memorialising Mani the heresiarch; a portrayal that drew on established literary templates for rubbishing the reputations of public figures. And yet the devotional biographies of Mani composed by his followers were no less contrived in their portrayal of Mani than those that were hostile to him. They served in particular to transpose their own sense of communal belief and identity onto their imagined sense of Mani's 'personality', thereby highlighting the fact that ancient biography almost always primarily reflected the immediate concerns of the author, rather than a desire to impart in an uncomplicated manner the 'facts' of the subject's life.

2. Mani the Unknowable?

It has become something of a convention for modern studies of Manichaeism to contain at least one chapter entitled 'The Life of Mani' (or variations thereof).[1] Such biographical treatments share an almost identical template, their main concern being to particularise – by reconstructing on the basis of evidence offered by the ancient sources – the life of Mani from birth to death, with an emphasis on the emergence of Mani's religious sensibilities, his travels and exploits in the cause of his message, and his relations with the powerful kings and princes of his day. The presence of a biographical component in Manichaean studies is certainly not inappropriate, as the evidence presented by the ancient sources indicates that Mani commonly resided at the very centre of his followers' concerns. In a liturgical Bema text from the Medinet Madi collection of Psalms, performed during the commemoration of Mani's life and death (styled by the Manichaean community as a martyrdom) at which his presence was symbolised by the placing of his portrait on a seat (Gk *bēma*) of judgement,[2] Manichaeans spoke aloud the following doxology:

> Glory to thee, our father Manichaios, the glorious one,
> (the joy of) the gods ..., the entire remission of sins,
> the preaching of life, the ambassador of they that are on high;
> glory to your *bēma*, your seat that gives ...[3]

In theological terms, both Mani himself and later Manichaean writers dwelt on formulating an understanding of Mani's centrality to the religion, in a manner which conveyed his identity relative to his place within the religion's dominant model of prophetology (see below). Manichaeism would appear therefore to have been a religious tradition in which the role of prophetic personalities was essential to the overall meaning of the religion's teachings.

Given this ancient concentration of interest in Mani's life, the modern writer seeking to present a biography of the prophet from southern Mesopotamia is presented with an extensive range of ancient sources that seemingly offer a treasure-trove of information about Mani, his family, his childhood, his influences and his activities and achievements. Within Manichaeism, there is a variety of largely fragmentary historical, homiletical and hagiographical materials that contain descriptions of Mani at various stages in his life, and that are of a varying historical character and quality. Accounts from non-Manichaean works,

---

[1] See esp. Puech 1949, 15–57; Klíma 1962; Widengren 1965, 23–42; Ort 1967; Decret 1974, 44–71; Merkelbach 1986; Tardieu 2008, 1–30.

[2] Klimkeit 1993, 145.

[3] Psalms of the Bema 222. 30–33; trans. I. Gardner and S.N.C. Lieu 2004, 240; an earlier version of part of the same psalm was unearthed in Kellis, see Gardner 1996, 33–41.

frequently hostile to the religion, may also be of use for biographical purposes if handled appropriately. Furthermore, certain Manichaean works have also been received as if they were intended incontestably by their ancient authors to serve as biographies of Mani: notable in this regard is the modern reception of the *CMC* utilised as the foundational text for supplying all that is essential in drawing modern biographical portraits of Mani. In such treatments, Mani is most frequently referred to as the institutor of a brand-new religion, the founder of the faith carrying his eponym. Influenced by dominant patterns in modern approaches to life-writing, Mani's biographers have also chosen to discuss this late-antique Mesopotamian by way of exposing his 'personality'.[4] However, should a modern biography of Mani make a claim to present a positivist account of its subject – i.e., the details of Mani's life as being incontestable – we probably have reasonable grounds to think of such an account as being somewhat misjudged. Evidently there is no deliberate intention on the part of authors to mislead readers of such studies: disciplinary fashion has dictated that, in the study of ancient religions, at least some consideration should be given to providing a biographical account of those individuals regarded as being instrumental in the formation or reformation of ancient traditions. Indeed, this impulse has proved to be especially dominant in the study of Late Antiquity, where certainly since the late 1960s an increasing interest in the ancient lives of both pagan and Christian sainted men and women has become apparent, particularly in defining and 'decoding' the symbolism and significance of those lives for ancient writers and their audiences.[5]

Indeed, as such research has indicated, modern biographers seeking to write the lives of figures from antiquity must be mindful of the problems that are likely to arise when ancient sources are handled as if they are 'treasure-troves' of information. A starting point in identifying some of these issues, therefore, is the need to recognise the cultural and intellectual trends which have come to dominate the contemporary composition of biography. Both popular and academic instances of 'life-writing' combine a number of elements which frequently stand in contradiction to one another: for instance, the striving on the part of the author to achieve a degree of objectivity in the presentation of a subject; an attitude of impartiality in the treatment of the life in hand; and the desire to explore the formation of personality and its psychological development.[6] It is in relation to these concerns that the aims and ambitions of modern biography begin to rub up against the concerns of ancient biography, which were really very different. Biography in its modern form is now very much a distinct genre in its own right, governed as we have seen by its own rules and conventions: in its ancient form, however, biography existed as a genre only in so far as it fulfilled a variety of literary and rhetorical functions, having been composed 'for praise or blame … for exemplary, moral purposes … for didactic or information … to preserve the memory of a great man … or simply to entertain.'[7] Such ambitions

[4] For instance, Williams Jackson 1938; Ort 1967; also Widengren 1965, 135–44.
[5] Cf. Dillon 2006.
[6] See Baker-Brian 2007.
[7] Burridge 2006, 38.

are indeed reducible to one basic observation: in ancient biography little else mattered other than the relationship which existed between the intention of the writer – i.e., the purpose which his work served – and the portrayal of his subject: thus, the intention of the ancient biographer is both discernable in and conveyed via the portrait of his subject's life.

From a modern biographer's perspective, this consideration is therefore likely to seem both foreign and unsettling. In the case of Mani the obvious implication is that the 'historical Mani' becomes unknowable, since following this line of interpretation the 'personality' we encounter in the ancient literature is the medium through which the writer's intentions were realised. Often this may be overcome in those exceptional instances when we have an ancient person who is able 'to speak for himself' through the survival of some sort of textual artefact, be it an inscription, a collection of aphorisms, a selection of letters, or an 'autobiography': however with regard to the latter, historians should be mindful that ancient 'autobiography' is no more likely to reveal the author *as he actually was* – what he thought and did – than ancient life-writing may be expected to convey an impartial treatment of its subject.[8] Nevertheless, this has not prevented modern biographers from handling ancient 'autobiography' as if it provided a window onto the private thoughts and actions of the individual: by far the best example in this instance is the *Confessions* of Augustine (d. 430), the Catholic bishop of Hippo in North Africa, which exerts a considerable influence on the shape taken by modern biographies of this apostate Manichaean, in addition to the material provided by his other writings which are quite astonishing with regard to both the quantity and the variety of material. The adoption of such material, however, is not problem-free.[9]

Indeed, Mani himself, in certain writings, disclosed 'personal details'. Alongside statements in the *Šābuhragān* and the *Living Gospel*, which shed light on Mani's own sense of identity as an apostle charged with the task of propagating divine teachings, Mani also imparted details about himself in the remains of his other works. In a recently edited letter written by Mani, surviving in Coptic translation, Mani recounts to the letter's addressee an ongoing bodily illness:

> I was very sick in the body. I did not find the way to spend a single hour to sit and hear it; nor also was I able to straighten out (?), because I was greatly pained. Indeed, further, when I listened to the words that you wrote for me in that letter, all my limbs slackened and worsened with me painfully in the anguish of my body (P.Kell.Copt. 53.31 – the *Epistle of the Ten Words*; trans. I. Gardner 2007a, 74; see also 74–83).

However, from the contents of the epistle it is apparent that Mani was attending to a pastoral problem that had lately beset his followers, and that in the letter he was purposefully drawing attention to his own physical fragility in order to console the sufferings of a nascent community of followers. Thus, what we take as being an instance of personal disclosure was in fact being put to the service of

[8] Baker-Brian 2007.
[9] Most recently, see O'Donnell 2005; cf. Chadwick 2009.

his community: an example of the sharing of personal information not unusual in the ancient world.

Nevertheless, there are evidently moments and incidents in the accounts of Mani's life which are historically transparent, disclosing his actual experiences and achievements: that Mani travelled, undertook missionary work, and met with and persuaded kings and dignitaries of high rank about the veracity of his ideas, are events in the history of early Manichaeism which should not be contested as actually having happened. Rather, what we should be scrutinising is whether those things occurred in precisely the way that we are told they did. Indeed, it is these very same events that were likely to become idealised in the service of later attempts to develop legendary narratives of Mani and Manichaeism. In this regard, we find ourselves in the complex world of the problems and issues thrown up by the Iranian Manichaean materials unearthed in Central Asia, over which Werner Sundermann has cast such a commanding presence; whilst many of Sundermann's specific findings about the legendary and historiographical habits of Manichaean writers remain largely unknown to English-language students of Mani, his overarching contribution to the historical treatment of Manichaean literature is nevertheless evident across the study of Manichaeism in the awareness that great care needs to be paid in the way that historians handle the historicity of biographical traditions about Mani and the early history of the church.[10]

With this in mind, it is necessary to note that, when approaching biographies of Mani as narrated in ancient Manichaean literature, fairly soon after his death we encounter a tendency to idealise all aspects of his life, but in particular of his childhood and early adulthood. The literary idealisation of a holy man's life is termed *hagiography* ('an account of a sainted one'), and Manichaean works recounting the life of Mani are replete with hagiographical themes and motifs. Evidence of this early idealisation is present throughout the *CMC*, where a central preoccupation of the text is to present Mani as being under the constant guidance of heavenly powers from a very early age, and to relate accounts of the revelations granted to Mani by a specific heavenly figure referred to as Mani's 'Twin' (Gk *syzygos*) who, appearing to Mani notably on two occasions at 12-year cycles of 12 and 24 years of age, instructs the young man not simply about his role as a teacher of profound spiritual truths, but also about his 'real identity' as a spiritual being granted an earthly existence in order to fulfil the will of God.

> He (the Syzygos) drew (me away to one side) ... and (showed me) who I am and what my body is, in what way I came and how my coming into this world happened, and who I have become among those who are most distinguished in pre-eminence, and how I was born into this fleshly body, or through what woman I was brought to birth and delivered into this flesh, and by whom I was begotten (*CMC* 20.16-21.16; trans. J.M. Lieu and S.N.C. Lieu, in I. Gardner and S.N.C. Lieu 2004, 50).

Thus the Twin discloses to Mani that they are in fact one and the same, with the Syzygos serving as Mani's *alter ego*, the residue of his spiritual personality which

---

[10] See Sundermann 2009a, for a concise explanation of his ideas.

had become separated from Mani at the time of his fleshly embodiment: the inference emerging from such a description is that Mani had an earlier, spiritual existence before his incarnation in the body of the Mesopotamian teacher.[11] With the appearance of the Twin, the two sides of the same personality are now reunited – Mani finally recalling who he is as if coming round from the stupor of drunkenness (*CMC* 22.14) – and his apostolic mission can now begin. The *CMC* serves as an important witness to what we can imagine was the reasonably early transformation of Mani into something other than a human prophet and teacher in terms of how his followers thought and spoke about him, a transformation evidently suggested to Mani's later follows by Mani's own earlier claims of having received a divine commission for his teachings. For instance, cited within the *CMC* is the opening portion of Mani's work the *Living Gospel*, which provides clear evidence of Mani's own sense of self:

> I, Mannichaeus, apostle of Jesus Christ, through the will of God, the Father of Truth, from whom I also came into being. He lives and abides for all eternity. Before everything he is, and he remains after everything. Everything which has happened and will happen, is established through his power. From him I have my being, and I exist also according to his will. And from him all that is true was revealed to me and from (his) truth I exist (*CMC* 66.4-20; trans. J.M. Lieu and S.N.C. Lieu, in I. Gardner and S.N.C. Lieu 2004, 156–7).

In another section from the *Living Gospel*, also preserved in the *CMC*, Mani announced the appearance of his Twin, and the nature of the teachings which the Syzygos disclosed to him:

> When my father showed favour and treated me with pity and solicitude, he sent from there my never-failing Syzygos, the complete fruit of immortality, who might ransom and redeem me from the error of those that rule. He came to (me and) brought to me (the) noblest hope, the (redemption) of immortality, true instructions and the laying on of hands from my father. He came and chose me in preference to others and set me aside, drawing me away from the midst of those of that rule in which I was brought up (*CMC* 69.9-70.9; trans. J.M. Lieu and S.N.C. Lieu, in I. Gardner and S.N.C. Lieu 2004, 158–9).

Mani's own sense of divine election, the account of his revelatory experiences with his divine companion, and the resulting decision to withdraw from the religious rule (Gk *nomos* = Law) of the community in which he had been raised, provided inspiration for the development of advanced theological speculation about the actual person of Mani, and which, in one sense, is the distinguishing feature of the *CMC*. The *Codex* should therefore be regarded as something *more than* a biography of Mani: rather, it is the literary expression of his followers' convictions about the significance of Mani's person, a significance that moved

---

[11] See Sundermann 2009a.

beyond his historical appearance to account for his role in the wider, cosmic reality which he had expostulated during his lifetime.

Even after these brief remarks about the nature of ancient biography, it should be apparent that the possibility of composing a positivist account of Mani's life – one which judges the variety of source material to hand in an empirical fashion as if its main role is to offer up facts about Mani's life and times – seems (at least in the opinion of this writer) remote. This is not to suggest, however, that we do not glimpse some fixed details of Mani's life and personality, but any discussion needs to recognise the limitations of the available ancient source material, and to identify the aims and ambitions of writers in their portrayals of Mani. This chapter will therefore be mainly interested in examining the ways in which portraits of Mani were constructed during Late Antiquity within both Manichaean and anti-Manichaean literature, and in particular during the period following the death of Mani and his immediate disciples at the end of the third century and into the 300s, the time when Mani's teachings began to achieve a wider geographical distribution beyond the religion's Babylonian 'homeland'. Thus the Manichaean church was developing both institutionally and doctrinally in this period, and was witness to the production of many of its great creative monuments, among them theological treatises, biographies and histories, homilies and liturgical texts which together reflected on the phenomenon of Mani (see Chapter 1) in such a fashion that not only did he become a focal point for his followers' devotions but he was also transformed from a historical apostle to a legendary and quasi-divine figure. At the same time, Manichaeism's opponents were undertaking a concerted response to this newly emergent tradition and, because of the increasing importance placed on the person of Mani by Manichaeans in the formation of the religion's historical memory, Mani became the straw man of Christian heresiology, attacked on the one hand for his ideas and teachings, and utilised on the other as a foil in the determination of orthodox Christian identities. The reputation of Mani as a teacher, author, apostle and Christian, therefore, took centre stage in this clash of Christianities.

3. Disinformation and Information

So, what sources have been employed by modern biographers to compose lives of Mani? For very nearly sixteen centuries, the foremost portrait of Mani was considered to be the one contained in the anti-Manichaean work, the *Acts of Archelaus*.[12] *Acts* exerted a disproportionate influence on both patristic and medieval accounts of Mani and the religion associated with him, the work customarily being brought into service in order to inform and reinforce the common historical representation of Mani as a heresiarch, namely as the founder of a heretical Christian sect.[13] Although detailed consideration will be given to

---

[12] The work's principal 'Mani-vita' is to be found in the *Acts of Archelaus* 62.1–65.9; trans. M. Vermes 2001, 140–7.

[13] See Puech 1949, 99, nt. 10.

this work later in this chapter, it is worth outlining at this stage some salient points about the character and the influence of *Acts*.

Composed in the first quarter of the fourth century by Hegemonius, an author who is otherwise unattested in ancient traditions, *Acts* is a work that has intrigued scholars for centuries. Whilst purporting to serve as a record of a series of debates – presented as quasi-judicial interviews – between Mani and a Christian bishop named Archelaus in a Roman Mesopotamian frontier town called Carchar at some time during the reign of the emperor Probus (ruling 276–82), the historicity of the work, i.e., its reliability as a documentary source for the events it describes, has been called into question from the time when Manichaeism began to be scrutinised with a degree of historical objectivity during the early eighteenth century.[14] Indeed, questions remain open in relation to a range of issues, for instance: the *actual* date of the work's composition, which is very likely later than the (imagined) time at which the debate took place (it is *very likely* that *Acts* belongs to the first half of the fourth century);[15] the original language in which *Acts* was composed, the work now surviving only in its entirety in a Latin version, with additional material preserved in the heresiological works of the fourth-century Greek writers Epiphanius and Cyril of Jerusalem;[16] and, the supposed location of the work, which – if it is possible to talk about an 'academic consensus' – presently seems to favour Carrhae (Harran) in the northern Mesopotamian region of Osrhoene.[17]

Consensus also suggests that *Acts* is largely a work of fiction – a conclusion arrived at because of the weight of uncertainty in the areas mentioned above – and the cold, hard reality of such an assessment is that the meetings between Mani and the sacred and secular dignitaries of Carchar at some stage in the mid-third century most likely never actually took place. Nevertheless, Hegemonius evidently drew from a number of genuine Manichaean works as he set about creating his literary disputation. The treatments of Manichaean cosmogony and scriptural exegesis appearing in the mouths of Mani and his disciples have long been regarded as drawing on primary sources written by Mani and his immediate followers. Furthermore, it is apparent that Hegemonius was also attempting to present his work as an authentic account of events – in order to provide his audience with irrefutable proof of Mani's errors – by paying attention to the 'political' realities of the day, namely the causes of the tensions between Catholic and Manichaean Christians, and by setting his work in an imagined environment that nevertheless employed a sufficient number of cultural and racial stereotypes which would be recognisable to Roman Christians, thereby leading them to assume that what was described by Hegemonius as having taken place reflected to some extent what they believed to be happening in religious and political terms at the very eastern limit of the Roman empire. However, it should also be noted that questions about the genuineness of *Acts* were never actually raised by those authors who instead turned to the work down the centuries in order to

---

[14] See Ries 1988, 36–42.
[15] See BeDuhn and Mirecki 2007b, 9.
[16] See S.N.C. Lieu 2001, 13–16.
[17] See S.N.C. Lieu 2001, 16–23.

access a portrait of Manichaeism that corroborated their views concerning the erroneous nature of the religion. Critical appraisals of the work only belong to the early decades of the previous century, and stand within the wider cultural assessment of Manichaeism as worth investigating as a faith in its own right.

However, what is not the subject of any uncertainty is the character of the work: it is squarely anti-Manichaean, its purpose being to demonstrate the indefatigable nature of Roman Christianity in the face of the menace of Mani, by exposing the irrationality and indefensibility of Mani's teachings on a range of doctrinal issues, foremost among them being dualism, theodicy (i.e., the nature of evil in relation to the goodness of God), Christology and the exegesis of the Bible: namely, the very points over which the two rival (Roman and Mesopotamian) versions of Christianity held different views, and which served as the issues over which they were most likely to clash during the late-antique period (see Chapter 1). The challenge to and subsequent destruction of Manichaean teaching is achieved within the narrative of *Acts* by setting Mani against Archelaus within the context of two debates, the first held in front of the citizens of Carchar, presided over by a jury of the leading gentile citizens of the city – gentile here meaning pagan; arguably a contrived attempt on Hegemonius' part to demonstrate the lack of partiality to either the Christian (= Archelaus) or Manichaean cause.[18] In both instances, Mani is thoroughly humiliated, and after leaving Archelaus in the town of Diodoris, he goes 'on the run' for a period of time before being arrested by the 'king of Persia' who, in revenge for Mani's failure to cure his son of a disease, had the prophet flayed and his skin stuffed and displayed on the gates of the royal city.[19]

One of the work's dominant approaches in constructing its anti-Manichaean strategy lay in its parodying of those doctrinal concerns and historical events which were central to the early historical identity of Manichaeism as reflected in both the early and the later literary sources for the religion. For instance, the portrayal of both Mani and his disciples' endurance in propagating his teachings among the regions west and east of Sasanian Mesopotamia, which takes on a legendary dimension in Manichaean historiography, is consciously inverted by the author of *Acts*. For instance, upon his arrival in Carchar brandishing Mani's letter of introduction addressed to Marcellus, the leading citizen of the city, the disciple Turbo (otherwise unknown as a Manichaean disciple) simply cannot be bothered to return to Persia where Mani is said to be residing, due to the hardships that Turbo is said to have encountered during his journey to the city: indeed, the sluggish Turbo later converts to Archelaus' version of Christianity and is ordained a deacon. Furthermore, Mani's immediate successor as the leader of the Manichaean church, Sisinnios, who was martyred during the perse-cution of Manichaeans and Christians by Vahram II in the late 280s, and whose memory was sainted in later Manichaean literature, is portrayed by Hegemonius as a turncoat, who 'leaks' to Archelaus the secret details of Mani's life and lineage, which forms the basis for the biography of Mani in the work. Thus, *Acts* proceeds on its anti-Manichaean course by supplying slander and disinformation about

---

[18] *Acts of Archelaus* 15.5; trans. M. Vermes 2001, 59.
[19] *Acts of Archelaus.* 66.3; trans. M. Vermes 2001, 148.

its subject, and presenting an ersatz portrait of Mani as if it were genuine: most cunningly, the work's authenticity is reinforced by its principal literary form as a stenographic record, which memorialises the debate between a Christian bishop and an alien 'heretic'.[20]

This strategy – disinformation masquerading as genuine detail – is most keenly pursued by Hegemonius through his biography of Mani towards the end of the work. It is this life that has carried a most significant influence in the informing of later writers about the life of the Mani the arch-heresiarch. Furthermore, it is the details of Mani's life within *Acts* that have been regarded by many writers as supplying the foundation for detecting the errors of Manichaeism. During the fourth century, heresiologists such as Cyril, Bishop of Jerusalem, and Epiphanius, Bishop of Salamis in Cyprus, both borrowed extensively from the Greek version of the *Acts of Archelaus* (preserving bits of information and sections which are not transmitted by the Latin version), and in particular from the tendentious biography which they looked to first in order to identify and locate Mani's errors within the larger landscape constructed by orthodox Christians for creating a history of heretical errors: therefore, to later Christian writers the errant life of Mani as supplied by *Acts* was the best explanation for the erroneous nature of his theological ideas. As we will see in the final section of this chapter, Hegemonius lavished great care and attention upon situating Mani's life within the context of an 'anti-biography', by manufacturing an account of his life and achievements that was filled with vice, intrigue, double-dealing and an impoverished lineage (*Acts* styling Mani as a slave boy bought and then manumitted by a wealthy widow), a strategy which not only made use of numerous heresiological commonplaces, but also reveals the author's familiarity with the rules of ancient rhetorical theory for crafting works of blame and censure.

With these issues in mind, the other fascinating consideration raised by *Acts* and more specifically by its biography of Mani is the possibility that it was written as an orthodox answer to the idealised accounts of Mani's life and upbringing which were being composed by Manichaeans themselves in the late-antique period, of which the *CMC* is perhaps the only surviving example. The fundamental elements in the *CMC*'s presentation of Mani, his self-identity as an apostle of Jesus Christ, his willingness to be placed within a genealogy of divinely-sanctioned prophets and apostles, the centrality and sincerity of his Christian faith to the message he sought to proclaim, and his efforts to secure powerful patrons to assist him in this regard, are all parodied within the *Acts'* biography. Although problems concerning the precise dating of *Acts* and the *CMC* (see below) makes it difficult to suggest that in specific terms the former emerged as a response to the latter, it should be noted that the attack on Mani and his reputation in *Acts* is intensely personal, which at the very least indicates the author's awareness of the central role played by Mani in shaping the theology and religiosity of his followers, a role which was mediated through the biographical and historical tendencies in Manichaean literature.

Acts' lengthy influence on perceptions of Mani and Manichaeism finally began to unravel during the nineteenth century. Ancient sources that made detailed

---

[20] See esp. Scopello 1995.

reference to Manichaeism, which had been composed under quite different cultural and political circumstances than the *Acts of Archelaus*, began to emerge in Europe around this time, being translated by a handful of scholars proficient in a number of oriental languages relevant to the source material, primarily Syriac and Arabic. Among the most important of these sources for Manichaean studies is the Arabic historical and computistical work, *The Chronology of Ancient Nations* (following C.E. Sachau's translation of the title from 1879, *Athar-ul-Bakiya*) by al-Biruni, which dates from the eleventh century and which, as we noted in the previous chapter, preserves portions from Mani's *Šābuhragān*; and the Arabic encyclopaedia from the tenth century, the *Fihrist* by al-Nadim. Although both authors appear to divest themselves of the type of overt slander which characterised the Christian heresiological treatment of Manichaeism, it should be noted that neither al-Biruni nor al-Nadim were wholly impartial in their portraits of Mani and his teachings: they were, after all, working within a well-established tradition of Islamic heresiology, and as such were not likely to be favourably disposed towards sects that espoused dualism of a theological and ethical nature. The other crucial point about both these authors is that they had had access to Arabic translations of Mani's own works, which had been made during the final decades of the Umayyad period by, among others, the translator and civil servant Ibn al-Muqaffa (d. ca. 759), in addition to using the detailed compendia by earlier Islamic writers on the religion, such as the one composed by ninth-century figure Abu 'Isa al-Warraq, which formed a central influence on the approach and information provided in al-Nadim's *Fihrist*.[21]

Following the testimony supplied by Mani himself from his *Šābuhragān* in the chapter entitled 'On the Coming of the Prophet', al-Biruni relates the details of Mani's birthplace: born in the village of Mardinu on the Kutha canal in southern Mesopotamia, 'in the year 527 of the era of the Babylonian astronomers [following the Alexandrian era], in the fourth year of the king Adharban [i.e., the last Arsacid monarch Artabanus V]', a date equating to AD 216, Mani became the recipient of his first divine revelation in AD 228 at the age of 13 (cf. Al-Nadim, 'at the completion of his twelfth year').[22]

Whilst such precise details are absent from al-Nadim's account, his extended section on Mani and Manichaeism in the ninth chapter of his work nevertheless contains a much fuller anecdotal treatment of Mani's youth than is presented in the *Chronology*, so much so that, along with its detailed statements on Mani's teachings drawn from Mani's own writings, the *Fihrist*'s entry on Manichaeism is viewed as being the most complete heresiological account of the religion in any ancient tradition (Christian, Zoroastrian or Islamic).[23] Prior to the publication of the edition and commentary of the Manichaean section of the work by Gustav Flügel in 1862 (*Mani, His Teachings and His Writings*), the details provided by al-Nadim about Mani, his life, his career and the religion's early history were

---

[21] See Widengren 1965, 127–32; S.N.C. Lieu 1992, 113–14; Browder 1992, 328–33; de Blois 2005, 37–45.

[22] *The Chronology of Ancient Nations* 208; trans. C.E. Sachau 1879, 190; see Tardieu 2008, 1–2.

[23] Tardieu 2008, 98.

largely unknown. Leaving aside the claims for Mani's dubious lineage typically reproduced by Western Christian sources, al-Nadim presented fresh and startling material about Mani's early years, including the names and details of his parents: thus, we learn that Mani's father was called Fatiq (Gk Pattikios; Lt. Patticius), that he was a citizen of Hamadam (Gk Ecbatana), the old Iranian capital of the Medes, and that his mother was called Mays (or Marmaryam), who is said by al-Nadim to have been a descendent of the Ashkanian, the ruling Arsacid dynasty.[24]

Whilst al-Nadim's entire entry on Mani and Manichaeism is of great importance, we should draw attention to three descriptions provided by him that have assisted commentators in filling out their impressions of Mani's formative years, and which would prove absolutely invaluable in making sense of the evidence provided by the *CMC* from the early 1970s onwards. Beginning with information concerning his father, al-Nadim writes:

> It is said that his father was originally from Hamadan and had moved to Babylon, settling in al-Mada'in [i.e., the 'Twin Cities' of Seleucia and Ctesiphon], in the place called Tisfun (Ctesiphon) which had a temple (a house of idols). Fatiq attended this temple, like everyone else, when one day, a voice called to him from the inner sanctum of the temple saying: 'Fatiq! Do not eat meat, do not drink wine and abstain from intercourse with anyone.' Fatiq heard this call repeated many times over three days. Having witnessed that, Fatiq attached himself to a group of people in the vicinity of Dastumisan known as the Cleaners (al-Mughtasilah). Their remnants persist to this day in that place and in the marshes [Arabic: *Bata'ih*]. These people were (thus) of the sect which Fatiq was ordered to join when his wife was pregnant with Mani. Once she gave birth (to him), they claimed that she had had lovely dreams about him. And (once) she gained consciousness she had a vision of him being taken up into air by a force which then returned him, after perhaps a day or two (aloft). And then, having returned, his father came forth and took him to his place of residence to raise him and care for his community (following the translation in I Gardner and S.N.C. Lieu 2004, credited to M. Laffan, 46–7; cf. B. Dodge 1970, II.773–4).

As many commentators have noted, al-Nadim's source(s) for this passage was most likely to have belonged to a Manichaean hagiographical tradition that commemorated Mani's life in explicit, celebratory terms: Mani's parents' royal lineage, the religious conversion of his father from a Mesopotamian pagan cult,[25] Fatiq's revelations presaging Mani's own divinely-inspired experiences, and Mani's ennobled nativity, are all details which point to a tradition that idealised Mani's early years in conventional, hagiographical terms. A case may even be made to suggest that al-Nadim had to hand directly or indirectly a late-antique biography of Mani of the type which the *CMC* represents.[26]

---

[24] *Fihrist* 9.1; trans. Dodge 1970, II.773.
[25] See Tardieu 2008, 3.
[26] See Luttikhuizen 1985, 168–72.

The group to which Fatiq attached himself, and into which he also inducted his infant son, was the Mughtasilah ('those who bathe themselves'), an Arabic name which equates in Greek to the designation 'Baptisers'. Al-Nadim provides a brief description of the Mughtasilah in a later passage:

> These people are very numerous in the regions of al-Bata'ih; they are called the Sabat al-Bata'ih [lit. 'the Sabians of the Marshes']. They observe ablution as a rite and wash everything which they eat. Their head is known as al-Hasih and it is he who instituted their sect. They assert that the two existences are male and female and that the herbs are from the likeness of the male, whereas the parasite plants are from the likeness of the female, the trees being veins (*Fihrist*, 9.1; trans. B. Dodge 1970, II.811).

Al-Nadim's testimony informs us, therefore, that the Mughtasilah were southern Mesopotamian baptists, that they practised cleansing rites on the food they were to consume, and that they were led by al-Hasih. Whilst the reliability of some details in this passage has been questioned,[27] its importance lies in providing the distinguishing ritual aspect of the group to which Fatiq attached both himself and Mani, namely the practice of ablution, a feature which forms an important element in the life of Mani as conveyed by Manichaean sources appearing after the publication of Flügel's edition of the *Fihrist* in the late nineteenth century (see below).

Finally, al-Nadim informs his readers about the circumstances surrounding Mani's separation from the Mughtasilah, again likely relying on a Manichaean hagiographical tradition for Mani's early years:

> Mani acquired the art of wise words at a very young age. And at the completion of his twelfth year, he was inspired from above by (a being) he called the King of the Gardens of Light, (for) it was God Almighty who addressed him. And the angel that brought him (this) revelation was called al-Tawm, from the Nabatean word meaning 'companion'. And the angel said to him: 'Abandon this community, for you are not of them. You must be unblemished and abstain from desire. The time is not right for you to appear, for you are still young.' (So) when he turned twenty-four, al-Tawm brought him forth saying: 'Now is the time for you to appear and call (others) to your cause.'
>
> What al-Tawm told Mani: 'Peace be with you, Mani, both from myself and from the Lord Who sent me to you and Who chose you for His message. He has commanded you to invite (others) in your own right and to preach on His behalf the Truth, laying it upon you to do so with your utmost effort.' (*Fihrist*, trans. I. Gardner and S.N.C. Lieu 2004, credited to M. Laffan, 47; cf. B. Dodge 1970, II.774–5.)

The community that fulfilled the austere demands placed on Fatiq by the voice from the temple's inner sanctum failed nevertheless to impress the young Mani,

---

[27] Notably Luttikhuizen 1985, 165–72.

who, under the guidance of his divine companion (al-Tawm) sent by the highest God, sought to make a break from his father's baptists. As valuable as this information was to the developing discipline of Manichaean studies, many questions remained unanswered, including identifying with greater precision the tradition to which the baptisers belonged, discovering more details about their leader al-Hasih, and finding out what led to Mani's final break with the community. With these questions remaining for the large part unanswerable, a vacuum appeared at the centre of the study of Manichaeism during the best part of the twentieth century, which made it difficult to reconcile the prevailing essentialist assumptions about the origins and character of the religion (the main options being Iranian, Gnostic, Zoroastrian or Christian) which were developing as work on the Turfan materials progressed, with the evidence for Mani's beginnings from the Arabic sources. At the forefront of the analytical charge of those commentators attempting to fill this gap was Geo Widengren who, residing at the end period of the 'motif' approach to the historical study of religions (see Chapter 1), tried to reconcile these dominant strands of research with Mani's derivation from the Mughtasilah. As far as Widengren was concerned, the result was so certain that 'we may confidently assume that Patik [Fatiq] joined a Mandaean group in southern Babylonia and that Mani was brought up in this baptist community'; and further, 'Mani grew up in a southern Babylonian, gnostic, and more explicitly Mandaean, baptist community and there received impressions crucial to his future.'[28] However, one difficulty for Widengren was where to assign the Christian components in this heady mix of influences, a problem his thesis experienced very acutely as a result of Mandaeism's well-documented 'sibling rivalry' with Christian traditions.[29] Widengren, like so many others before and after, thus fell into the ancient heresiological trap of regarding Manichaeism's Christian elements as simply convenient 'add-ons', an argument which, as we saw in Chapter 1, is easily overturned, not only given the role of Christian teachings and practices in Mani's own writings, but also in relation to the codification of his teachings by his later followers. The English-language translation of Widengren's *Mani and Manichaeism* appeared in 1965, and in one sense marked off a specific period of research into the religion. With the emergence five years later of the *CMC*, a new era in the history of Manichaean studies began.

4. The Greek *Life* of Mani (*CMC*)

In the now famous article published in 1970 entitled 'A Greek Mani-Codex (P. Colon. inv. nr. 4780)' (the number referring to the catalogue number of the *Codex* in the Cologne collection), the *CMC*'s early editors, Albert Henrichs and Ludwig Koenen, announced to the world the wonders contained within the diminutive parchment codex. An important concern for Henrichs and Koenen was the reconciliation of this 'new data' about Mani's life in the *CMC* with

[28] Widengren 1965, 25–6.
[29] Buckley 2002, 150.

existing knowledge of his early years, and their attentions inevitably fell on the testimony of al-Nadim from the *Fihrist* and his disclosure concerning Mani's upbringing among a baptising faction from southern Mesopotamia. A concatenation of evidence drawn from the *CMC* that casts light on the characteristics of the sect in which Mani was raised – the striving on the part of the community's adherents for physical purity achieved through a daily round of ablutions of their own bodies and the foods which they consumed, the presence of both Jewish and Christian themes and texts within the community and in the work itself, and most significantly the appearance on p. 94 of the *Codex* of the name Alchasaios (cf. al Nadim's al-Hasih) referred to as the founder (Gk *archēgos*) of the baptists' Law – all of which led the editors to the conclusion that the baptists in the *CMC* were a sect of Elchasaites, followers of Elchasaios (Elchasai).

Elchasaios appears as a shadowy figure in a number of heresiological reports, portrayed variously as a man appearing in the reign of the emperor Trajan (AD 97–117), who was of Jewish origin but who nevertheless turned his back on Jewish observances. He is credited with writing a mysterious, apocalyptic book introduced into Rome by Alcibiades of Apamea,[30] and his name is associated with a sect known to Origen that displayed Jewish-Christian tendencies, by living according to select precepts from Jewish and Christian scriptures, although rejecting absolutely the letters of Paul.[31] In a later article from 1978, Henrichs and Koenen set out 12 points of agreement which they had identified linking the beliefs and practices of the baptists in the *CMC* and those of the Elchasaites as related by the patristic witnesses.[32] Such an endeavour demanded great detective work and historical skill, and has not surprisingly failed to convince some scholars, notably Gerard Luttikhuizen who doubted first of all the associations made by Henrichs and Koenen between the Mughtasilah and the Elchasaites, in addition to the connections claimed between the historically-reconstructed Elchasaites and the baptists of the *CMC*.[33]

The findings of Henrichs and Koenen have nevertheless won through, and their identification of Mani's early years as having been spent among a community of Jewish-Christian baptists in southern Mesopotamia forms an intrinsic part of the received historical narrative of Manichaeism as reconstituted in modern scholarship. Thus, in the recent English translation of Michel Tardieu's masterful short book, *Manichaeism*, in the *Que sais-je* series, a narrative of Mani's early formation is presented with seamless transitions between the disparate and troublesome pieces of ancient evidence, including the difficulties involved in establishing the line of historical continuity between the heresiologists' Elchasaites, the *CMC*'s baptists, and al-Nadim's Mughtasilah:

By the beginning of the second century of our era, Elchasaitic Judeo-Christianity was firmly established in Transjordan and very active in

[30] Cf. Jones 2004.
[31] Patristic testimonies concerning Elchasai and Elchasaites are collected in Klijn and Reinink 1973.
[32] Henrichs and Koenen 1978, 183–4.
[33] Luttikhuizen 1985.

Arabia. At the beginning of the third century, when Mani's father joined one of its Babylonian communities, Alcibiades of Apamea became its proponent in Rome. In the middle of the same century, Origen noted its 'recent' progress in Palestine under [the Roman emperor] Philip the Arab (224–249). In the following century, Epiphanius, an authority on religious movements in Palestine and Syria, noted that the baptist communities of Jordan had almost everywhere been assimilated by Elchasaitism. It was therefore a powerful movement. Some six hundred years later, Ibn al-Nadim, writing in the fourth century of the Hegira, confirmed its continuing presence under the name Mughtasila in the marshlands of Mesopotamia.[34]

However, in their utilisation of the *CMC* as a primary source of information for assembling the biography of Mani, modern commentators often overlook the religious and literary significance of the work to ancient Manichaeans. It is reasonable to suggest that its compilers were not concerned to provide a historically accurate account of Mani's early life, nor even indeed one of Mesopotamian Elchasaitism: that the *CMC* is frequently employed in such a manner should probably be reconsidered on the basis that it constitutes too optimistic a view of the work's service to modern readers seeking to write positivist accounts of Mani. Thus, whilst the *CMC* probably does indeed present 'the essential origins of Mani and his gnostic world religion',[35] a concern more germane to the work's original purpose can likely be seen in its specific portrayal of Mani – acting and reacting in a particular manner to a range of contrived dilemmas and situations – as a way of conveying those characteristics that were central to the overall identity of the religion in the late-antique period. It is to these considerations that we now turn.

The literary form of the *CMC* is complex, containing many layers of narration detailing the life and times of Mani within and beyond his involvement with the Elchasaites. Sections in the work, very many of which purport to contain sayings and statements by Mani in which he reflects upon his experiences, are introduced via the names of some of Mani's earliest disciples, who appear to serve as the transmitters of Mani's experiences and teachings. These testimonies may indeed date from the mid-to-late third century and constitute genuine 'sayings' of Mani, although the compilation and redaction of the *CMC* occurred much later, likely stretching into the fifth century and even beyond.[36] In this sense, therefore, the *Codex* probably had many authors and numerous editors, although the extent to which the authors of the work had any sense of being anything other than transmitters and compilers of the teachings and sayings of Mani is a moot point.[37] The *CMC*'s literary form appears to have shared in the format of the largely lost Manichaean church history in Coptic, a putative account of the primitive church which followed the deeds and exploits of Mani

[34] Tardieu 2008, 8.
[35] van Oort 2001a, 30.
[36] See Henrichs 1979.
[37] For Manichaean conceptions of authorship, see Baker-Brian 2009, 144–60.

and his disciples' earliest missions.[38] That the *CMC* formed the first part of such a history, a theory proposed by some commentators, appears to be substantiated by the types of details and events recounted in the *Codex*, beginning with Mani's earliest (pre-natal?) experiences with his Twin, and ending amidst a very damaged series of leaves (*CMC* 144–8) detailing Mani's journey from the Persian port of Farat to India.

An overwhelming concern within the *CMC* is the establishment of Mani's apostolic credentials: that these had been doubted at some stage during or after Mani's lifetime is made clear by the following statement conveyed under the testimonial guidance of the early disciple Baraies the Teacher, which comes at the end of a long section containing citations from a number of apocalyptic works credited to key Hebrew patriarchs, all of whom had experienced similar divine raptures to Mani, brought about in Mani's case through the interventions of his Twin. Mani's own experiences in this regard are included in the following section of the *CMC*, along with the citations from the *Living Gospel* (see above) and also from Mani's letter to the Manichaean community in Edessa:

> In the books of our father [i.e., Mani] there are very many other extraordinary events similar to these, which make known his revelation and the rapture of his mission. For great is this magnificent coming which comes to (us) through the Paraclete, the spirit of Truth. For what purpose and what reason have we dealt with such things, when we have been convinced once for all that this mission excels in its revelations? It is because of the reasonings of those who have clothed themselves with unbelief and think nothing of this revelation and vision of our father, that we have repeated from our forefathers their rapture and each one's revelation, so that they may realise that the commission of the (earlier) apostles was likewise of (this nature). For when each of them was seized, (everything he saw) and heard he wrote down and made known, and himself became a witness of his own revelation; while his disciples became the seal of his sending (*CMC* 69.23-72.4; trans. J.M. Lieu and S.N.C. Lieu, in I. Gardner and S.N.C. Lieu 2004, 58).

The incorporation of Mani's revelatory experiences alongside the raptures experienced by the patriarchal forebears mentioned in the *CMC* thereby introduces a prophetic genealogy – termed a 'prophetology' by Tardieu – a concern which resided at the very centre of the religious identity of late-antique Manichaeism. The *Codex*'s prophetology constitutes one instance of a concern first given a voice by Mani himself in the biographical portion from the *Šābuhragān* cited by al-Biruni, from the chapter in the work entitled 'On the Coming of the Prophet' (see Chapter 1). The model of prophetology on display in the *CMC* and in other Manichaean writings – the repeated appearance of prophets who, under inspiration from the divine figure named the apostle of light (who in turn acts under the aegis of the Light-Nous and Jesus the Splendour: see Chapter 4), makes known to humanity profound truths through the instituting of their own

[38] See Koenen 1978, 164–6.

'churches' – is likely a Manichaean adaptation of a Jewish-Christian concern with the notion of the 'True Prophet', a concern which was especially prominent among the Elchasaites. In an episode crucial to the *CMC*'s portrayal of Mani as a manifestation of the prophet, it is during a meeting of the baptists' council (Gk *sunedrion*; cf. NT: sanhedrin) that Mani discloses the nature of what had been revealed to him by the Syzygos, and the implications that the revelations would have for Mani's ideas about reforming Elchasaite beliefs and practices. On the basis of this disclosure, Mani's suitability as a prophet and teacher (i.e., the two main roles of an Apostle of Light), according to Elchasaite estimations, was proclaimed by some members of the council. In the following passage, Mani recalls the reaction of the baptist sanhedrin:

> Some of them treated me as a prophet and teacher; some of them said: 'The living word is sung through him. Let us make him teacher of our doctrine.' Others said: 'Has a voice spoken to him in secret and is he saying what it revealed to him?' Still others suggested: 'Has something appeared to him in a dream and is he saying what he saw?' Others asked: 'Is (this) he concerning whom our teachers prophesised when they said, "A young man will (rise up from) our (midst) and will come (forward) as a new (teacher) to call into question our whole doctrine, just as our forefathers have spoken of the 'rest of the garment'?" However, others said: 'Is not that which is voiced by him error, does he want to lead astray our people and split the doctrine?' Others of them were filled with malice and wrath and some of them voted for death. Others said: 'This is the enemy of our (rule).' (*CMC* 86.1-87.6; trans. J.M. Lieu and S.N.C. Lieu, in I. Gardner and S.N.C. Lieu 2004, 61).

Thus, an ancient, apocalyptic prophecy that spoke enigmatically about the 'rest of the garment' is brought forward by the Elchasaites themselves in order to locate Mani in the familial genealogy of the true prophet.[39] However, from the perspective of the writers/compilers of the *CMC*, together with the Manichaean audience apprehending the work, Mani's identity as an apostle was determined by the fact that he was precisely not the type of prophet anticipated by orthodox Elchasaite teachings; a fact acknowledged by a section of the council who noted that the ancient prophecy in question predicted the arrival of one who will 'call into question' the teachings (Gk *dogma*) of their community. Indeed, according to the *CMC*'s narrative of events, the indication of Mani's qualification as a heavenly prophet lay in his overturning of all aspects of the Elchasaite rule.

With this in mind, it is worth noting a number of further points with regard to the Manichaean presentation of Mani's apostleship in the *CMC*. First, in citing the divine raptures experienced by the biblical forefathers Adam, Seth, Enosh, Shem and Enoch (*CMC* 45–60) – all drawn from apocalyptic texts which had been presented as if composed by these primeval, legendary figures (referred to as pseudepigraphic literature)[40] – the *CMC* was placing Mani's experiences

[39] See esp. Koenen 1986, 285–91.
[40] See Reeves 1996, *passim*.

and revelatory teachings squarely within a model of prophetology which Jewish-Christians would have had little difficulty in acknowledging as valid. Such an approach provided a foundation for the claim that what Mani taught adhered to prophetic precedent, having also been 'experienced' by other similarly inspired figures. Therefore, the Mani of the *CMC* is no innovator, guided by novel or revolutionary claims: rather he is a conservative reformer, desiring the unsullied translation of divine knowledge to humanity by adhering to the precedent of those memorialised in ancient Jewish lore. He is the restorer of divine knowledge among the aberrant Elchasaites.

And yet, the *Codex* subverts this model by introducing a number of controversial elements. Immediately after the testimonies of the Jewish forefathers, sections from Paul's letters (Gal. 1.1; 2 Cor. 12. 2–5; Gal. 1. 11–12) are brought forward to highlight the divine nature of Paul's commission as an apostle of Jesus Christ: on the Damascus road (Acts 9), Paul experienced a divine rapture through the appearance of the risen Christ which is recounted by him (2 Cor. 12) in order to highlight the derivation of his sense of apostolicity. The inclusion of Paul's experience in the *Codex* is a bold move: Paul's writings, which had questioned the need for believers of Jesus to maintain a relationship with the ritual laws of Jewish traditions, had for that very reason probably led to his rejection as a religious authority by the Jewish-Christian Elchasaite community of Mani's formative years. This rejection was indicated not only in the reports of the heresiologists (e.g., Origen in Eusebius; see Klijn and Reinink 1973, 147), but also in the jibe levelled at Mani by the Elchasaite community that, in abiding by Paul's writings, '[Mani] wishes to go to the gentiles and eat (Greek) bread'.[41] However, the *CMC* appears to suggest that Mani had incorporated Paul into the Elchasaites' very own model of prophetic succession.

The boldness of Mani's actions grew in the context of the controversy surrounding Mani's disclosure before the Elchasaite council of the teachings that had been revealed to him by his Twin. In the main controversial episode in the *CMC*, ranging from pages 80 through to 101 of the *Codex*, and culminating in a description of a violent attack on Mani instigated by the disgruntled members of the council, the *Codex* sets out the complaints of Mani towards the baptists, and the counter-accusations of the baptists towards their young initiate. Mani's challenge to the Elchasaites drew its focus from his objections to their conception of ritual purity (Gk *katharotēs*) which they sought to achieve through a daily round of ablutions. The point of disagreement lay not in the need to achieve purity *per se*; rather, the Mani of the *CMC* sought to relocate the focal point of what purity is from a bodily to an ethical context. Indeed, in a vignette dealing with the temptation of Mani by Sitaios ('the elder of the Council'), the value of the ritual preoccupations of the Elchasaites is reduced to nought, as highlighted by the inability of their leader to act in an ethical manner (e.g., *CMC* 74–7).

[Sitaios] seized (me) by the hand while no one else (was) with us, and going forward he (dug up) and showed me great treasures which he had secretly stored away. He said to me: 'These treasures are mine and I have

---

[41] *CMC* 87.19–21: see Gardner and Lieu 2004, 61–2, nt. 42.

control over them. From now on they will be yours; because I love no one else like you, to whom I shall give these treasures.' When he had uttered these words to me I said in my mind: 'My most blessed father took me first and gave me an immortal and unfading treasure. Whoever inherits this will (earn) from it (immortal) life.' Then I said to Sitaios (the) elder: 'Our (forefathers) who possessed these earthly treasures before us, and who inherited them, where are they? For behold, they died and perished and did not keep them as their own, nor yet did they take them with them.' I said to him: 'What use are these treasures to me since they introduce errors and faults to everyone who possesses them? For the treasure of God is very great and very valuable and provides everyone who inherits it with life.' When Sitaios saw that (my) mind was not induced to (accept) the treasures he had shown me, he was utterly amazed at me (*CMC* 74.8–77.2; trans. J.M. Lieu and S.N.C. Lieu, in I. Gardner and S.N.C. Lieu 2004, 59).

Thus the message of the work is clear: the baptists may have achieved purity of the body, but not of the mind that controls it (cf. *CMC* 14. 4–12). That many commentators have read these sections from the *Codex* as a 'gnostic' repudiation on Mani's part of religious ritual, particularly those pertaining to the care of the body, is understandable: however, as Jason BeDuhn has noted, and as we will discuss in Chapter 4, Manichaeism did indeed reconfigure the ritual usefulness of the human body by subjecting it to stringent ritualised practices.[42]

However, the real significance of the episode ranging over pages 80–101 lies in the subtle way in which the *CMC* presents a clash between two rival Christian traditions, both claiming to uphold the teachings of Jesus. On the one side are the beliefs and practices of the Jewish-Christian baptists, prominent among their rituals being 'the rest', namely observance of the Sabbath; and on the other the ablutionary activities undertaken by the baptists in order to achieve a sanctified state, which included the rinsing of food and the washing of the body. Whilst these practices evidently drew from the diverse prescriptions set out in the Pentateuch, the Elchasaites most likely received them in modified forms, which had emerged among the sectarian Jewish groups whose origins lay in the Second Temple period of Jewish history.[43] As the *CMC* presents the matter, these 'Jewish' elements were considered by the baptists to be reconcilable with 'the command-ments of the Saviour', namely Jesus, and in fact were regarded by them as having derived from Jesus himself. Thus, Mani's attempts to undermine the Elchasaite idea of physical purity elicited the following response:

[T]hey summoned me to their assembly and said to me: 'From your youth you have been with us and have lived correctly by the ordinances and customs of your rule. You had been like a modest bride in our midst. What has happened to you now or what has appeared to you? For you are (opposing) our (rule), and invalidating (and) abolishing our (doctrine). You have taken a different path from ours. We hold your father [Patticius; cf.

---

[42] BeDuhn 2002, 209–33.
[43] See esp. Gruenweld 1983; also Jones 2004.

Fatiq in al-Nadim] in great honour: why then do you now declare invalid the ritual washing of our and our father's rule by which we have long lived? *You are invalidating the commands of the saviour (CMC* 90.8–91.11; trans. J.M. Lieu and S.N.C. Lieu, in I. Gardner and S.N.C. Lieu 2004, 62).[44]

Mani, clearly horrified by this accusation, responded by saying that he would never undermine the commandments of the saviour. Indeed, as he understood affairs, Mani himself was upholding the authentic teachings of the saviour, as communicated directly to him by his Twin. It was his mission to correct the aberrant practices of the Elchasaites by reinforcing among them that 'this is in truth the most righteous purity which you have been exhorted to practise'.[45] These truths, espoused by Jesus and now by Mani, are presented as being concerned with 'knowing about' (Gk *gnosis*) what amounts to the fundamental tenets of the Manichaean religion: thus, the Mani of the *CMC* presents his teachings in very general terms, as a recognition of the need to divide 'light from darkness, death from life, and living waters from poisoned waters (*CMC* 84.12–17)', namely teachings which are life-giving as opposed to death-bringing. Thereby, a broad, doctrinal statement is projected retroactively into the mouth of Mani as the defining revelation of his apostolate. Furthermore, whilst the statements made by Mani in the presence of the Elchasaite elders are, on one level, a way of demonstrating Mani's isolation from the community in which he was raised, an isolation brought about by the revelations which highlighted the doctrinal errantry of the baptisers, they also serve as a way of reaffirming Mani's identity in the specific sense as a true prophet, whilst also reinforcing the Manichaean church's sense of exclusiveness, an important feature of Manichaeism's identity within the market place of Christianities in Late Antiquity, as highlighted in Chapter 1 by the community designations evidenced in the letters from fourth-century Kellis. The *CMC* thereby not only recounts in an idealised manner the story of Mani's own personal odyssey, but it reaffirms contemporary Manichaean identity through its portrayal of the apostle.

Mani's apostolate, as the *CMC* suggests, is characterised by the recognition of his identity as the Paraclete, 'the Spirit of Truth' (*CMC* 46; 70), the figure that Jesus himself promised would come to fulfil his teachings (e.g., Jn. 14.16), and which in the *CMC* serves as an additional identity for Mani's Twin. That the identification of Mani with the Paraclete was an indication for Manichaeans that the apostolate of Mani represented the final turn in the cycle of prophetic revealers can also be seen in other Manichaean writings, and possibly also in Mani's own *Gospel*, as related by al-Biruni in his *Chronology*: 'In his gospel, which [Mani] arranged according to the twenty-two letters of the [Aramaic] alphabet, he says that he is the Paraclete announced by Messiah [Jesus], and that he is the seal of the prophets (i.e., the last of them).'[46] The implication of this claim for

---

[44] My emphasis.

[45] *CMC* 85. 1–4; trans. J.M. Lieu and S.N.C. Lieu in Gardner and Lieu 2004, 61.

[46] Al-Biruni, *The Chronology of Ancient Nations* 207; trans. C.E. Sachau 1879, 190. For discussion of the passage and the Manichaean appropriation of the Johannine Paraclete, see Koenen 1978, 167–76. The expression 'Seal of the Prophets' is discussed in Stroumsa 1986.

late-antique Manichaeism in the *CMC* is clear: as no other prophet will arrive after Mani, his church is therefore the culminant tradition founded on the religious principles taught by Jesus.

The imperative nature of Mani's appearance as the final apostle is thus communicated by the *CMC* through its characterisation of the Elchasaites, a group that, whilst professing allegiance to Jesus and his commandments, had nevertheless polluted those same teachings unnecessarily with Jewish practices. It is in this context that the inclusion of Paul alongside the other legendary forefathers becomes clear. Paul was viewed by certain Christian groups in Late Antiquity as the teacher who had maintained a distance between the Gospel of Jesus from the legalism of Jewish traditions, a concern which had achieved greater definition from the second century onwards through the writings of Marcion,[47] who regarded the letters of Paul as a guide to rooting out Jewish teachings which, in his estimation, had been added to the gospel narratives by Christians who nevertheless remained partial to Jewish customs. Those Christians who upheld this Pauline division were unwilling to accept the textual legacy of classical Jewish traditions, namely the Old Testament as received by orthodox Christianity, and both Marcionite and Manichaean Christians adhered to a model that isolated the memory of Jesus from contact with all classical Jewish laws, prophecies and traditions. There was, therefore, a strong although largely unacknowledged influence of Pauline ideas – as mediated through the Marcionite Christian churches of Mesopotamia and Syria – on early Manichaean theology. The interpretive position which arose from this influence, referred to as antinomianism (the rejection of the laws and customs of the Jewish scriptures) characterised the Manichaean exegesis of the Bible, and formed one of the main areas of contention between Manichaean and Catholic Christians in the Roman empire.[48] Whilst such explicit details are absent in the *CMC*, they nevertheless underpin the text's central idea about Mani as an apostle whose authenticity is confirmed by his unfailing adherence to the 'commandments of the Saviour', stripped of the Jewish legalism that the Elchasaites had introduced.

Whilst the *CMC*'s portrayal of Mani is complex, it is unfailing in its attempts to demonstrate that the apostolate of Mani is the immediate heir to the apostolate of the historical Jesus, the religious leader from Nazareth, both of whom according to Manichaean tradition were direct recipients of the divine revelations whose ultimate source was the archetypal revealer, Jesus the Splendour (see Chapter 4). Whilst the *Codex* certainly contains biographical data about Mani which confirmed the testimonies from Islamic heresiological sources, it should also be apparent that the writers and editors of the work were looking to do much more than simply document Mani's remarkable life: rather, their portrait of Mani served as a way of conveying the dominant self-identity of the religion in Late Antiquity as *the* authentic Christian tradition.

---

[47] See Lampe 2003, 241f.
[48] See Baker-Brian 2009, 1–79.

5. The 'Mani-biography' in the *Acts of Archelaus*

As the *CMC*, through its portrayal of Mani, provides clear statements about the collective identity of late-antique Manichaeans, so the *Acts of Archelaus* also presents its judgement about the religion on the basis of what it has to say about the lineage and life of Mani. Whilst these details are drawn, on the whole, from an established template for the portrayal of heresiarchs, it would be a mistake to think that Hegemonius, the putative author of the work, was not also fully aware of the distinguishing features of the Manichaean tradition, not least in the prominent role taken by Mani himself as the putative founder of Manichaeism.

The 'biography' of Mani stretches from chapter 61 to chapter 66 of *Acts*, nestling amidst the second address delivered by Archelaus, the Catholic bishop of Carchar, against Mani in the town of Diodoris which, as with Carchar, is also unattested elsewhere in ancient traditions, although it is evidently meant to represent a Romanised civic environment in Mesopotamia close to the frontier separating Roman from Sasanian territory. As the narrative indicates, Mani had fled to Diodoris after his initial defeat at the hands of Archelaus in Carchar. As noted by Hegemonius, alongside the population of Diodoris, the inhabitants of the entire province and 'the neighbouring areas' had come to the town in order to listen to Archelaus' denunciation of Mani: an evident rhetorical device within the narrative to suggest widespread popular support for the Christian teachings of the bishop of Carchar. Indeed, that the audience for the text is being led to understand the work as detailing a battle between two rival Christianities is clear from the statement outlining the Catholic position with regard to ecclesiastical tradition and the notion of apostolicity, made by Archelaus in chapter 61 of *Acts*:

> We are called Christians due to our desire for our Saviour, as the whole world testifies and the apostles teach; moreover the best architect Paul both laid down our foundation, that is the foundation of the Church, and handed down the law, and ordained ministers and presbyters and bishops within the Church. He described in special passages the manner in which ministers of God ought to be appointed and the kind of people needed, the kind that should become presbyters and in what way, and the kind of men that should seek the office of bishop. All of these good and proper arrangements have maintained their standing right down to today, and the observance of this formality remains with us (*Acts of Archelaus* 61.7–8; trans. M. Vermes 2001, 140).

What is likely to strike the modern reader of this passage are the doctrinal similarities that appear to exist between the Catholic position as outlined by Archelaus and the theology and institutional traditions of the Manichaeans: an attachment to Jesus the Saviour, the role of Paul in defining tradition, and the institutional structures of the church based on the transmission of teachings through a line of apostles, were all concerns shared by both Manichaean and Catholic Christians alike, although formulated according to very different cultural traditions of ancient Christian theology. If we were indeed unaware that Archelaus was speaking about Catholic Christianity at this point, then we would not be off the mark in ascribing these words to a spokesperson for Manichaean Christianity. However, the very point of this introductory salvo fired by Archelaus was to reclaim ground that Manichaean Christianity had already successfully claimed for itself in both the Mesopotamian and Roman worlds.

Hegemonius demonstrates his familiarity with the accepted way of under-mining an individual's or a community's reputation through the composition of a speech that drew attention to the principal faults and failings of its subject. A speech of blame (Gk *psogos*) was one of the main ways of attacking an opponent in antiquity, and stood in contradistinction to a speech of praise (Gk *enkōmion*), both of which formed elements in the wider subject of epideictic rhetoric: a higher educational discipline which the elite classes of the Roman world – politi-cians, lawyers and educators – took over from their Greek cultural ancestors and made their own. The appropriation of the discipline was also one of the distinguishing features of late Roman Christianity, as the 'new elites' – Christian bishops, theologians and heresiologists – made extensive use of rhetorical techniques to denigrate the ideas of opponents, foremost among them being those who in the process were branded as 'heretics'.[49] The construction and subsequent success of a speech of either praise or blame depended on the skills of the writer in following a prescribed list of virtues or vices that determined the rhetorical persuasiveness of his argument: i.e., the extent to which a speech actually affected a change in the listener's mind about a person. With regard to ancient invective, items of necessity that contributed to an overall 'negative' portrayal of the subject at hand included references to low birth (direct or indirect, and usually involving connections to slavery), instances of criminal activity (theft) and sexual impropriety (the more depraved the better): in its characterisation of Mani and his 'religious ancestors', *Acts* makes very effective use of the first two in the list.[50]

As members of the elite literary class in Late Antiquity, heresiologists followed the model of classical rhetoric, but not necessarily the examples (Gk *topoi*) – historical personalities and events – used by their rhetorical predecessors to establish parallels between the moral character of their subject and those of stock historical persons, heroes and, on occasion, gods. In the case of *Acts*, Ester Spät has demonstrated the way in which Hegemonius lent heavily on the portrayal of Simon Magus, the other arch-heresiarch (besides Mani) in early Christian apocryphal literature, in order to build a series of parallels between the fictional life of Mani and his predecessors.[51] Additional heresiological commonplaces are also in evidence throughout the biography, not least in terms of the stylisation of Mani as an arch-syncretist, which Hegemonius in turn was able to associate with the nature of the religion based on his teachings.

And so, Hegemonius' assessment of Mani's worth governs and runs alongside his assessment of the Manichaean religion, his intention being to show that the errors and failings of Mani are reflected in enlarged form in the character

[49] For an introduction to ancient rhetoric, see Pernot 2005, *passim*; for an up-to-date analysis of Late-Antique Christian attitudes to rhetoric, see Quiroga 2007.
[50] More detail on this subject may be gleaned from Knust 2006, 17–50.
[51] Spät 2004.

of Manichaeism. That Mani was not privy to divine revelations, and that by association he was neither (as he claimed to be) the 'Apostle of Jesus Christ' nor indeed the Paraclete (*Acts of Archelaus* 65. 6; Vermes 2001, 147), is established by Hegemonius through his exposure of the very human roots of Mani's dualist ideas about the universe. By way of establishing an anti-apostolic tradition – most likely assembled in full knowledge not only of the importance of providing an antithesis to the apostolic tradition of Catholic Christianity in the patristic representation of heresy, but also with the awareness of how important the idea of apostolic succession was to Manichaeism's reflection on Mani's identity – *Acts* posits that Manichaean dualism first appeared through a certain Scythianus who 'came from the race of the Saracens' (*Acts of Archelaus* 62. 4; Vermes 2001, 141). The ultimate source for Scythianus' ideas, however, was held to be the Greek philosopher Pythagoras, an important connection for Hegemonius to make since, according to heresiological tradition, Christian teachings were judged likely to become contaminated (i.e., heretical) at the point when philosophy was allowed to intersect the revelations of Christ: thus the polluting of divine teachings with human, 'pagan' speculation was held to create an 'ancient syncretism'.[52]

Acts adds layer upon layer of heresiological characterisation to Mani's unsavoury genealogy: Scythianus marries a woman prisoner, who in the Greek version of *Acts* used by Epiphanius (*Medicine Chest* 66.2.4) is a beautiful but licentious prostitute whom Scythianus rescues from a brothel, a detail which appears to have been borrowed from patristic traditions surrounding Simon Magus's consort Helen, variously styled as a prostitute and prisoner who, in the heresiological retelling of certain gnostic mythologoumena, represents a shamed and fallen Wisdom (*Sophia*) or 'First Thought of God'.[53] In making reference to this woman as Scythianus' companion, Hegemonius may have wanted to align Manichaeism with other 'gnostic' heresies that displayed mythopoeic tendencies, as described in earlier patristic literature, or, as is more likely, he wanted to strengthen the connections between Mani's teachings and their perceived origin within the Simonian tradition. Scythianus is also given by Hegemonius a connection with Egypt which would have carried dual significance for *Acts*'s ancient readers: not only was it an area of early Manichaean missionary activity and home to various Manichaeans, some living in monastic environments, others in Romanised villages and towns (e.g., Kellis), but, in heresiological terms, Egypt was also synonymous with magic ritual, the performance of which was a standard accusation levelled against heretics by patristic traditions.[54] As Hegemonius sarcastically remarks, this is the 'wisdom of the Egyptians' that eventually found its way into Mani's teachings.

Mani's other dualistic predecessor, Scythianus' disciple Terebinthus, is credited by Hegemonius as the author of four books, the titles of which are drawn from writings associated with Mani (see Chapter 3):

[52] See Scopello 1995, 216–17.
[53] See Pearson 2007, 26–33; also Spät 2004, 12.
[54] See Spät 2004, 7.

[Scythianus] was, to tell the truth, very gifted in intellect and in abilities, as those who knew him have also testified to us in the account handed down. He had a particular disciple, who wrote four books for him, one of which he called the book of the *Mysteries*, another that of the (*Chapters*), the third the *Gospel*, and the last book of all he called the *Thesaurus* (*Acts of Archelaus* 62.5–6; trans. M. Vermes 2001, 141–2).

Whilst Scythianus was planning to visit Judea and exchange ideas with the learned men there (see Epiphanius, *Medicine Chest* 66.3.1–7, for an expanded version of his visit), he passed away; Terebinthus, sensing his opportunity for fame and fortune, stole the books which he had authored, and fled to Babylonia. Arriving in Persian territory, Terebinthus changed his name to Buddha, and engaged in dialogue with 'a prophet called Parcus and Labdacus the son of Mithras' (*Acts of Archelaus* 63. 3; Vermes 2001, 142): however, they condemned his statements in which 'he would declare to them what existed before the present era, and about the sphere and the two luminaries, moreover about where souls depart to and how, and in what way they return to bodies again, and many other things of this nature and still more evil things than these, for example that war was caused for God with the elements …'.[55] In this regard, Hegemonius is evidently supplying an outline of Mani's teachings concerning the stages of co-eternity, war and eventual separation of the powers of the Light and the Darkness (the so-called 'Three Lessons': see Chapter 4), whilst claiming that Terebinthus' (= Mani's) dualism was so misguided that it even deviated from the orthodox teachings (as Hegemonius perceived them) of Zoroastrianism, represented by the figures of Parcus and Labdacus. The ignominious end for Mani's final predecessor came when, after moving in with a widow, Terebinthus fell from a high roof which he had ascended in order to invoke by magic the 'princes of the air', and thereby achieve physical flight. As Spät has demonstrated, Hegemonius in this instance was clearly following a tradition from the apocryphal *Acts of Peter* which recounted a similar ambition on the part of Simon Magus, and which also ended in an identical fate.[56] However, as with countless other elements in *Acts*'s 'biography', a genuine Manichaean tradition probably also lay behind the parodical technique of Hegemonius. Thus Paul Mirecki has noted: 'The exhibition of spiritual power evidencing the ritualist's access to heavenly secrets was apparently a common feature in the proselytizing methods employed by Mani … Hegemonius … defused Manichaean proselytizing intent by identifying the Manichaean use of such rituals with demonic magic, charlatanism, insincerity, failure and – in the case of our poor Terebinthus – death.'[57]

Feeling lonely, the widow purchased as a slave a small boy 'about seven years of age' named Corbicius (*Acts of Archelaus* 64.2; Vermes 2001, 143–4). Upon reaching adulthood (aged twelve), Corbicius received as his legacy from the recently deceased widow the books passed on from Scythianus to Terebinthus. Young Corbicius grew up to become the mature Mani who, changing his name

---

[55] *Acts of Archelaus* 63. 3–4; trans. M. Vermes 2001, 142–3.
[56] Spät 2004, 8–11
[57] Mirecki 2007, 155.

along the way, set about engineering the institution of the Manichaean church by sending out disciples to Egypt and Scythia (the lands from the Danube to the Volga and Caucasus). Again in imitation of hagiographical traditions that portrayed Mani as a physician, the prophet attended the court of an unnamed Persian king who charged him with curing his son of an illness. However, the child died and Mani was imprisoned (*Acts of Archelaus* 64.8–9; Vermes 2001, 145–6).[58]

Whilst languishing in prison, Mani was visited by his disciples who recounted their lack of success in winning converts. In order to obtain credibility for his missions, he ordered his disciples to purchase 'the books of the Christians', from which Mani artificially christianised his dualism by locating scriptural passages from the Bible that supported his claims. Furthermore,

> ... he pretended to adopt [the name of Christ], so that in all the cities when they heard the holy divine name of Christ they would not abhor or banish his disciples. Moreover when he found the verse in the Scriptures about the Paraclete, he supposed that he was the one ... (*Acts of Archelaus* 65.5–6; trans. Vermes 2001, 147).

The illusion of popularity offered by Christ's name profited Mani little, however, and he incurred the wrath of the Persian king who, presumably through fear that Mani was now a Christian proselytiser, inflicted even greater punishments on him. Mani, however, succeeded in fleeing prison, only to fall foul of Archelaus. Thus, Hegemonius' narrative of Mani's life ends 'in real time' with his appearance in Diodoris (*Acts of Archelaus* 66; Vermes 2001, 147–8), and the presentation of his 'biography'.

Thus, *Acts* follows the template of portraying heretics as being guilty of contaminating divine revelations with human artifice motivated by greed and vanity: the work locates Mani as a syncretistic Christian, as one in a line of opportunists seeking greater exposure for his teachings. Hegemonius' portrayal of Mani and his teachings carries, nevertheless, greater significance than other patristic treatments of heresiarchs due to the centrality of Mani's claims to be an apostle of Jesus Christ and the Paraclete, claims which Hegemonius succeeded in uncoupling from the twin foundations on which they rested, namely the Manichaean notion of apostolic succession and the Christian identity germane to Mani's teachings and those of his church. This was achieved by establishing an alternative genealogy for Mani: a model that had its origins in the heresiological version of apostolic succession which grew out of patristic imaginings of atrocities committed by Simon Magus, the Samaritan visionary from the *Acts of the Apostles* 8.9–24.

Whilst the historical value of the *Acts of Archelaus* as a documentary source for the life of Mani is rightly challenged, the representation of Mani in the *CMC* should prove no less challenging to those commentators who are seeking 'facts'

---

[58] See Gardner and Lieu 2004, 84–5, for an English translation of the Middle Persian fragment M3, recounting Mani at the court of Vahram I.

about Mani's life, his deeds, and the nature of his personality from the text. As this chapter has suggested, however, such a reading of both of these works constitutes a basic misunderstanding of the nature of ancient literature which, although demonstrating a preoccupation with the lives of either meritorious or nefarious individuals, nevertheless had very different concerns to those of modern authors and their audiences who engage with biography in the expectation of being able to 'get under the skin', so to speak, of an individual. In a devotional, hagiographical work like the *CMC*, that which can be securely known about Mani the third century visionary in a positivist sense is concealed by the overwhelming aim of the writers(s), who sought to present an image of Mani to the Manichaean community that would reinforce not only the primary cultural memory of Mani as the final apostle, but also the dominant sense of Manichaean community identity, which had been founded on this very same claim.

Chapter 3

Manichaean Theology I: Theology and Text

1. Introduction: Mani the Literary Apostle

Mani was readily associated by his opponents at an early stage with the production of writings. The apostle's first appearance before Marcellus in the *Acts of Archelaus* is of an image of Mani with a 'Babylonian book' tucked under his left arm (*Acts of Archelaus* 14.3; Vermes 2001, 58). The association was certainly not unwarranted, since Mani himself looked to present many of his central ideas in written form, 'my living books' as he referred to them in one fragmentary text (M5794 I etc., trans. I. Gardner and S.N.C. Lieu 2004, 109). This chapter will discuss the contribution of Mani to the literary traditions of late-antique Christianity by investigating what we know about Mani's writings, none of which, however, have survived in their entirety. Indeed, an awareness of how scholars over the years have sought to re-establish the form and content of Mani's books will also be a concern of this chapter.

The emergence of a canon of Mani's writings also goes hand in hand with the issues raised in this chapter. One trend in Manichaean studies is to regard the canon as the work of Mani himself, posited on the representation and words of Mani in works such as *The Chapters* as a self-consciously literary figure who valued the canonisation of his writings as a way of guaranteeing the longevity of his teachings and revelations. Whether or not Mani himself was responsible for this process is an important, although perhaps unanswerable, question. The little we do know about Mani's works indicates a pragmatic approach to writing in a manner not too dissimilar from the epistolary habits of Mani's hero, Paul. Mani was the figurehead for his nascent communities, and what he wrote undoubtedly reflected this position in the way that the sparse evidence for his many works suggests that they were used to instruct, cajole and console his new followers.

2. 'Write all these secrets on tablets of bronze': The Preservation of Mani's Message

The oft-repeated statement found in modern studies that the tenets and practices of Manichaeism appeared systematised from the very beginning – i.e., emerging fully formed at some point during or soon after Mani's own lifetime – constitutes a misunderstanding in thinking about the development of the Manichaean church in Late Antiquity. Such an assumption is nevertheless understandable since the institutions and practices of the church took their inspiration from the ideas, pronouncements, plans and expectations of Mani himself. Whilst the early period of the religion was marked by the consolidation of Mani's message, achieved primarily through its strategic dissemination among the ruling elites within and beyond Mesopotamia, the ritual character and the communal structures of the religion survived as barely realised ideas in the mind of Mani and in the burgeoning endeavours and practices of his immediate disciples and followers. Returning again to the *Epistle of the Ten Words* discussed briefly in the previous chapter – the recently discovered letter by Mani unearthed as part of the Kellis cache and painstakingly restored by Iain Gardner – we are given an insight into Mani's own role in securing an institutional future for his revelations. By way of some context – which is nevertheless difficult to pin down throughout the epistle – the letter itself appears to carry a sense of consolation, perhaps in the face of someone or something disrupting the peace of the nascent community in question, and Mani appears concerned to reassure the recipient about his chosen religious convictions:

> Remember your first faith that you had in your youth: How I laboured in the congregations of the sects at the time when there was yet no catechumen or church. You have become people made better by blessed poverty. Now, since you have been bringing forth catechumens and churches – you proclaimed and they listened to you – you are obliged the more now to perfect the blessing of this poverty, by which you will gain victory over the sects and the world (P.Kell.Copt. 53.51.1–14; trans. I. Gardner 2007a, 75).

Whilst pre-empting ourselves a little here in raising details about the structural operations of the Manichaean community that will nevertheless be covered in a more in-depth manner in the following chapter, it is worth offering some introductory remarks at this stage in order to contextualise the practical issues at stake in this letter by Mani. One half of the Manichaean church in its normative form was represented by the presence of a catechumenate, otherwise known as the Hearers. They were the linchpin for the ritualised activities pursued by the Manichaean Elect, the remaining other half of the community. The Hearers took care of the Elect by supplying all that was necessary for their daily needs, which included gathering food as alms for the Elect, in order to shield the Elect from in any way compromising the immaculate nature of their highly ethical lifestyle. The establishment of this bicameral (two-fold) structure was regarded by Manichaeans themselves as the major institutional achievement of the Manichaean church, since it made possible the ultimate rationale of an institutionalised Manichaeism, namely the performance of a ritual meal by the Elect that stood as the religion's central act of salvation (see Chapter 4). As Mani notes in the letter, those to whom it was addressed are called upon 'to perfect the blessing of this [blessed] poverty' precisely because a body of catechumenate is now in place in order to assist them in their ascetic endeavours.

In common with other significant cultural figures from the late-antique period, Mani engaged enthusiastically with the practice of letter writing. Al-Nadim in his *Fihrist* (Dodge 1970, II.799–800) provides a long list of the titles of letters authored by Mani 'and of the Imans [i.e., heads of the post-Mani church] after him' (totalling 52), and a further list 'in addition to these' (totalling 21), whilst failing nevertheless to make a more clear distinction between those letters authored by Mani and those written by his successors; furthermore, his list probably represents an incomplete catalogue of the total number of letters that Mani actually authored.[1] At some stage – perhaps even during Mani's own lifetime – the letters of the apostle were gathered together to form a single authoritative collection, as evidenced by their short-lived reclamation from among the Coptic works of Medinet Madi:[2] indeed, collections of Mani's letters are also attested in texts from Turfan.[3] For Mani, the writing of letters went hand in hand with the missions conducted by his nascent movement, most likely acting as the means by which he initially introduced himself and his disciples to would-be converts, and almost certainly served as the most appropriate way for him to keep abreast of developments within early Manichaean communities. In this sense, a comparison between Mani's use of the 'communicative technology' of letter writing and the epistolary practices of St Paul is very appropriate, it being a commonplace in Manichaean studies to suggest that Mani was imitating Paul in this regard. Like Paul, Mani's letters were likely to have been prompted by moments of crisis within his communities, an example of which is hinted at tantalisingly in the *Epistle of the Ten Words*. Although what actually remains of letters authored by Mani is sparse, the evidence indicates that the addressing of pastoral issues was a significant feature of Mani's concern with letter writing; however, it should also be noted that the most famous letter by Mani to have circulated in the Roman empire, *The Foundation*,[4] which may be the same as the 'long letter to Futtuq' mentioned by al-Nadim – the letter's fame arising from Augustine's response to it[5] – was effectively a concise statement of Mani's main cosmogonic tenets for use by his disciples (i.e., Patig) among the Romanised provinces of Palestine and Egypt.[6]

Mani's industriousness as a letter writer is the clearest sign of his wider concern with the communicative role of the written word as a pastor and theologian. A tradition emerged within late-antique Manichaeism which held that Mani himself had insisted upon the importance of writing down his teachings for the sake of posterity. In the introduction to *The Chapters*, Mani is presented as associating the success of his teachings with the act of committing them to a written form, whereby success equates to the notion that the writing down of revelations guarantees their longevity within the world: as Mani notes in that work, his illustrious apostolic predecessors – Jesus, Zoroaster and Buddha – taught and established churches but 'did not write their wisdom in books ... [and as a result]

---

[1] Sundermann 2009b, 260.

[2] Gardner 2001, 98–100.

[3] Sundermann 2009b.

[4] See Stein 2002; English translation in Gardner and Lieu 2004, 168–72.

[5] Augustine, *Answer to the Letter of Mani known as The Foundation*; trans. R.J. Teske 2006, 234–67.

[6] Cf. Gardner 2001, 103–4.

their righteousness and their church will pass away from the world.'[7] Whilst such a claim was evidently used by authors in the post-Mani period to also justify the existence of their own works alongside those written by Mani himself (an especially prominent concern in the introduction to *The Chapters*), the seeds of the idea concerning the inviolability achieved when religious teachings are set down in the form of a text are present in Mani's own writings. From the opening address of his *Living Gospel*, Mani notes: 'I have proclaimed hope and revealed this revelation: and have written this immortal gospel, in which I have put down these pre-eminent secret rites [Gk *orgia*] and declared great deeds, indeed the greatest and holiest of supreme deeds of power.'[8] Such a statement suggests that as far as Mani was concerned the immortal nature of the revelations experienced by him could only be, in his estimation, most appropriately and most reverentially received by offering those teachings the closest thing to an immortal existence in this world, namely their enshrining in the written word.

What lies behind the notion of longevity beyond the lengthy but still finite materiality offered by the written text was the desire to preserve Mani's teachings from contamination by the teachings of the *dogmas* – a term favoured by Greek Manichaean writers to denote errant religious sects – a problem which to the Manichaean mind had been experienced acutely by the traditions that had been established under the names of Mani's apostolic predecessors. For example, the Gospel of Jesus had, in Manichaean estimations, experienced very great contamination – understood primarily in relation to the four canonical gospels – by 'Judaisers', an idea that was meant to suggest the deliberate mixing of Jewish traditions with the teachings of Jesus: a judgement that may have arisen as an original challenge by Mani himself to the scriptural tendencies and ritual activities of Jewish-Christian (Elchasaite) groups in Mesopotamia. In concrete terms, this meant that Manichaeans condemned material in the Gospel which looked as if it was extraneous to its overall message, such as those sayings (Gk *logia*) whereby Jesus was heard to uphold the law of the Pentateuch at the expense of his own antinomian message, e.g., 'Do not suppose that I have come to abolish the law and the prophets; I did not come to abolish, but to complete' (Mt. 5. 17). One of the earliest missionaries sent by Mani to the Roman world called Adda – nicknamed Adimantus ('The Fearless One') in the Western tradition – was particularly concerned in one of his works (*The Disputations*) to cut away the polluting influence of the 'classical' Jewish scriptures, i.e., the Pentateuch and the Prophets (certain Jewish traditions being regarded negatively by Manichaeism: see below), on the way in which Christian groups contextualised the prophetic status of Jesus.[9] For Adda and later Manichaeans in the Roman world, the theological themes of promise and fulfilment linking the Jewish scriptures (The Old Testament) with the Gospel (The New Testament) constituted a heinous theological error of judgement. As far as Manichaeans were concerned, the only

[7] *The Chapters* 8.8–10: trans. I. Gardner 1995, 13.

[8] *CMC* 67.11–21; J.M. Lieu and S.N.C. Lieu, in. Gardner and Lieu 2004, 157. Quite what Mani meant by 'secret rites' in the context of his decision to publish details about them is a moot point.

[9] See Baker-Brian 2009.

prophetic context needed to identify the significance of Jesus was to place him within the true prophetology that Mani himself also claimed membership of in his own writings and pronouncements.

Indeed, this leads us onto a crucial consideration concerning the role that Mani and the Manichaeans placed on the importance of writings in their religion. As a result of who Mani himself and consequently his followers believed him to be – i.e. the Paraclete and the apostle of Jesus Christ – it was regarded, in a sense, as part of Mani's 'apostolic duty' to commit his revelations and teachings to writing. Whilst the 'national apostles', Zoroaster (Persia), Buddha (India) and Jesus (the 'Western world'), had failed (according to the introduction to *The Chapters* 7.18–8.28) to leave written accounts of what they had taught and had 'left things to chance', so to speak, by depending on their disciples to write down their teachings, Mani was also very likely aware of a rich scriptural tradition that consisted of writings that were credited to some very archaic figures. The apocalypses of the biblical forefathers – Adam, Seth, Enosh, Shem and Enoch (cf. *CMC* 45–60) – derived via detailed adaptation by Manichaeans from an 'extrabiblical' tradition of Jewish pseudepigraphic literature (the term *pseudepigraphicum* denotes a literary work given an assumed name), which had its roots in the so-called Second Temple period of Jewish history.[10] The presence of portions of these 'apocalyptic' texts in the *CMC* has reinforced the already well-established awareness among modern commentators that Mani and his followers borrowed, adapted and transformed key works of Jewish pseudepigrapha, for the purposes of developing their own theological ideas about the world and its relationship to the wider universe, referred to as a *cosmogony*; and for situating the central religious claim for Mani as a member of a divinely-elected 'family' of divine apostles, i.e., the concept of prophetology discussed in Chapter 2. That Mani appears to have read and been influenced by Jewish pseudepigraphic literature is apparent from the inclusion of a work entitled the *Book of Giants* in the Manichaean scriptural canon as having been authored by Mani himself, an earlier and highly fragmentary recension of which formed part of the Qumran collection of texts – the so-called 'Dead Sea Scrolls' – which in turn represented a discrete and extended exegetical treatment of the pseudepigraphic work, 1 Enoch chs 6–11 (see below).[11]

The association made in the *CMC* between the biblical forefathers as divinely-commissioned apostles and the apostolic identity of Mani is therefore established through the obligation that apostles are charged with *writing down* teachings revealed to them at moments of divine inspiration, as the best way of securing their longevity and immunity from corrupting influences. The *CMC* reflects an idea important to Manichaeism – likely deriving from Mani himself – that religious authority derives in large part from texts: as Balsamos, 'the greatest Angel of Light', called upon Adam to 'receive from me and write these things I reveal to you on the purest papyrus which is not perishable or liable to worm',[12]

---

[10] For a highly useful introduction to the history and literature of the Second Temple period, see Helyer 2002.

[11] On 1 Enoch and its influence on early Christian writings, see Helyer 2002, 77–92. Mani's relationship to previous traditions of the *Book of Giants* is the main concern of Reeves 1992.

[12] *CMC* 49.3–12; trans. J.M. Lieu and S.N.C. Lieu in Gardner and Lieu 2004, 54.

and as Enosh was commanded similarly by an angel to 'write all these secrets on bronze tablets',[13] so Mani must also write if he is to realise his role as an apostle of God.

3. The Writings of Mani and the Manichaean Canon

Building on the claims made in works like *The Chapters* linking the production of writings with the development and consolidation of an uncorrupted religious authority, many commentators regard Mani and Manichaeism as having played an important role in influencing one of the more distinctive aspects of late-antique religious identity: the emergence of traditions that accorded a central role to the production of sacred texts as a way of establishing claims to being authoritative bearers of divine law, a trend which has been referred to as a 'Scriptural Movement', although is more widely known in the idea of the rise of the 'Religions of the Book'. Whilst the latter expression itself has a long, and not entirely unproblematic, history in the study of ancient religions, it is only in recent times that more concentrated study has been undertaken aimed at unpacking the various layers according to which religious authority was achieved by textual means.[14] Christianity, Manichaeism and Islam – and indeed other traditions including the philosophical schools (e.g., Neoplatonism) of the late-antique period – all sought to promote whilst simultaneously defend their teachings by engaging with the new developments in the production of texts, in forms such as the codex which certain traditions (notably Christianity) took over and made their own: recall indeed the Manichaean partiality for amulet codices, as seen in the miniature dimensions of the *CMC* (see Chapter 1). Whilst these different traditions utilised the written word in order to establish the supremacy of their own teachings in a variety of different ways – Manichaeism and Islam locating themselves as culminant authorities in the history of revealed religions with their own books (Mani's writings and the Koran) forming an essential element of this claim – the notion of the 'Religions of the Book' is nevertheless chiefly bound up with, indeed is only really conceivable in relation to, the process known as scriptural canonisation: in other words, the decision to fix in a collected form a body of scriptural texts which have been regarded – consensually or otherwise – as representing the normative teachings of a tradition.

When and why Mani's writings became fixed in a canon remains something of a mystery. The earliest indication that a collection of the apostle's writings were regarded as forming an essential component in the legacy of Mani's teachings to the Manichaean church is found in a number of works from Medinet Madi. In one of the sermons belonging to the great collection of Coptic *Homilies* from Narmouthis called 'The Sermon on the Great War', ascribed to an early disciple named Koustaios – a work that represents a sustained meditation on Mani's teachings about the great and final conflict presaging the end of times[15]

---

[13] *CMC* 54. 11–12; trans. J.M. Lieu and S.N.C. Lieu in Gardner and Lieu 2004, 55.

[14] See Stroumsa 2008; and Stroumsa 2009, 28–55.

[15] See esp. Pedersen 1996, 399–403.

– the writings of Mani are listed as a *Heptateuch* (a collection of seven books),[16] although in other sources the canon is reduced to a *Pentateuch* (a collection of five books; *The Chapters* 148. 355.4–25[17]). The Heptateuch runs as follows:

1. Gospel (Living Gospel)
2. Treasury of Life
3. Pragmateia
4. Book of Mysteries
5. Book of Giants
6. Epistles
7. Psalms and Prayers

All of the above works were originally composed in Syriac (i.e., Mani's native language), although it should be noted that what remain of these writings are largely translations (e.g., in Greek, Latin, Coptic, Arabic and the many Iranian languages), having been preserved for posterity for no other reason than because they provided testimony of 'Mani's error' for those Christian and Islamic heresiologists who wrote refuting his theological ideas and those of his later followers. However, evidence from Turfan and Kellis have brought to light – and indeed continue to do so – translations of Mani's writings as read by his followers in both the late-antique and medieval Chinese worlds. Despite some variation in the order of individual works in other references to the canon in Manichaean literature, a considerable degree of uniformity in its representation is evident throughout the religion's history.[18]

It is noteworthy that two works do not appear in classical formulations of the canon, one being the exegetical-cosmogonic-eschatological *Šābuhragān* (see below), the other called the *Image*. The former was probably not included in such lists since those responsible for canonising Mani's writings were likely to have been first- or second-generation Mesopotamian Manichaeans, for whom Syriac rather than Pahlavi (Middle Persian) was their 'living language' (see below). The latter work, appearing after the list of seven writings in the *Homilies* (25. 5) under its Coptic-Greek title *Eikōn* (Middle Persian title, *Ārdhang*), has intrigued generations of Manichaean scholars. Older opinions about the function of the *Image* linked it squarely with the contents of the *Living Gospel* as a type of illustrated companion volume, an idea that has since fallen out of favour. More convincing is the idea that the *Image* contained illuminated scenes depicting Mani's cosmogony, the images serving as mnemonics in the imparting of the elaborately woven cast of divine characters and events that went to make up Mani's dramatic account of the universal clash of Light and Darkness.[19] If the work is to be regarded therefore as a companion volume to Mani's core works, the allusions to the work suggest that its 'natural' companion would have been the *Pragmateia*, the work that laid out the central cosmogonic teachings of

[16] *Manichaean Homilies* 25. 2–5; ed. and trans. N.A. Pedersen 2006, 25.
[17] See Pettipiece 2009, 209.
[18] See Tardieu 2008, 48–51.
[19] See Tardieu 2008, 43–4.

Mani. Discussion of one part of the work's contents raised in *The Chapters* (92. 234.24–236.6: I. Gardner 1995, 241–2) reveals that the *Image* depicted scenes from the final times, in relation to the judgements passed on the Elect and the sinner respectively. The work also appears to have carried with it a commentary, with explanatory remarks accompanying individual illustrations.[20] That Mani valued pictorial art as a way of communicating his teachings is an indication of his commitment to a medium that he regarded as being of equal value to the written word, an attitude which almost certainly influenced later traditions of illuminated Manichaean works.[21]

The appearance of a seven-fold collection of Mani's writings in the context of 'The Sermon on the Great War' may shed some light on understanding the decision of the Manichaean community to collect Mani's writings into a canon. As Nils Arne Pedersen (1996) has demonstrated in his commentary on 'The Sermon on the Great War', the historical context for the homily lay in the period of intense persecutions of Manichaean communities in Sasanian-controlled lands, in the later half of the third century. The persecution of Manichaeans soon after the death of Mani and subsequent stop-start persecutions stretching all the way to the end of the third and into the fourth century brought moments of genuine crisis for Manichaeans in what was, in effect, their homeland of Mesopotamia: that these persecutions were regarded by Manichaeans themselves as being religiously motivated, brought about through the machinations of the Zoroastrian clergy in the Sasanian court, is evident in the homily through the alignment of the theological concept of Error (Gk *planē*) with the malign intentions of the Magi, the ruling Zoroastrian priestly elite. The immediate consequences of the persecutions for followers of Mani would therefore have included both imprisonment and execution, or flight to territories beyond Sasanian rule, for those standing by their Manichaean allegiances; or, for those wishing to escape punishment, the renouncing of Mani's name and the shame of apostasy.

During such periods of crisis, dramatic ruptures in the ritual and cultural traditions of Mesopotamian Manichaean communities must have been inevitable, and therefore the desire to consolidate the elements intrinsic to 'Manichaean' identity was likely experienced very keenly, one aspect of which should be seen in attempts to collect, order and close off (i.e., the stages of canon formation) Mani's writings. In this sense, the development of a canon extends one of the principal roles of writing itself as 'a medium of memory',[22] in the sense that the canon protects in a move towards memorialisation those teachings regarded as revelatory and normative, their normativity increasing during the process of canonisation. Furthermore, amidst the tumultuous events of the late third century, the development of a Manichaean canon represented undoubtedly 'a desire for permanence, the longing for eternity amid ephemeral phenomena and the transitory world'.[23] Indeed, it is in this context that the

---

[20] See Henning 1943, 71–2; although note the cautions sounded by Sundermann 2005.
[21] See esp. Gulácsi 2005.
[22] Assmann 2006, 87.
[23] Assmann 2006, 79–80.

remark ascribed to Mani in *The Chapters* concerning the permanency brought about by his move towards writing down his revelations (as against the orality of Zoroaster, Buddha and Jesus) should be regarded *not* as the words of Mani himself, but rather as a statement by the authors/editors of *The Chapters* concerning the rationale for creating a canon of the apostle's writings: '[Mani speaks] ... [Buddha] unveiled to them his hope. Yet, there is only this: that he did not write his wisdom in books. His disciples, who came after him, are the ones who remembered somewhat the wisdom that they had heard from Buddha. They wrote it in scriptures (*The Chapters* 8.3–7; trans. I. Gardner 1995, 13).'

The statement from the introduction is of particular importance since *The Chapters* probably derived from the same time and the same troubled Mesopotamian environment as the *Homilies*, and as such it is very likely that the canonisation of Mani's works dates from this period in Manichaeism's early history. Whilst the closing-off of the canon may, in theory at least, have protected Mani's teachings from corrosive influences, it did little to resolve the ambiguities raised by Mani's own writings. Canonisation thus encouraged the production of 'sub-canonical' literature within Manichaeism, the best example of which is probably *The Chapters* itself, a work which served a 'scholastic' purpose by adding commentary and clarifying opaque aspects of Mani's teachings.[24] That the author(s) of *The Chapters* felt the need to systematise the ideas of Mani is an indication that what Mani wrote was determined by the events and circumstances which he found himself involved in during his day-to-day experiences as a peripatetic teacher and religious reformer: he wrote as a teacher, responding to the needs of his followers, and always with one eye on expanding his church, having little care or time to create a 'systematic theology', which he is so often credited with developing.[25] The influence of the canon on early and later developments in Manichaean theology and literature was therefore uniquely powerful: it created a pronounced sense of cultural identity among Manichaeans, influencing their own forms of religious expression, much of it in imitation of what Mani wrote, such as the extensive tradition of psalms and hymns from nearly all periods of the religion's history.

Many modern discussions of Mani's writings begin with the claim that the canon of his works formed an important part of his own legacy to the Manichaean church. L.J.R. Ort's observation is typical in this regard: '[Mani] chose to bestow to his church a clearly defined canon of books.'[26] Others have mistakenly regarded Mani's success in spreading his message so successfully in such a relatively short period of time as arising from 'his creation of a canon of authoritative writings'.[27] Such claims nevertheless form one aspect of a larger misunderstanding in the apprehension of Manichaeism's historical development, which as we saw above stems from the by now familiar desire – formulated intentionally or otherwise – to deny the possibility that the religion developed

[24] See Pettipiece 2009, 79–91.
[25] Cf. Rudolph 1987, 334–6.
[26] Ort 1967, 115.
[27] van Oort 2004, 282.

historically, through the imposition of the notion that Manichaeism instead appeared ready-formed in the person and teachings of Mani, thus implying a process of ahistorical generation. Indeed, the emphasis in discussions on the Manichaean canon has also meant that scrutiny of the individual writings that went to make up the Manichaean Heptateuch has been less thorough than it should have been. *However*, concentration on the canon rather than on the writings is one of legacies of the practical situation facing those studying Manichaeism, since so very little of the individual works of Mani survive intact, as a result of the many persecutions endured by the religion through the centuries and the inevitable attempts at the cultural eradication of Manichaeism that were part of such oppressive actions. Indeed, one of the great ironies in the study of Manichaeism concerns the fact that, whilst the canonisation of Mani's writings may have protected the apostle's teachings from corruption, it could do little to save them from almost total destruction.

In this regard, some interesting observations have been made by Jan Assmann – a prominent academic in the application of the theories of cultural anthropology to the disciplines of history and archaeology, and who has written in broad terms about the phenomenon of textual canonisation – noting that ancient developments in canon formation encourage shifts in modern academic perspectives away from the critical scrutiny of the individual works that collectively comprise a canon, to the consideration of 'the forces that motivate the development, growth, coming together, and sanctification of the texts.'[28] The expression 'sanctification of texts' through canonisation is especially relevant with regard to modern studies of Mani's writings, since his works not only tend to be viewed from a canonical rather than an individual perspective, but as a further consequence they are also regarded as theological writings of a peculiarly rarefied kind.

However, Mani's own approach to writing was almost certainly a much more gradual and pragmatic affair than is suggested by the apprehension of his works through their presence in the Manichaean canon. Indeed, one way in which we would be able to better understand the background and purpose of Mani's writings on a case-by-case basis – even in their highly fragmented states – would be to keep in mind Mani's principal (and self-styled) roles as an apostle and teacher during discussions of his writings. These roles demanded of Mani an entirely practical approach to the propagation of his teachings, particularly in light of the claims made in the fragmentary texts (M5794 I + M5761) which likely formed the point of orientation for the revelations of Mani's apostolate, and which may have been part of his *Šābuhragān*:

> [Mani speaks] This religion which was chosen by me is in ten things above and better than the other religions of the ancients. Firstly, the older religions were in one country and one language; but my religion is of the kind that it will be manifest in every country and in all languages, and it will be taught in far away countries (trans. S. Lieu, in I. Gardner and S.N.C. Lieu 2004, 109).

[28] J. Assmann 2006, 65.

Forming an essential aspect of the Christian character of Mani's teaching, the plan of the apostle from the outset was for his religion to be determined by a thoroughgoing sense of mission, realised in the linguistic and cultural acts of translating his teachings. Alongside the early Manichaean disciples who themselves brought about these translations through their abilities as teachers and linguists – Mani choosing for himself a number of urbane, multi-lingual disciples from cosmopolitan towns and cities such as Seleucia–Ctesiphon, the famous 'twin cities' of Mesopotamia, and Palmyra, the rebellious client kingdom of the later Roman empire – was the role taken by his own works in the communication of his message. Thus, text and mission were closely intertwined during the religion's earliest times. Mani's desire to enhance the effectiveness of the written word as a medium of communication is evident from his adaptation of the existing Iranian Pahlavi script to accommodate characters from the Syriac alphabet, in order that his works could be made accessible to Iranian audiences. Michel Tardieu notes the seismic historical–cultural significance of this achievement:

> ... Mani occupies a central place in Iranian culture and, more generally, in the history of writing. In casting his prophecy in a modern and clearly written language, he resolutely turned his back on the custodians of linguistic hieraticism who served the state religion (archaicizing language being the sign of outmoded religious practice) and prepared the way for the adoption of the Arab script in Iran following the advent of Islam. The prophecies of Mani and Muhammad each constituted a religion of the book. Such a religion, in order to give voice to God, must possess clarity of language and writing.[29]

We should perhaps envisage two scenarios for the role of Mani's writings in the diffusion of his teachings. The first scenario involves the place taken by them as a feature inherent in the nature of the missions themselves, with disciples taking copies of the writings with them for the purposes of teaching target audiences, and for leaving with nascent communities once the vanguard missionaries had departed, as the symbolic presence of Mani's authority despite his absence from them. Evidence for this suggestion may be seen in a fragment (M2) in Middle Persian recovered from Turfan detailing the early history of the church, which provides a priceless insight into the involvement of Mani himself in overseeing the course of missions in the Roman world, whilst he remained in Mesopotamia:

> [The disciples of Mani] went to the Roman Empire and saw many doctrinal disputes with the religions. Many Elect and Hearers were chosen. Patig was there for one year. (Then) he returned (and appeared) before the apostle. Hereafter the lord [Mani] sent three scribes, the [*Living*] Gospel and two other writings to Adda. He gave the order: 'Do not take it [the mission] further, but stay there like a merchant who collects a treasure

(trans. J.P. Asmussen 1975, 21; reproduced in I. Gardner and S.N.C. Lieu 2004, 111).

The *Living Gospel*, the work residing at the head of the religion's canon lists, evidently played an indispensable role in the advancement of the religion in the West. However, as the Iranian fragment suggests, Mani may not have actually finished writing the work when the western mission was initially sent on its way. From the same text is to be found an account of another early mission (both taking place at some period in the early 260s), this time, however, sent in the opposite direction further east into Abarshahr in the western reaches of Khorasan, where Adda's eastern counterpart Mar Ammo also had the need to consult one of Mani's books during his encounter on the border of the Kushan empire with Bagard, the spirit of the East. Although the account in question is evidently of a semi-fabulous nature – indeed both accounts, whilst based upon ancient historical recollections of the events they record, nevertheless show signs of being transformed by the legendary tendencies of later Manichaean historio-graphical traditions – it manages to convey an impression of the central teaching role taken by Mani's writings in the early missions:

> When they came to the watchpost of Kushan, lo, there appeared the spirit of the border of the East in the form of a girl. And she asked me, Ammo, 'What do you want? Where have you come from?' I said, 'I am a believer, a disciple of the Apostle Mani.' The spirit said, 'I will not accept you. Return to where you have come from!' Then it disappeared after me. Thereafter I, Ammo, stood in prayer to the sun for two days of fasting. Then the Apostle appeared to me and said, 'Do not be faint-hearted. Recite (the chapter) "The Collecting of the Gates" from *The Treasure of the Living*.'
>
> Then on the following day, the spirit appeared again and said to me, 'Why did you not return to your country?' I said, 'I have come from afar because of the religion.' The spirit said, 'What is the religion you bring?' I said, 'We do not eat meat nor drink wine. We (also) keep away from women.'
>
> It said, 'In my kingdom there are many like you.'
>
> I recited (the chapter) 'The Collecting of the Gates' from *The Treasure of the Living*. Then it (the spirit) paid respect to me and said, 'You are a pure righteous one. From now on I shall no more call you "possessor of religion" but "the true bringer of religion", for you surpass all others' (trans. H.-J. Klimkeit 1993, 204).[30]

The second scenario relates to the genesis of these works, and the likelihood that the decision to produce writings occurred whilst Mani was engaged in travelling throughout the regions that lay within and also beyond the control of the Sasanian empire. However, what is known about Mani's own early missions is fragmentary, a situation compounded by the presence of two seemingly different traditions suggesting alternative routes for these first journeys. One

---

[30] See S.N.C. Lieu 1992, 219–20.

tradition, as preserved in *The Chapters*, records an immediate push by Mani into the far eastern limits of Iranian territory and beyond into India soon after his decisive encounter with his Twin (1. 15.24–16.2; trans. I. Gardner and S.N.C. Lieu 2004, 75; cf. chapter 76, 'Concerning Lord Manichaios, how he journeyed'; trans. I. Gardner 1995, 193–7). *The Chapters* describes Mani's journey to India in proselytising terms: 'I crossed to the country of the Indians. I preached to them the hope of life. I chose in that place a good Election [i.e., founded a community].' The other tradition, found in the *CMC* (107.1–147.12; trans. I. Gardner and S.N.C. Lieu 2004, 66–73), hints at a more complex and far-reaching Western mission in Iran, prior to his departure for the East and India.[31]

Furthermore, the details of the later travels of Mani, including his involvement in the retinue of Shapur I, are patchy, and can only be surmised about at best.[32] A more balanced assessment of early Manichaean mission is certainly required, one which rightly acknowledges Mani's skills as a promoter of his teachings, his aptitude evident in the range and number of missions that he is credited with commissioning, whilst also emphasising the pragmatic nature of many of these ventures, some of which indeed may not have been of a missionary nature at all.

One of the main hurdles in reconstructing the missionary history of early Manichaeism concerns the nature of the later Iranian source material from which our impressions are drawn, much of which presents a triumphalist portrait of Mani and his disciples' activities in the provinces and regions within and beyond Sasanian territory, converting rulers, performing miracles and overcoming the teachings of the other 'dogmas' and 'false faiths'. One particular incident, involving Mani's conversion of the Shah of Turan, 'a small Buddhist kingdom in what is today Baluchistan',[33] and narrated in fragments in Parthian (M48; trans. H.-J. Klimkeit 1993, 206–8), demonstrates the complexities involved in assessing the documentary value of the central-Asian Manichaean material. Werner Sundermann's discussion of the account, which narrates Mani's disputation with 'a righteous one' (perhaps signifying a Buddhist teacher), followed by the instruction and conversion of the Shah that includes a confession by him of Mani as *the* Buddha, acknowledges that a conflicted assessment of the incident is almost inevitable:

Mani is himself described as a Buddha, and it is probably not going too far to assume that Mani here regards himself as the Buddha Maitreya, the eschatological saviour of Mahayana Buddhism, as whom he is often referred to in the later Central Asian Manichaean texts. Admittedly, the story of the conversion of the Turan-sah displays many of the hallmarks of Manichaean hagiographical stylization. However, the name Turan and the title and the very existence up to the middle of the third century of a Turan-sah are historical, and there is no geographical or chronological

[31] See esp. Römer 1994; also Deeg and Gardner 2009.
[32] See S.N.C. Lieu 1992, 70–80.
[33] Klimkeit 1993, 206.

reason why Mani should not have visited this area and even converted a king.[34]

Thus, even in a relatively early work like *The Chapters*, a tendency to prioritise 'high-status' missions, notably Mani's journey to India, is clearly apparent, which appears to distort, historically-speaking, the actual route of Mani's primary journeys.

Therefore, in the accounts of Manichaean missionary history, it is arguable that the historiographical (the memorialisation of the past), and the hagiographical (the idealisation of Mani's person and activities) tendencies of the religion obstruct an appreciation of some of the slightly more fundamental concerns of Mani's early years. Mani's travels likely involved just as much, if not more, education and disputation with other sects and traditions than proselytising activities. With regard to Mani's fabled journey to India, about which Manichaeans were justly proud, Max Deeg and Iain Gardner have challenged the religion's historical memorialisation of this expedition, together with academic assessments of the journey's missionary purpose:

> The circumstances of Mani's journey to India have to be collected from different rather fragmentary sources but it seems clear that it took place between 240 [and] 242. This was a crucial and formative period, as Manichaean tradition in [*The Chapters*] reports that Mani received his decisive 'revelation' in 240. Thus one may well, supposing in reality a more gradual development of Mani's teaching than asserted by later tradition, suggest that the years after this date still belonged to the formative period of his religious system; and that what came to be stylized as a mission journey by the Manichaeans themselves was rather an 'educational' trip to the then accessible regions east of the Iranian homeland.[35]

However, as Werner Sundermann has noted (see above; 1986), the evidence in favour of Mani initiating some sort of community foundation in India is too considerable to be simply dismissed.

The *CMC* (107.1–147.12) records an alternative westward orientation for Mani's early travels than the impression given in *The Chapters* of a direct push eastwards into India, and purports to preserve Mani's contact with baptist groups (see, e.g., 140.8–143.12) which were probably linked 'genetically' to the Elchasaites of his formative years. The extent to which Mani experienced opposition to, but also acceptance of, his alternative ideas to baptismal law is not known, although from a strategic point of view it made good sense to start with what was familiar: thus, Mani began his mission among baptists, as Jesus (Mt. 4.23), Stephen and Paul (Acts 6.8ff.; 9.20) had begun their teaching in synagogues.[36] Among other religious groups, however, Mani's teachings were not always well received: one particular incident, forming part of the biogra-

---

[34] Sundermann 1986, 13.
[35] See Deeg and Gardner 2009, 12–13.
[36] Henrichs and Koenen 1981, 276.

phy's poorly preserved final pages, narrates an exchange between Mani and a religious leader of an assembly (Gk *sunagōgē* = synagogue) during his travels at the southernmost limit of Mesopotamia, which Mani, in true hagiographical style, succeeds in winning:

> (... [Mani is speaking] I came) into (a) village called S(...) and went (into the) assembly of the (...), the so-(called sons) of the truth. The head of the (sect of) unrigh(teousness) said (to me: 'The) exact understanding of the teaching (of our fathers ...)' *10 lines lost* He conducted (a) disputation with me before the men of his faith. In all points he was (defeated) and (drew) laughter on himself, so that he was filled with (envy) and malice (*CMC* 137.2–138.9; trans. J.M. Lieu and S.N.C. Lieu, in Gardner and Lieu 2004, 71–2.)

The fragmentary nature of this portion of the text has prevented any firm identification of which sect this was – possibly Magi, possibly Jews[37] – and whilst its place in the *CMC* should alert us to its propagandistic value in a text that was concerned to construct an idealised biography of Mani (see Chapter 2), it nevertheless raises the important consideration that Mani was required on occasions to defend and adapt his teachings. That these processes were pursued using the written word, i.e., through his writings, in addition to the model of orality on display in the *CMC* is an issue of importance in the evolution of Mani and Manichaeism's religious development.

Evidence for the idea that Mani's writings reflect early concerns of the sect with sectarian controversies can also be seen in the remains of those works. Most significantly, the testimony supplied by al-Nadim for Mani's *Book of Mysteries* (Dodge 1970, II.797–8; cf. M. Tardieu 2008, 38–41) indicates that Mani's challenge to the more established religious traditions of Mesopotamia and Syria was an important concern of the work (see below). Therefore, whilst it is a challenge to date the composition and appearance of individual works – although, as the testimony from M2 suggests, the *Living Gospel* and the *Treasury of Life* had already been written by the 260s – it is reasonable to assume that some of Mani's writings were inspired by, and to an extent reflected his direct experiences in the propagation of, his teachings among individuals and communities who were probably inimical to his message. The suggestion, therefore, that some of the works of Mani at least took the role of apologies – as defences of his ideas in the face of opposition – for his teachings is rarely remarked upon in studies of Manichaeism.

Following the order of works from the canon lists in the Coptic writings (e.g., *Homilies* 25. 2–5; *The Chapters* 5. 23–6), the subsequent section will consider what we know about Mani's writings, whilst also bearing in mind the complex textual problems which surround their reconstruction, an approach taken by many Manichaean scholars, including Widengren and Tardieu, in their own introductions to the religion. However, we start with the work not included in 'Western' canonical formulations of Mani's writings, the *Šābuhragān*, which is

---

[37] See S.N.C. Lieu 1994, 1–21, for a discussion.

nevertheless named as one of Mani's works by authorities such al-Nadim, who states simply that 'Mani wrote seven books, one of them in Persian [i.e., the *Šābuhragān*] and six in Syriac, the language of Syria' (trans. B. Dodge 1970, II.797).

Šābuhragān

Whilst discussion of the *Šābuhragān*'s teachings has been raised in Chapter 1, and will be discussed further in Chapter 4, the following points of interest should be noted. The importance of the *Šābuhragān* for appreciating Mani's embracing of text as the medium for the communication of his message is taken one stage further in his dedication of a work to the ruling Sasanian monarch, in what was presumably an attempt to gain or to consolidate the patronage of Shapur I for his nascent teachings. Manichaeans celebrated the relationship between prophet and king, as evidenced in al-Nadim's description in the *Fihrist* (Dodge 1970, II.776) recounting the change of mind which came over Shapur on seeing Mani for the first time: intending initially to have Mani killed, Shapur saw something like two lamps of light shining above Mani's shoulders and recognised his pre-eminence.[38] A way of introducing himself to Shapur, the remains of the *Šābuhragān* indicate a work in which the apostle sought to place himself at the very centre of his own teachings: al-Biruni in his *Chronology* (207–8; trans. C.E. Sachau 1879, 189) notes that Mani informed his royal readership not only about his earthly origins ('born in a village called Mardinu on the upper canal of Kutha'), but also about his divine derivation, as the final messenger in a line of apostles who have brought 'wisdom and deeds always from time to time … to mankind by the messengers of God'.[39]

Composed by Mani in Middle Persian, an orthodoxy challenged by Mary Boyce, who held that Aramaic was the original language of the work,[40] five different manuscripts from Turfan contain fragments from the *Šābuhragān*, two groups of which – M470 etc., and M49 – are secure identifications, whilst the remaining three – M98 I and M99 I, M7980 and M506 – have been assigned on the basis of shared terminology.[41] The 'eschatological' fragments (M470 etc.) of the work have been edited and translated by David MacKenzie in two articles from 1979 and 1980, which include the apocalyptic scenes of the final judgement taken from the canonical Christian gospels (see Chapter 1). Manfred Hutter (1992) has assigned the 'cosmogonic' fragments (M98 I, M99 I, and M7980–M7984) to the *Šābuhragān*, in which we witness Mani's adaptation and development of Jewish-Christian ideas about the creation and purpose of the cosmos (see Chapter 4). Should the assigning of these cosmogonic texts prove secure, the *Šābuhragān* evidently sought to supply Shapur with a colourful yet comprehensive description of Mani's message about the origins, purpose and

[38] See S.N.C. Lieu 1992, 76–8.
[39] On this passage, see Reck 2010.
[40] Boyce 1983, 1196–7.
[41] See esp. Reck 2010.

eventual dissolution of the world. The reach of the work's influence was certainly long, and whilst not appearing in 'Western' formulations of the Manichaean canon, it nevertheless did appear to influence the important eschatological homily 'The Sermon on the Great War', which was transmitted in the Roman world as a Coptic translation ascribed to Koustaios, one of Mani's earliest followers.[42]

Living Gospel

In recalling the scriptural traditions of Manichaeism, Christian and Islamic heresiology displayed considerable scepticism towards Manichaean claims to the possession of a gospel, a scepticism expressed in the comparative language typical of heresiological discourse contrasting the 'gospels of heretics' unfavourably with the canonical gospels of the New Testament. In his *Chronology*, al-Biruni wrote:

> Every one of the sects of Marcion, and of Bardesanes, has a special Gospel ... Also the Manichaeans have a Gospel of their own, the contents of which from the first to the last are opposed to the doctrines of the Christians; but the Manichaeans consider them as their religious law, and believe that it is the correct Gospel, that its contents are really that which Messiah thought and taught, that every other Gospel is false, and its followers are liars against Messiah (*The Chronology of Ancient Nations* 23; trans. C.E. Sachau 1879, 27).

Unfortunately al-Biruni's lack of precision prevents us from identifying the 'Gospel' in question here, and his discussion of this work is concerned primarily with its corruption as 'The Gospel of the Seventy [Apostles]'.[43] However, further on in his work, al-Biruni supplies what is arguably the essence of Mani's *Living Gospel* via a terse description of the work: 'In his gospel, which he arranged according to the twenty-two letters of the [Syriac] alphabet, he says that he is the Paraclete announced by Messiah, and that he is the seal of the prophets.'[44] Whilst al-Biruni's concern in the eighth chapter of his work was with false prophets and prophecies in general ('On the eras of the Pseudo-Prophets and their Communities who were deluded by them'), his emphasis on the prophetological context of the *Living Gospel* is corroborated by other witnesses to the work. Portions of the text appear in the *CMC*, 66-70 (trans. I. Gardner and S.N.C. Lieu 2004, 156–9), notably its opening formula of address ('I, Mannichaeus, apostle of Jesus Christ'; see Chapter 2), and the prevailing theme of these citations concerns Mani's testimony – presented in the first person – describing the nature of his prophetic commission by 'God, the Father of Truth' through the agencies of Jesus and his (Mani's) Twin. Michel Tardieu suggests that Mani's claims in the *Living Gospel* were patterned on the Christian Gospel's

---

[42] See the discussion by Pedersen 1996, 115–52.
[43] See Puech 1991, 380–1.
[44] *The Chronology of Ancient Nations* 207; trans. C.E. Sachau 1879, 190.

presentation of Jesus as the fulfilment of Old Testament prophecies, with Mani presenting himself as fulfilling the person and teachings of Jesus, a presentation achieved through the exegetical treatment of key passages from the four canonical Gospels and the letters of Paul.[45] Whilst not denying the possibility that the work engaged in an exegetical treatment of Christian scriptures as a way of locating the apostolic identity of Mani – compare the interpretive kernel of the *Šābuhragān* (see Chapter 1) – the *Living Gospel* appears nevertheless not to have followed exclusively the literary format of the New Testament gospels, in the sense of being dominated by a narrative account of Mani's life and deeds; rather, it is the contents of the work, its proclamation of the 'good news' of Mani's teachings rather than its literary form, which determines its evangelical status. In this regard, therefore, it may be compared to the homiletical role that commentators have ascribed to the Valentinian work the *Gospel of Truth* unearthed at Nag Hammadi.[46]

The *Living Gospel* represented Mani's statement of qualification as an apostle of truth, and the work that set forth the divine origin of his teachings within a revelatory context. For these reasons, it is clear why this work stood at the head of the Manichaean canon, and why it appears to have been indispensable in the libraries of his disciples. Indeed, the range of its diffusion may be seen in evidence for its translation into Middle Persian (M17) and Sogdian (M172), fragments of which were recovered from central Asia (trans. I. Gardner and S.N.C. Lieu 2004, 157–8). The Iranian fragments of the *Living Gospel* are also prefaced by a doxology to key deities in the Manichaean pantheon, including Jesus the Splendour and the Maiden (Virgin) of Light, which suggests that parts at least of the work were read aloud during the Bema festival, forming part of its extensive liturgy.[47]

As al-Biruni also notes, the internal division of the work followed the 22 characters of the Syriac alphabet, from Aleph to Taw: a fragment of the teaching imparted under Aleph is given in the Turfan text M17.

Although very much an example of 'work in progress', research on the least well preserved codex from Medinet Madi, the *Synaxeis* codex, is moving towards a clearer assessment that that work contains very many citations from the *Living Gospel*, and indeed is even more closely associated with the work than simply acting as a commentary on the text, which had been the prevailing view up to point when Karen King (one of the work's many transcribers and editors) floated the suggestion that the codex is 'the *Living Gospel* itself, presented in a form meant for liturgical reading. The number of the *synaxeis* [i.e., Gk for 'meetings', referring to the 'sub-divisions' in the work] – roughly fifty – may indicate weekly readings of an annual cycle.'[48] An article from 2009 by one of the work's principal editors, Wolf-Peter Funk, has brought to light some of his own startling translations from the codex, which shed further light on the possible contents of the *Living Gospel* itself, with the early divisions or 'discourses' (following the

---

[45] Tardieu 2008, 36.
[46] See Robinson 1990, 38–9.
[47] See Klimkeit 1993, 146.
[48] King 1992, 286.

letters of the Syriac alphabet) containing details of Mani's mythological ideas, and the later discourses appearing to indicate Mani's concern with highlighting the teachings (and errors) of other, competitor faiths: one passage in particular recounts details of Mani's journey to India, and his encounter with the sects and castes of an unnamed region, including a measured yet critical assessment of 'the caste of the Brahmans ... I took a close look at their [law] and found that the leaders and the teachers ... in prophecy and [asceticism], in special skills ... the hair on their head. It is to their own teachers that they listen – even since their prophets, their fathers.'[49]

Treasury of Life

The *Treasury*, the work that central Asian Manichaeans regarded as having assisted Mar Ammo in forging a path for the religion into the far east (see above), survives in a limited number of fragments (originally a work comprising no less than seven books), the central theme of which appears to have been concerned with imparting the elements of Mani's cosmogonic teachings. Al-Biruni, in his 11th century work *India* (*Tahqiq mā lil-Hind*) quotes a portion of the *Treasury* in which Mani appears to have discussed the nature of the forms (angelic hosts) brought forth by the Third Messenger, one of the gods responsible for orchestrating the salvation of the Living Soul (= light particles: see Chapter 4), in language reminiscent of Paul's epistle to the Galatians (3. 28).[50] The role of the Third Messenger in the soteriological process is also evident in a portion of the work cited by Augustine in chapter 44 of his anti-Manichaean epitome *On the Nature of the Good* (trans. I. Gardner and S.N.C. Lieu 2004, 159–60), which relates the cosmogonic episode that has come to be referred to as 'The Seduction of the Archons': an incident whereby the Third Messenger exposes his divine forms to the evil archons (powers) who, captivated by the forms' beauty, ejaculate the living soul (as semen) which they had held captive. Mani's use of sexually evocative imagery predictably raised the ire of heresiologists such as Augustine: incidentally, such imagery may lie behind one particularly slanderous attempt to portray Manichaean ritual as involving the consumption of human semen, determined by a heresiological strategy that intentionally associated mythological language of a sexual nature with ritual practices (raised by Augustine, *On Heresies* 46. 9; trans. I. Gardner and S.N.C. Lieu 2004, 144):[51]

> When reason demands that they should appear to males they show themselves in an instant in the form of beautiful virgins. Again, when they have to come to women they put off the appearance of virgins and take on that of beardless boys. At this comely sight, their ardour and concupiscence grow, and in this way the prison of those evil thoughts is broken, and the living soul which was held bound in their members of those same (beings)

---

[49] Funk 2009, 123.
[50] *Alberuni's India* 3.19; trans. C.E. Sachau 1910, I.39.
[51] On this issue, see Goehring 2000.

is by this opportunity released and escapes and mingles with the purest air which is its native element (Augustine, *On the Nature of the Good* 44, trans. J. Burleigh, in Gardner and Lieu 2004, 159–60).[52]

An additional fragment from the *Treasury* is also preserved by Augustine in his *Answer to Felix*, a record of a public debate held in Hippo between Augustine and Felix, a Manichaean teacher, in AD 404. This fragment from the *Treasury* is of particular importance since it highlights Mani's commitment to the idea that man is able to exercise a choice as to whether or not he desires to be saved (an aspect of the doctrine of Free Will), a feature of Mani's theology that was often lost under the weight of Catholic polemicising that sought to characterise Manichaean teaching on human nature as being defined by an immovable sense of being fixed on a course of sinfulness, influenced by the corrupting influence of matter (= the human body) on the will (referred to as *Determinism*: see Chapter 4):

> But because of their negligence these souls did not permit themselves to be purified from the defilement of the previously mentioned spirits and did not obey the commandments of God in their entirety and were unwilling to observe fully the law given them by their deliverer and did not govern themselves as they ought to have ... (Augustine, *Against Felix* 2.5: trans. R. Teske 2006, 301).

In the Coptic work *The Chapters* (91.230; trans. I. Gardner 1995, 237–8), Mani makes reference to the *Treasury* during a question-and-answer session with a disciple concerning the destiny of an idealised Hearer who, through his unfailing commitment to the precepts of the religion (see Chapter 4), achieves direct salvation, thereby avoiding the usual destiny for Hearers which entailed the soul's rebirth into an improved form (i.e., the body of an Elect), as one stage closer to the final liberation of the soul. Mani makes reference to this idealised Hearer as an 'archetype' (Gk *tupos*), 'Just like the good pearl [cf. Matthew's gospel 13.45–6], about which I have written for you in the *Treasure of Life* and which is beyond price' (91.230.7–9; trans. I. Gardner 1995, 237). In addition, Mani also notes that, in the *Treasury*, he had laid out what all Hearers (i.e., the ones who are not idealised 'types') needed to do in order for their souls to be finally released and purified (*The Chapters* 91.230.20–3).

Trends in Manichaean research during the twentieth century (see Chapter 1) meant that the title '*Treasury*' was regarded as offering a point of comparison between Mandaean and Manichaean literary traditions, since Mani's work shared a similar title to the Mandaean scriptures, the *Ginza* (i.e., *Treasure*).[53] However, increased awareness of Mani's Christian (and indeed biblical) roots has meant that a scriptural influence for the title of the work is not beyond the realm of possibility (cf. Mt. 6. 19–21).

---

[52] See Moon 1955, 226–34.
[53] Widengren 1965, 77.

Pragmateia

Little can be said with certainty about this work. In pentateuchal accounts of the Manichaean canon, the *Pragmateia* is placed together with the *Book of Mysteries* and the *Book of the Giants*: 'these three holy writings are a single one, the gifts of the light Twin [i.e., *Syzygos*]'.[54] In previous attempts at identifying its contents, a range of suppositions have been proposed, one of which has aligned the *Pragmateia* with the 'Great Letter to Patticius' (i.e., 'the long letter to Fattuq' from al-Nadim; see above), which itself has been linked with Mani's letter *The Foundation* (the letter that circulated in the Roman world, creating a considerable impact), perhaps with some degree of justification. Basing his judgement of the work on the ideas of the great Augustinian and Manichaean scholar Prosper Alfaric (author of a still indispensable, two-volume, French-language work, *The Manichaean Scriptures*, from 1918 to 1919), Francis Crawford Burkitt was able to refer interchangeably to the *Pragmateia* and the 'Great Epistle to Patticius' as one and the same work.[55] Other commentators have been more cautious, an attitude of restraint typified by Geo Widengren's statement that: 'The contents were probably of a practical ethical kind, but in the absence unfortunately of fragments, quotations or statements about its contents nothing definite can be said by way of comment on this work ...'.[56]

Puzzlement has surrounded the Greek title of the work (*Pragmateia* = Treatise), which was faithfully transmitted in Coptic, Arabic (*Fihrist*: Dodge 1970, II.798) and Chinese (Gardner and Lieu 2004, 155–6) accounts of the canon. Did Mani himself give a Greek title to this Syriac work? Michel Tardieu has taken the work's title as the starting point for his theory about the *Treatise*, handled by him in relation to the use of the term *pragmateia* by classical historians (e.g., in the Greek *Histories* of Polybius) to denote a systematic treatment of past events and personalities, and in particular the legendary accounts of events from pre-history: 'Thus it is that in the Greek of the preclassical period, the (grammatically singular) expression *troikè pragmateia* signifies not a "treatise" relating to the Trojan War but legendary accounts – or, more simply, legends – of the Trojan War. These legends (*pragmateia*) were therefore synonymous with the myths (*muthoi*) or mythological inventions (*muthologika*).'[57] This explanation for the work's title indeed chimes with the evidence for the *Pragmateia* provided by the so-called Chinese *Compendium* (S3969) that describes the *Pragmateia* (Chin po-chia-ma-ti-yeh) as the 'book of instruction which testifies the past.'[58]

Thus, the legendary material treated by the *Pragmateia* must have been – so Tardieu argues – Mani's cosmogony, a disparate collection of narrative ideas which offered Manichaeans a comprehensive explanation for the origin and nature of the universe. It is this legendary material from the *Pragmateia* that Tardieu holds was cited extensively and refuted by the eighth century Nestorian

---

[54] *The Chapters* 148.355.11–14; Gardner and Lieu 2004, 154.

[55] Burkitt 1925, 32; 66.

[56] Widengren 1965, 77–8.

[57] Tardieu 2008, 42.

[58] Trans. I. Gardner and S.N.C. Lieu 2004, 156.

Christian, Theodore bar Koni: thus, Tardieu's judgement is that evidence for the contents of the *Pragmateia* can be found in this late Christian work.[59] The 11th chapter (Syr. *memra*) of Theodore's Syriac work, the *Book of Scholia*, sets out in direct quotations the teachings of 'Mani the Wicked' on the events and circumstances surrounding the great cosmic conflict between the Light and the Darkness, ending with the 'gnostic-style' awakening of Adam by Jesus the Splendour (see Chapter 4).[60] Since Mani and Theodore both shared in the literary usage of Syriac, it is also assumed that Theodore's work faithfully transmits the same or similar names and terms employed by Mani himself to denote the identities of his chief gods, powers and emanations.[61] As John C. Reeves (1992, 197) has demonstrated, the Manichaean work excerpted by Theodore provides a clear demonstration of Mani's interest and usage of Jewish Enochic traditions concerning the legends of the Watchers and the Giants (1 Enoch 6–11), based on the sixth chapter of Genesis. Accepting Tardieu's identification of the *Pragmateia* with the passages in Theodore's *Book of Scholia*, it should also be noted that Mani appears in this work to have been concerned with providing only the legendary material surrounding the Beginning and Middle times of the Manichaean periodisation of the cosmos.[62]

Should Tardieu's argument be valid – and there is little reason to doubt otherwise – the *Pragmateia* is arguably the most historically significant work written by Mani, for the reason that it has been towards the Manichaean cosmogonic drama that very many of Manichaeism's opponents have been drawn during their efforts to challenge and undermine the religion. Therefore cultural representations of Mani and Manichaeism down the centuries have focused almost exclusively on the legendary elements of Mani's teachings, and it is accounts such as that of Theodore's which have informed the dominant impression of Manichaeism as recalled especially in the historical memory of the Western world.

Moving in the opposite direction to Tardieu is the appearance of references to Mani's *Pragmateia* in Iain Gardner and Samuel Lieu's source-book from 2004, *Manichaean Texts from the Roman Empire*. In their chapter on the scriptures of Mani (151–75), Gardner and Lieu supply, under the cautious heading '*From an unnamed work of Mani, probably* The Pragmateia', excerpts of a Manichaean work cited and refuted by Severus, patriarch of Antioch during the early sixth century, in his 123rd homily (composed in Greek, but surviving now in a Syriac translation).[63] There is a notable difference between the nature of the

---

[59] The historical context for Theodore bar Koni is discussed by Hunter 2005, 165–78.

[60] For an English translation with a comprehensive commentary, see Reeves 1992, 189–205. The commentary by Williams Jackson 1932, 221–54, with the translation of Theodore's resume by A. Yohannan, remains important.

[61] Cf. S.N.C. Lieu 2005, 245–54.

[62] Although as Sundermann 2005, 382, points out, the Shorter Greek formula for the renunciation of Manichaeism (ed. Adam 1969, 94) has the title of the work as the 'Treatise of All Things'.

[63] Trans. I. Gardner and S.N.C. Lieu 2004, 160–3. An English trans. with detailed commentary is also available in Reeves 1992, 165–83.

Manichaean work as presented in Severus's homily, and the Manichaean work cited by Theodore bar Koni three centuries later: the debt which the latter work owes to the Enochic tradition for supplying the mythological names as they appear in the Manichaean list of *dramatis personae* stands in contrast to the 'abstract, almost philosophical flavour' (Reeves 1992, 173) of the work cited by Severus. Curiously, Gardner and Lieu provide no explanation for their choice of Severus's homily as a possible candidate for the lost *Pragmateia*, and one can only assume that, in the minds of these editors, there was an association to be made between the Greek title of the work and an unspoken supposition on their part that the title reflected the intention of the work as they conceived it, namely an attempt on Mani's part to provide a rationalistic account of his complex Jewish-Christian myth that was more in keeping with the intellectual sensibilities of a Hellenic audience. However, taking Tardieu's definition of *Pragmateia* as concerned with the exposition of legendary material, it would seem that the Manichaean work cited by Severus is not a likely candidate for Mani's influential cosmogonic work, since the eschewing of the legendary for the rationalistic is the Severian-Manichaean work's most striking feature.[64]

Book of Mysteries

As noted above, the extent to which the themes and issues raised by Mani in his writings were influenced by his life as a Christian teacher who had been made privy to a series of revelations from a divine source, and in particular the peripatetic sense of religious vocation that Mani envisioned was an essential element of his life as an apostle, is rarely discussed in studies of Manichaeism. However, considering the religiously diverse nature of the late-antique Sasanian empire – a diversity in evidence on all sides of the frontiers that marked out Persian territory – it is to be expected that Mani came up against other living faiths and traditions, and that *something* of these interactions came to be reflected in the subjects covered by his writings. It appears that evidence for such religious and cultural exchange is discernable in the testimonies for Mani's *Book of Mysteries*, provided by writers in the Arabic tradition.

In the entry on the writings of Mani in the *Fihrist*, al-Nadim provides the chapter headings (Arb. *bāb*: Dodge 1970, II.797–8; cf. Tardieu 2008, 38–41) of the work that he refers to as the *Safar al-Asrār*, i.e., the *Book of Mysteries*. Following the testimony of the *Fihrist*, therefore, Mani's *Mysteries* comprised 18 chapters in total. The detail supplied in the case of this work by al-Nadim far exceeds the details supplied by him for Mani's other writings – except with regard to the epistolary titles of Manichaean letters – and this attention may in part be explained by the likely target and subject matter of the *Book of Mysteries*. The work must have held especial interest to Muslim intellectuals who demonstrated a preoccupation with 'creation and with the soul', as a result of their intercessory role as guardians of classical philosophy.[65] Eye-catching

---

[64] See Reeves 1992, 170–4.
[65] Drijvers 1966, 200–7.

in this regard were chapters one, twelve and thirteen of the work, all of which were devoted to refuting the teachings of the Bardesanites, a sect that held by the ideas of Bardaisan, on the nature of the soul and its fate after the death of the body. Bardaisan (d. AD 222), frequently styled as a late-antique 'Renaissance Man',[66] remains nevertheless an inscrutable character of the second century, although his high birth and his close connections with the ruling family of Edessa, acting for a time as a courtier of Abgar IX ('the Great', ruling 179–216), belong to a relatively secure biographical tradition. After the fall of Edessa to the Roman emperor Caracalla (ruling 198–217), Bardaisan may have gone into exile in Armenia, dying in 222.[67] Al-Nadim demonstrates a fascination not so much with Bardaisan himself, but rather with his followers, including a short entry on the Bardesanites (*al-Dayṣānīyah*) immediately after his treatment of the Manichaeans, observing the extent to which they were similar to but not wholly identifiable with the Manichaeans, and noting their historical location in the area of al-Bata'ih in the marsh regions between Wasit and al-Basrah, the area which al-Nadim also indicates was the origin of the Mughtasilah (Dodge 1970, II.806).

The relationship of Mani and Manichaeism with the teachings of Bardaisan remains far from clear. However, evidence for the influence of certain aspects of Bardaisan's dualistic-cosmogonic teachings on Mani's thinking is held by commentators,[68] in spite of the fact that, as the *Book of Mysteries* indicates, Mani was concerned to refute Bardaisan's teachings on the nature of the soul, and the relationship between the soul and the body. Indeed, one of the champions of Christian orthodoxy in the fourth century, Ephraim, in his attack on Mani in his *Discourses addressed to Hypatius* (I. 122.26–31) was keen to style Bardaisan as one of Mani's teachers (the other being Marcion), adding: 'Because Mani was unable to find another way out, he entered, though unwillingly, by the door which Bardaisan opened.'[69] However, we need to be wary here of yet another heresiological commonplace, namely the linking together in one great chain of corrosive influence the 'heretics' of the day, a concern with its roots in the patristic notion of the 'anti-apostolate' (see Chapter 2). The facts remain that Mani set himself in direct opposition to the teachings and followers of Bardaisan, and that, as Ephraim indicates, Bardaisan had written a 'book of mysteries' (now lost) which suggests that Mani's similarly-named work offered a critical reappraisal of Bardesanite teachings, with his instruction on 'the mysteries' supplanting those offered by Bardaisan.[70]

Four fragments have been identified by Tardieu from al-Biruni's *India* as belonging originally to Mani's work, three from chapter 13 (entitled 'Refutation of the Bardesanites Concerning the Living Soul') and one from chapter 15 (entitled 'The Preservation of the Cosmos'). The fragments belonging to chapter 13 expose one of the main areas of controversy between Mani's and Bardaisan's

[66] Cf. S.N.C. Lieu 1992, 55.
[67] See Drijvers 1966, 217–18.
[68] Cf. S.N.C. Lieu 1992, 59.
[69] Trans. in Drijvers 1966, 225.
[70] Cf. Drijvers 1966, 163.

teachings concerning the relationship between the soul and the body, which in turn is suggestive of different opinions concerning the *nature* of the two forms. In contrast to the Manichaean idea of the 'mixed heritage' (BeDuhn 2002, 89) of the human body and the soul, which conveys a largely (although not absolutely) pessimistic view of the body as an impediment in the soul's purification and release (see Chapter 4), Mani's criticism of Bardesanite anthropology reveals a tradition which ascribed to the body a central role in the liberation of the Living Soul. In this sense, therefore, Bardesanite teaching on the body is unusually optimistic, an idea that emerges from a decision not to ascribe to matter a role in the generation or continuation of evil in the world (*contra* Mani):

> For in another place, [Mani] says: 'The partisans of Bardesanes think that the living soul rises and is purified in the carcase [i.e., the body], not knowing that the latter is the enemy of the soul, that the carcase prevents the soul from rising, that it is a prison, and a painful punishment to the soul. If this human figure were a real existence, its creator would not let it wear out and suffer injury, and would not have compelled it to reproduce itself by the sperm in the uterus' (*Alberuni's India* 5.27; trans. C.E. Sachau 1910, I.55).

The extent to which the *Book of Mysteries* was entirely dedicated to challenging the theological heritage of Bardaisan is, however, difficult to discern. The other core concern of the work involved yet again Mani's exegetical treatment of key apocryphal writings, which assisted in the contextualisation of his own claim to reside at the end-point of the line of divinely-sanctioned apostles: the titles of chapters six ('Beginning of the Testimony of the al-Yamin after His Conquest': al-Yamin = 'the just' = Enoch? See M. Tardieu 2008, 39) and ten ('The Testimony of Adam about Jesus') likely indicate treatments of the pseudepigraphic writings ascribed to Enoch and Adam, in their roles as apostles of light, that may have been similar if not the same as the apocalyptic works cited in the *CMC*. The historian al-Ya'qubi noted that the *Mysteries* contained an attack on 'the signs of the prophets', presumably a challenge to those figures who were considered not to be part of the Manichaean prophetological family of apostles, including perhaps Moses (see below), a concern on Mani's part which may have found a place in chapter 17 on 'The Prophets'.[71]

With the *Mysteries*' treatment of apocalypses in mind, it is also worth noting Mani's citation of a saying ascribed to Jesus, drawn from the fragments of the work preserved by al-Biruni, which probably also belonged to its 13th chapter. The quotation in question concerns Jesus instructing his disciples about the transmigration of souls, and the fate of those souls which have not been receptive to divine teachings: 'Whereupon [Jesus] said "Any weak soul which has not received all that belongs to her of truth perishes without any rest or bliss."'[72] Al-Biruni prefaces the saying with the explanation: 'When Mani was banished from Eranshahr [i.e., the Iranian empire], he went to India, learned metem-

---

[71] See Reeves 1996, 52, nt. 29; also Tardieu 2008, 41.
[72] *Alberuni's India* 5.27; trans. C.E. Sachau 1910, I.55.

psychosis from the Hindus, and transferred it into his own system.'[73] However, against al-Biruni, whose gloss has been taken over by modern commentators as proof that Mani drew from the Indian tradition of metempsychosis, Sundermann has argued that the quotation is more likely drawn from an apocryphal Christian gospel, indicating parallels with the third century Coptic work the *Faithful Wisdom* (*Pistis Sophia*).[74]

Book of Giants

Mani's familiarity with the language and imagery of writings which reside in the Enochic tradition is evident from the colourful cosmogonic scenes and cast of characters appearing in his *Šābuhragān*, and in likely witnesses (i.e., Theodore bar Koni) for the *Pragmateia*. The considerable influence on the mind of Mani of texts whose origins lay in the Second Temple period of Jewish history becomes fully apparent when we approach the fragmentary evidence for his creative reimagining of one of the principal components (the 'Book of the Watchers') of the work known as 1 Enoch: an imagining better known as the Manichaean *Book of Giants*. The extrapolation of the legendary account of the watchers (Gk *egrēgoroi*) – the angelic 'children of heaven' (1 En. 6.2) who came to earth and coupled with the 'beautiful and comely daughters' of men (1 En. 6. 1)[75] producing gigantic offspring (cf. Gen. 6. 1–4) – from the Enochic tradition, and its transformation into an extended discourse on the related issues of cosmogony and the nature of evil that characterises Mani's *Book of Giants*, was not something original to the genius of the apostle. The major source for Mani's work, from which it now appears that he made considerable borrowings, has been identified via the joining together of fragmentary texts as an earlier *Book of Giants*, a work which was once in the possession of the sectarian Jewish movement responsible for the library unearthed at Qumran on the western shores of the Dead Sea.

The attraction of a work like the *Book of Giants* for Mani lay in its depictions of the visceral consequences that occurred when the heavenly realm collided with the mortal world: Mani's abhorrence at the mixing of the two worlds is an indication of a strong Jewish influence on his cultural outlook, an influence that was undoubtedly present among the 'world-view' of the Mesopotamian baptist community of the Elchasaites. Indeed, that Enochian literature, and more specifically the Qumranic *Book of Giants* (or at least a later version of it), found a place in the Elchasaite canon of scriptural texts should at least be entertained as a strong possibility, knowing as we do something of their apparent partiality for Jewish apocalypses: thus, Mani likely grew up with this literature, although it should also be noted that its significant – although largely unacknowledged – influence on the theological contours of early Christianity probably also meant that Mani and his immediate followers

---

[73] *Alberuni's India* 5.27; trans. C.E. Sachau 1910, I.54.

[74] Sundermann 1986, 16.

[75] Trans. M. Black 1985, 27.

came across religious communities who were also familiar with these Jewish legendary texts.[76]

Whilst it was known for some time that Mani had authored a Book of Giants, the title being attested in both Manichaean and ancient heresiological canon lists, together with the tentative attempts by early modern Manichaean scholars (notably Isaac de Beausobre) to flesh out the Enochic connection with Mani's speculative theology, it was the work of Walter Bruno Henning which provided detailed evidence for the existence of a Manichaean work that built on the lore contained in 1 Enoch.[77] Henning's work on the Iranian fragments from Turfan culminated in 1943 with a reconstruction of the *Kawān* (the Middle Persian title for *Giants*) comprising transliterations with an accompanying English translation of fragments in Middle Persian, Sogdian and Uighur (with corresponding Manichaean texts in Coptic and the witnesses supplied by Arabic sources) published in the *Bulletin of the School of Oriental and African Studies*. As Henning claimed in the article, '[i]n their journey across Central Asia the stories of the *Book of the Giants* were influenced by local traditions':[78] a statement of some significance in light of his previous assessment that the appearance of names drawn from ancient Turfan Iranian lore to designate the Aramaic names of the two giants Ohya and Ahya – the giant offspring of Shemihaza (the chief apostate Watcher from 1 Enoch) – as Sahm the giant (*kavi*) and Pat-Sahm in the Sogdian version of the work,[79] represented an attempt by Mani to fuse together Jewish and Iranian legendary material. However, along with evidence for other alterations appearing in translations of the work, Henning concluded that Mani's later disciples in Asia had altered the work in order to add a local 'flavour' to it, presumably for proselytising purposes (see also his comments on 52–3: '[Mani] did not make use of the Iranian mythological tradition'). Nevertheless, arguments continued to emerge which presented the *Book of Giants* as prime evidence of Mani's syncretistic abilities and ambitions: notable in this regard is the assessment of the work by Widengren (1965, 78–80): '... nothing can be more natural than that [Mani] should have tried to blend the Iranian mythical-historical tradition with the Syriac-Christian historical outlook.'

As John C. Reeves notes (1992, 30–1), Henning's work led to the assumption that Mani, in the composition of his *Book of Giants*, had had access to an Aramaic version of the relevant portions of 1 Enoch. However, with the discovery and decipherment of the scrolls from Qumran, and in particular through the research of one of the early pioneers of Qumranic studies, Józef T. Milik, it became clear that an earlier, prototypical *Book of Giants* had been in existence.[80] Comparison of the Aramaic fragments from Qumran alongside the Manichaean Turfan fragments indicates that the latter 'was based, at least in part, upon a text very similar to that recovered in

---

[76] See Sundermann 1994.
[77] See Reeves 1992, 9–49.
[78] Henning 1943, 55.
[79] Henning 1943, 70.
[80] See Milik 1976, 298–310.

Qumran',[81] although precisely how Mani adapted the work to suit his own ends remains largely hypothetical.[82]

However, as Henning noted in his article from 1943, the theodicy developed by Mani which served as his defence of the immaculate goodness of God could not permit the apostate angels (Watchers) to have their origin in the Kingdom of Light (i.e., in Heaven).

> Therefore [Mani] transformed them into demons, namely those demons that when the world was being constructed had been imprisoned in the skies, under the supervision of the *Rex Honoris* [King of Honour = a demiurgical figure]. They rebelled and were recaptured, but two hundred of them escaped to the earth. Mani also used the term *egrēgoroi* (preserved in Coptic, see texts L, M, P, S), or rather *yr* ['Watcher'] in Aramaic (once in a Middle Persian fragment, text D), but in eastern sources they are mostly referred to as 'demons' ...[83]

Due to the fragmentary nature of the evidence on both the Jewish and the Manichaean sides, we cannot fully inform ourselves about the manner of Mani's adaptive handling of the work; nor can we know for certain what attracted Mani to the existing *Giants* tradition. Was it, as Guy Stroumsa suggests, a result of Mani discovering something of 'religious value' in the work, which prompted him 'to develop a *Gnostic* understanding of the giants – the pervasive myth of the lustful archons and their wicked deeds throughout history'?[84] Or was it, as Stroumsa (1984) also suggests, an indication of Mani's efforts to provide a 'true exegesis' of the original biblical text from Genesis (representing perhaps 'the severing of its [i.e., the narrative of the Watchers] links with the Hebrew Bible': 153)? Certainly the religious value of the work, coupled with Mani's self-awareness as an apostle of light, meant that in his own mind he could 'take over and complete' a longstanding work of a legendary nature in a manner not dissimilar to his appropriation and reimagining of certain gospel texts, as evidenced in his *Šābuhragān* (see Chapter 1).

What we do know for certain, however, is the primary place assigned to the *Book of Giants* in the Manichaean tradition as a work authored by Mani, indicated by the comments on its canonisation in *The Chapters* (148.355.11–14; Gardner and Lieu 2004, 154) and its alignment with the *Pragmateia* and the *Book of Mysteries*. Furthermore, like the *Living Gospel* and the *Treasury of Life*, the *Book of Giants* was one of the essential items for early disciples of the religion: a Parthian epistolary fragment (M5815 II) from Turfan records the actions of a church official (assumed to be Sisin (= Sisinnios), Mani's immediate successor as Head of the church) based in Merv in Parthia to send to Ammo (see above) a copy of the work: 'And to dear brother Zurvandad I am very, very grateful because he in his goodness has watched over all brothers. And I have now

---

[81] Reeves 1992, 127.
[82] See the discussion in Reeves 1992, 51–164.
[83] Henning 1943, 53.
[84] Stroumsa 1984, 165.

despatched him to Zamb, and sent him to dear Mar Ammo and to (the province of) Khorasan. He has taken (the *Book of*) *the Giants* and the *Ardahang* with him. And I have made another (copy of the *Book of*) *the Giants* and the *Ardahang* in Merv.'[85]

The final word on the *Giants* should perhaps be given over to a consideration of the pragmatic value of the work, expressed by Michel Tardieu's original and intriguing suggestion about the latent 'political radicalism' of the work:

> Mani's successors at the head of the church, like him Aramaeans, retained the *Book of Giants* in the canon of scriptures while excluding from it the *Šābuhragān*, which no longer served any purpose since the kings of Iran had now become the active enemies of the church. One might even consider the *Book of Giants* to be a sort of anti-*Šābuhragān*. It is not impossible, in fact, that at the end of his life, writing a stronger version of the Jewish book 'for the Parthians',[86] Mani (like his readers), confronted with the hatred of the powers of this world, had seen and read in the violence and corruption of the original giants the fate of failure and death befalling historical empires and their princes – and this all the more readily as the Middle Persian word for 'giants' [*kawān*] was, during the Sassanid period, synonymous with 'tyrants'. The Manichaean *Book of Giants* was therefore conceived and perceived as a political pamphlet in the guise of allegory and myth.[87]

Epistles

The dynamic nature of Mani's self-appointed mission as an 'apostle of Jesus Christ' is evident also in the remains of his letters. However, as with all of Mani's writings, sizeable problems exist in relation to the fragmentary nature of the remaining source material, a problem compounded by the appearance of letters purporting to derive from Mani's hand which are likely nevertheless to be forgeries, instances of which include:

- The possibly spurious 'Letter to Menoch' attributed to Mani, which appears in a work by Julian of Eclanum, arguably Augustine's most savvy opponent;[88] the letter was utilised by Julian in order to embarrass Augustine by drawing out the remains of what in Julian's mind was evidence of a Manichaean influence on Augustine's formulation of sin.[89]

---

[85] Trans. J.P. Asmussen 1975, 23.

[86] The title of a work in the enumeration of the Manichaean canon in *The Chapters* 5. 22–6, taken by some commentators to be an alternate title for the *Book of Giants*; see Tardieu 2008, 45.

[87] Tardieu 2008, 46–7.

[88] See Lössl 2001, *passim.*

[89] Trans. in I. Gardner and S.N.C. Lieu 2004, 172–4; see Stein 1998, 28–43; also Harrison and BeDuhn 2001, 128–72.

- Four letters attributed to Mani but belonging to the fifth century – including one sent to Mani's 'western disciple' Adda – intended to tar another heretical church (the Monophysites) with the Manichaean brush by portraying their christological position (that Jesus had only one nature) as deriving from Mani's ideas about Jesus.[90]
- The attempts by the eastern schismatic Manichaeans, the Denawars,[91] to bolster their rigorist claims by appropriating for their cause the memory of the famed eastern disciple, Mar Ammo, by fabricating a letter (Parthian) sent by Mani to him, in which Mani charges Ammo directly to labour in the cause of the eastern Manichaean church.[92]
- The letter to Marcellus attributed to the Mani of the *Acts of Archelaus* (5. 1–6), whilst evidently fabricated within the context of the work's malign intentions, nevertheless shows many signs of having been written with a detailed knowledge of the epistolary conventions used by Mani, which again suggests that Hegemonius was concerned with presenting his work as an authentic encounter with the Manichaean religion.[93]

The effort that went into producing epistolary forgeries bearing Mani's name is a clear indication of the formidable reputation that Mani had established for himself as one of the most prolific letter writers in Late Antiquity. As texts from Medinet Madi and Turfan indicate, Mani's letters were gathered together and circulated in collections, although what remains of such anthologies is now severely diminished.[94] What we do have, however, are fragments from various epistles in translation, arguably the most remarkable of which appear among the writings from Kellis. Published as P.Kell.Copt. 53 (inventory no. 'ex P93C et al.') in 2007(a) by Iain Gardner and Wolf-Peter Funk are the remains of a collection of Mani's letters in Coptic translation: furthermore, the themes and style of a further text, P.Kell.Copt. 54 (inv. no. 'ex P30/P55/P59B') suggest that it was also once part of one of Mani's letters.[95] With reference to P.Kell.Copt. 53, Gardner notes that it would seem that the fragments together constitute parts of at least three individual letters, one of which is the *Epistle of the Ten Words*, its assigned title taken from al-Nadim's list of Mani's epistles (Dodge 1970, II.799), which corresponds with Mani's consolatory statement in the letter: '[I] have written for you these ten words that I would comfort your heart, my child.'[96]

---

[90] Trans. in I. Gardner and S.N.C. Lieu 2004, 174–5; see S.N.C. Lieu 1994, 109–12.

[91] See S.N.C. Lieu 1992, 220.

[92] The letter is part of the historicising text (M5815 II) detailing Sisin's(?) intention to send the *Giants* to Ammo; see M. Boyce 1975, 50, text r; further comments and trans. H.-J. Klimkeit 1993, 259–60.

[93] See Gardner 2007b, 33–48.

[94] A description of the remaining 20 leaves of the letter collection from Narmouthis can be found in Gardner 2001, 97–100; for the central Asian epistolary tradition, see Sundermann 2009b, 259–77.

[95] Gardner 2007a, 84–93.

[96] P.Kell.Copt. 53. 52.17–19; trans. I. Gardner 2007a, 75.

As we noted in the opening section of this chapter, Mani's engagement with letter writing appears to have been focused on the day-to-day concerns of his early communities within and beyond Mesopotamia. Such concerns were met by Mani through his letters, which likely took on a range of homiletic, educational and exhortative guises.[97] Thus, Mani's letters carried clear statements of his authority, evident in the famous opening formula: 'Manichaios [Syr. 'Mânî hayyâ' = 'Mani the living'], the apostle of Jesus Chrestos [Gk: 'good'[98]], and all the brothers who are with me' (as in P.Kell.Copt. 53, 12.1–3; Gardner 2007a, 74). In this sense, therefore, it could be argued that Mani exploited the medium of letter writing – and other literary forms – in order to develop for himself a literary profile which served as his effective presence for his communities in his absence. The letters were therefore not only concerned to communicate his authority, but were also intended to act as reminders – monuments – of his achievements. The last letter that Mani wrote whilst in prison, called the *Letter of the Seal*, the evidence for which comes from fragments in Middle Persian, Parthian and Sogdian, was intended to be 'his legacy sent to his adherents'.[99] The memorialisation of this particular letter within a later Iranian Manichaean liturgical work, the *Book of Prayer and Confession* (M801), is a demonstration that Mani's letters remained treasured possessions for later manifestations of his church.[100] A reading of Mani's *Letter of the Seal* formed part of the annual Bema service, and the final part of the letter's opening greeting is preserved in the *Book*:

> … and from Ammo, my [most beloved] son, and from all the very dear children who are with [me]. To all shepherds, teachers and bishops and all the Elect [and auditors, to the brothers] and sisters, great and small ones, the pious, perfect and righteous ones, and to all of you who have received this good message from me and who have been happy with this teaching and these pious deeds that I have taught you, and who are firm in the faith and free of doubt. To everyone personally (M801; trans. H.-J. Klimkeit 1993, 134).

The opening introduction (Lat *exordium*) of Mani's letters forces us to think a little more deeply about the role of Jesus in the mind of Mani. Thus far, we have only really discussed Mani as an 'apostle of Jesus Christ', without qualifying in any great detail precisely what constituted the identity of Jesus in Mani and his followers' minds. It is worth noting, nevertheless, that the issue indeed impinges on how we should begin to understand the nature of Mani's authority, the relational manner of which stands either i) in an intermediary position between his followers in the Manichaean church and the divine agent who is the

---

[97] Sundermann 2009b, 267.

[98] Cf. Alexander of Lycopolis, *Critique of the Doctrines of Manichaeus*; trans. P.W. van der Horst and J. Mansfeld 1974, 91.

[99] See Reck 2009, 225–39.

[100] The text, edited by W.B. Henning and published in 1937, is also commonly referred to by its assigned German title *Ein manichäisches Bet- und Beichtbuch* ('A Manichaean Prayer and Confession Book'), and abbreviated as *BBB*.

ultimate source for his awakening and teachings – thus Mani is acting on behalf of Jesus; or ii) as an authority who supplants Jesus, by presenting his Gospel in its final form, in which case Mani's teachings update the Gospel for the times and circumstances applicable to his mission. Central to the issue of Mani's self-identity as an apostle of Jesus, therefore, is the question of which role Mani had in mind for his own understanding of Jesus, a complex problem bound up with the Christology of the religion, since Manichaean traditions record a number of 'Jesus figures', i.e., Jesus acting in a variety of roles, in a supernal capacity as 'Jesus the Splendour' (thereby giving rise to point i), or in a historical sense as 'Jesus the apostle' (determining point ii).

A related aspect of Mani's epistolary authority apparent in the fragmentary texts from Kellis concerns his handling of Christian biblical texts. As we have seen in other instances (e.g., *Šābuhragān*), Mani's interpretation of key gospel passages – in a manner which suggested that the teachings of Jesus had been fulfilled in his own thoughts and actions – was determined by Mani's own sense of being an 'apostle of Jesus Christ'. To put the matter in another way: what happened to Jesus will also happen to Mani. One fragment in P.Kell.Copt. 53, referred to as the 'Enemy Letter' by its editors, reveals Mani analogising his own betrayal (of which no details are given) with that of Jesus during Passover, a similarity conveyed by Mani in his citation from John's gospel 13.18 and Jesus's quotation from Psalm 41.9 ('He who eats bread with me has turned against me') within the context of an act of table fellowship:

> The word that our lord proclaimed with his mouth has been fulfilled with me, that 'one who eats the salt with me has set his foot upon me.' I myself also, this thing has happened to me: One who eats salt with me at the evening table, my garments upon his body, set his foot upon me; just as an enemy would do to his enemy (P.Kell.Copt. 53.41.5–13; trans. I. Gardner 2007a, 76).

With regard to Mani's epistolary style, in particular the habitual opening formula of his letters ('Manichaios, apostle of Jesus Christ'), Mani's imitation of Paul is clearly apparent. However, when Paul's influence on Mani is raised by commentators, rarely is any comment made about the two centuries that separate them both – a period of enormous significance that witnessed the development of a distinctive Christian literary culture, which suggests that the literary 'personalities' and subsequent intentions of the two men were very different from one another. For Paul, the idea of scripture as a body of authoritative teachings comprised the Torah, namely the Pentateuch and the Prophets, whilst his textual apprehension of Jesus was confined to a 'Sayings Collection' of Jesus's pronouncements that, during the first century, did not enjoy anything akin to scriptural authority.[101] Indeed, it is Paul's letters that kick-start the development of something like a Christian literary culture, pre-dating as they do the emergence of the first Christian gospels. Paul's own use of the Jewish scriptures tends towards an 'ecclesiocentric' interpretation, focused on his plan for a unified church of Jews and Gentiles, rather than being 'Christocentric', where the focus

---

[101] See Koester 1990, 31.

would be on the notion that Jesus as the Messiah fulfilled the ancient Jewish prophecies.[102] In contrast to the first century, Mani in the third century had at his disposal a diverse range of biblical traditions about Jesus, their influence evident throughout Mani's writings, in particular with regard to his extension of a 'Christocentric' model of interpretation to encompass his own claims as having fulfilled Jesus's teachings and actions. Whilst both Paul and Mani were experts at creating intertextual pieces of writing – i.e., the development and presentation of their own ideas using citations and allusions from prior scriptural works – the texts that in a sense were 'current' in their own times also determined significantly their respective understandings of Jesus, and the sense of their own relationship to him as the literary guardians of his teachings. Mani, therefore, appears in the remains of his letters as a product of a highly evolved Christian literary culture.

The variant form of Jn. 13. 18 – the substitution of salt for bread in the canonical version of John[103] – also highlights the important consideration about the biblical texts and traditions that Mani was familiar with. Alongside his reading of Paul, and the influence which Paul's representation of Jesus exerted on Mani's Christology,[104] it is also apparent that Mani knew the canonical Christian gospels, although whether he had read the four gospels, evangelist by evangelist, in Syriac translation (referred to as the 'Old Syriac' versions), or encountered the gospels in some sort of harmonised narrative of Jesus's life represented in its classical form by the *Diatessaron* (Gk lit. 'out of four [gospels]') attributed to the second-century theologian Tatian – a work comprising a patchwork text in which passages and saying from the four gospels were spliced together to form a continuous biography – is a contentious issue. Evidence for the Manichaean use of gospel harmonies has been found among the biblical citations offered by Manichaeans in the fourth century, including in Augustine's anti-Manichaean writings, and also in the finds from Turfan.[105] However, an indication of the early Manichaean use of the separate Old Syriac gospels is apparent from the circulation of Manichaean exegetical writings in the Roman empire.[106] But it is also likely that Mani's Christian library included apocryphal works such as the *Acts of Thomas*, which may have informed Mani about India and inspired his travels there,[107] in addition to certain apocryphal gospels which claimed to preserve the teachings of Jesus to his disciples (see above and the *Book of Mysteries*).

In summary, and as Iain Gardner has illustrated (e.g., in 2007a, 81, and in the use of Pauline imagery in Mani's 'Enemy Letter'), the remains of the canonical collection of epistles recovered from Kellis indicate Mani's tendency to write letters that were replete with a range of scriptural quotations, scriptural paraphrases and scriptural allusions. Mani's ability to create complex literary works, which were nevertheless able to be understood and employed by his

---

[102] See Hays 1989, 86f.
[103] See the comments by Gardner 2007a, 80–1.
[104] See Böhlig 1983.
[105] See Klimkeit 1993, 69–75.
[106] See Baker-Brian 2009, 58–61.
[107] Tardieu 2008, 31–2.

community, is a further demonstration of the biblically-literate character of the Manichaean church in Late Antiquity.

Psalms and Prayers

The collection of Coptic Psalms (the *Psalm-Book*) attributes to Mani two psalms together with 'his prayers' (Gardner and Lieu 2004, 164). Whilst the discoveries of Manichaean writings from Egypt and Central Asia illustrate that the religion developed a rich liturgical tradition comprising psalms, hymns and prayers – undoubtedly in imitation of Mani's own hymnic writings – none the less very little is known about the original contributions of the apostle. As we have seen with reference to the *Living Gospel* and the *Epistles* (i.e., *Letter of the Seal*), Mani's writings were incorporated into the liturgy of the Bema festival. It may have been the case that it was these or other works by Mani which were regarded as being 'psalms' in the minds of his followers, as a result of their role in the liturgical life of the community. The attribution of psalms and prayers, which he was not responsible for, to Mani is nevertheless another indication of Mani's supreme literary authority among his followers (cf. Turfan text M 842, trans. H.-J. Klimkeit 1993, 124).

Writing at the end of the nineteenth century, Konrad Kessler, a philologist of oriental languages and the author of a remarkably far-sighted study of Manichaeism from 1889, regarded Mani's religion as something that was unique in the religious landscape of antiquity. Eschewing the pejorative labelling of the religion as a Christian sect, signified by the German word *Manichäismus*, which suggested a derivative and deviant (= heretical) relationship to late-antique catholic Christianity (cf. Lim 2008), Kessler proposed the alternative term *Manithum* which, like *Christentum*, denoted a discrete faith, its independence linked with the ambitions and activities of its 'founder'.[108] Kessler's revision of the term *Manichaeism* chimes with modern approaches to the study of ancient Christianities, which are concerned with unpicking the influence of heresiological discourse on the 'naming strategies' applied to the many different Christian movements of Late Antiquity by a state-sponsored religious orthodoxy. However, the extent to which the literary products of Mani and his followers can be claimed as evidence for the early systematisation of Mani's teachings, which may in turn suggest Mani's uniqueness and independence from existing traditions, is a pressing point of debate in Manichaean studies. It is undoubtedly the writings of Mani, and principally their presentation as a canonical 'package' of texts by his later followers, which has led some commentators to make certain claims for the emergence of the Manichaean religion; for instance: 'Whereas Christianity took centuries to formulate its doctrines, and the controversies of the great councils seem far removed from the teachings of Jesus, Mani took great pains to establish a total religion based upon his own comprehensive scriptures and preaching ... There is less scope in the study of Manichaeism to trace the

---

[108] Kessler 1889, vii–xxvii.

evolution of doctrine, since all teaching was rigidly tied to the very details of the divine word in Mani's scriptures'.[109] However, as we have seen in this chapter, it is unlikely that Mani's writings prescribed 'a total religion', or indeed anything like a 'religion' in the modern sense of the word. The reality likely fell somewhere in the middle of this claim, whereby the guidance that the writings offered to Mani's followers was put to the service of building a system *out of* his teachings, an initiative which came about precisely because his devotees recognised that the works of Mani were not intended to address every single theological and pastoral issue which arose at any given time. However, as a result of the harsh realities facing Manichaeans in Sasanian and Roman territories as they entered the fourth century, moves towards preserving what Mani had written, and utilising those writings to develop a concrete formulation of his ideas, were to be expected.

[109] Gardner and Lieu 2004, 9–10.

Chapter 4

Manichaean Theology II: The Universe, its Rituals and its Community

1. Introduction: Mani's Myth and *Ecclesia*

This chapter considers Mani's mythological account of the cosmos. It provides a summary description of the myth, and argues that the narrative itself served as the fundamental feature of Mani's teachings, in the sense that it supplied the principal point of departure for Mani's theology. The myth, which included details of the way in which Light fought back against Darkness, narrated for his followers what had gone wrong in the universe and on a localised level within 'their world', and talked about the ways in which the problems facing humankind could be solved. However, the solution advocated by Mani on the basis of the myth was not confined simply to knowing about the 'true nature' of the world, nor indeed simply about informing an individual of his or her role in it. Rather, the myth existed in a reciprocal relationship with the religion's ascetic practices and the ritual performance of those practices via the hierarchy and the liturgical traditions of the Manichaean church. The Manichaean myth supplied the 'specific configuration of the universe'[1] necessary for the performance of the rituals prioritised by the Manichaeans, in terms of their successful repetition time and time again within Manichaean communities through history. This chapter integrates the significance of the myth for the practice of Manichaean rituals, through an introduction to the structural hierarchy and rituals of Mani's *ecclesia*.

However, Manichaeism's opponents focused on Mani's myth as a fable ripe for lampooning. The chapter begins by discussing some of these derisory responses on the part of both pagan and Christian writers hostile to Manichaeism, and in so doing builds a bridge backwards to some of the ideas raised in Chapter 1. Within the context of Mani's own time and environment, myth was one of the main ways in which religious truth was communicated to audiences: the Manichaean myth stood in an ancient Jewish-Christian tradition of enshrining within a story an account of cosmic conflict, which sought to provide both an explanation and solution to life's 'Big Questions', e.g., how to overcome evil, and the ways in which humankind could establish a meaningful relationship with God. However, those Christian traditions – predominantly in the Hellenised

---

[1] BeDuhn 2002, 70.

world of the later Roman empire – which had been formed under different theological and philosophical influences from those in west Asia, reacted strongly against Manichaeism's chosen method of communicating these concerns. Thus it is in the reception of Mani's myth by its opponents that we see most clearly the sizeable gulf dividing Roman Christianity from Mesopotamian Manichaean Christianity during Late Antiquity.

2. 'An Imperfect Beginning, a Flabby Middle, and a Ruined End': Mani the Mythographer

The reason I say this is that I know for a fact that [the Manichaeans], whenever deficient in proofs, bring together from all sides certain matters derived from poetry to use them as a defence of their private doctrines. However, they would not have done so if they had ever consulted any author you would like to suggest with any amount of care (Alexander of Lycopolis, *Critique of the Doctrines of Manichaeus* (ed. A. Brinkmann (1895), 16.21–17.2), trans. P.W. van der Horst and J. Mansfeld 1974, 71).

The author of this passage, the pagan philosopher Alexander, from Lycopolis in Egypt, was writing at a point in time when the third century met the fourth, and in a province which had become an important centre for Manichaeans during Late Antiquity.[2] Alexander was responding to the successes which Mani's early followers in the Roman world had enjoyed in shifting the allegiances of some of his fellow-philosophers away from the rationalistic teaching of his cherished Platonism to a range of ideas which, in Alexander's opinion, contained nothing of any recognisable philosophical worth.[3] The presentation of Mani's teachings in Alexander's Greek treatise, *Critique of the Doctrines of Mani*, represents an attempt, either on Alexander's part, or on the initiative of Mani's followers based in Roman Egypt, to transform Mani's 'astonishing doctrines' into something equating to a 'scientific' and ethical philosophy. Who, indeed, was responsible for this transformation is a crucial question for anyone considering Alexander's treatise, although it is apparent that Alexander's philosophical handling of the doctrines of Mani was intended to highlight their lack of logical coherency; a tactic that amounted to a common polemical strategy, since writers recognised that attempts to rationalise a particular tradition using approaches and terminology unfamiliar to that tradition usually led to it appearing to be even more irrational and nonsensical than it would have seemed in the first place, in its original mode of expression. Alexander's response to Mani and Manichaeism was evidently meant as a polemic against the religion, and as such it represents a highly valuable primary source for gauging the concerns of educated pagans with the interpretation of Christianity offered by Mani and his followers.

---

[2] On whether Alexandria or Lycopolis should be assigned as Alexander's sphere of activity, see Schenke 1997, 290–1.

[3] *Critique of the Doctrines of Manichaeus* (ed. Brinkmann (1895), 8.5–9.5); trans. P.W. van der Horst and J. Mansfeld 1974, 58.

Alexander's offering-up of Mani's teachings in 'Greek garb' led one distin-
guished scholar, Hans Heinrich Schaeder,[4] to lean heavily on the work in
the development of a thesis which held that Mani himself was a thoroughly
Hellenised thinker, who expressed the nucleus of his ideas in the kind of Greek
philosophical terminology – God, Soul, Spirit and Matter – found in Alexander's
work.[5] Whether or not Alexander's treatise contains evidence for an early form
of Mani's teachings remains an open question; what is important in this regard,
however, is the portrayal of Mani's central ideas about the origin (his *cosmogony*)
and workings (his *cosmology*) of the universe in Alexander's work, which is wholly
different from the way in which those ideas are expressed in other sources from
Late Antiquity conveying details of Manichaean cosmogony and cosmology.

The explanation given by Mani for the origin and workings of the universe
has become the cornerstone for the reception of Manichaeism in the modern
age, supplying nearly all of its most commonly acknowledged elements: the
essential drama of dualism, namely the primordial battle of Light versus
Darkness, Good versus Evil; the loss of the soul through the 'defeat' of the First
Man; the demonic creation of Adam and Eve; and the triumph of Good over
Evil and the liberation of the soul. Taken together, all of these features have
influenced popular definitions of Manichaeism: for instance, the renowned
ethicist Peter Singer, in his discussion of the apocalyptic tendencies in the ethical
pronouncements of George W. Bush, remarks: 'Seeing the world as a conflict
between the forces of good and the forces of evil is not … the orthodox Christian
view, but one associated with the heresy of Manichaeanism'.[6] However, beyond
the building-blocks of Manichaean dualism, the panoply of Mani's cosmogony
remains largely unknown to the modern, casual observer. This was certainly not
the case in the late-antique period, when it was the finer details of Manichaean
cosmogony – the cast of divine beings and the intricate plot of an unfolding
drama that held profound consequences for humanity – which were frequently
cited by opponents in order to pour scorn on the religion.

Indeed, such details are absent from Alexander's representation of Mani's
teachings, an absence explainable in part as a result of the philosophical prejudice
which Alexander shared with very many ancient critics towards cosmogonic
accounts that placed gods in competition with one another, and which also
portrayed divine beings as afflicted by emotions such as, e.g., anger and jealousy.
During the third and fourth centuries, Christians and pagans in the Roman
empire – the 'West' – memorialised Mani as the creator of a spectacular myth
detailing not only the origins of the universe but also its dissolution (i.e., the
Manichaean *eschatology*), as a result of which Mani became the mythographer –
the author of a myth – *par excellence*. The dominance of this characterisation has
disproportionately influenced prevailing cultural memories of Manichaeism in
the modern period, typified in the frequent prioritisation of Mani's cosmogony
in scholarly accounts of Manichaeism, above anything else which the religion
offered to its ancient adherents. However, for a religious thinker in antiquity, it

---

[4] Schaeder 1927.
[5] See Villey 1985, 27–32.
[6] Singer 2004, 209.

was not necessarily an honour to be recalled in this way. Alexander of Lycopolis's treatise epitomises neatly some of the concerns about Mani's ideas, concerns which were widely held by the philosophically-trained elites of the Roman empire, and which included of course Christians as well as pagans. Alexander's view of Mani's 'astonishing doctrines' was, in the main, determined by the central role which myth appeared to play in Mani's teachings.

> [The Manichaeans] surpass by far the mythographers who are responsible for the castration of Uranus or who wrote about the scheming against Kronos by his son, who wanted to gain possession of his father's dominion, or who, again, have Kronos swallow his sons and then have him make a mistake because of the appearance of a piece of stone. Their stories are undoubtedly of the same sort, since they describe a regular war of matter against God, but they do not even mean this allegorically, as e.g. Homer did, who, in his *Illiad*, describes Zeus' pleasure on account of the war of the gods against each other, thereby hinting at the fact that the universe is constructed out of unequal elements, which are fitted together and both victorious and vincible (*Critique of the Doctrines of Manichaeus* (ed. Brinkmann (1895), 16.9–21); trans. P.W. van der Horst and J. Mansfeld 1974, 70–1).

The ancient Greek poet Hesiod's narration of the origin of the universe – the emasculation of the sky-god Uranus by his son Kronos, the anxiety of Kronos that at some time he will be usurped by one of his own children, resulting in Kronos swallowing his offspring whole, the duplicity of Kronos's wife Rhea in keeping the birth of Zeus a secret from Kronos by passing her swaddled baby off as a stone, and the ensuing long war between the Olympians and the Titans – featured prominently amongst the myths that most scandalised ancient philosophy.[7] According to Alexander, the diminution of supernal potency, internecine rivalries and territorial aggrandisement were themes common to both Greek and Manichaean mythological traditions, resulting in descriptions of less than immaculate behaviours on the part of the gods. However, Alexander is clear that Manichaean myth went beyond the outrageous impieties of classical theogonies. A polemical extension of this argument, an example of which may be seen in the passage from the *Life of Porphyry* (§86) by Mark the Deacon discussed in Chapter 1, was the heresiological commonplace which suggested that Mani had obtained his 'blasphemous' ideas about the gods from Hesiod, and from other Greek poets and tragedians. Alexander would seem to be saying the same thing, although using the terminology of logic to do so, in his observation that the Manichaeans look to poetry when their attempts to argue their ideas in a rational manner fail.

Thus, certain trends in late-antique philosophy reacted in a specific way to classical portrayals where the gods appeared fallible, regarding them nevertheless as worth retaining so long as the crimes and misdemeanours of the gods yielded something that could be considered of cultural value, through an allegorical reading of the myths in question. Judgements concerning a mythology's impiety

---

[7] See Villey 1985, 247.

and its continued philosophical utility depended on the cultural assumptions of the myth's interpreter, whose decision to handle a particular account figuratively was an open admission that the contents of the myth in question did not map adequately on to the pattern of cultural norms (be they philosophical, religious or scientific) which influenced the attitudes and strategies of assessment of the interpreter.

However, in Alexander's estimation the situation with Manichaeism was very different, since the *mythopoeic* (i.e., the creative act of myth making) impulse in Mani's writings was totally different from the mythopoeia of classical mythology. Moving beyond the philosophical presumption which held that most classical authors of myth had meant for their work to be read according to the hidden meanings which they had buried deep within the text, Alexander remarked that the Manichaeans had meant for no such approach to be taken with regard to their own myth since they made it clear that no further meaning was hidden beneath its surface. Implicit within this particular criticism lay Alexander's understanding that Mani had indeed intended for his myth to be received as a genuine 'scientific' explanation for the origin and workings of the universe – i.e., that his myth was no allegorical fable, but a literal, descriptive account explaining why things are the way they are – a state of affairs that for Alexander was more scandalous than Mani's irreverent descriptions of his gods and divine powers.

It seems that this literal approach to the religion's cosmogony came directly from Mani himself, as suggested by the words of Ephraim that formed part of his discourse against Mani (210.30–6): 'For Mani forces one to understand him straightforwardly (even) when he speaks preposterously, (as when he says) 'Darkness loved Light, its opposite'.[8] Augustine, the religion's best-known apostate, also indicated that Mani's insistence on the literalness of his myth was determined by his apostolic identity: as the final apostle, Mani not only spoke in an open and accessible fashion about his own teachings, but he also disclosed what his predecessors had revealed in figurative language, in plain and literal speech:

> But when the Manichaeans abandon their imaginings of that shape, they cannot be Manichaeans. For they ascribe it to the praises of their founder as something proper and excellent when they say that the divine mysteries set forth in figures in the scriptures were left to be resolved and revealed by this man who was going to come last. And they say that no teacher will come from God after him precisely for the reason that Mani said nothing in figures and allegories. For he had made clear what the ancients had said in that way and plainly and openly revealed his own thoughts. The Manichaeans, therefore, do not have any interpretations to which they can have recourse when it is read to them from their founder: 'But next to one part and side of that bright and holy land was the land of darkness' (Augustine, *Answer to the Letter of Mani called The Foundation* 23.25; trans. R.J. Teske 2006, 250–1).

[8] Trans. J.C. Reeves 1997, 232.

Very many anti-Manichaean authors shared Alexander's opinions about Mani's myth, their judgements influenced by their own traditions of natural science and its expression in the philosophical language of rationalism, postulates and proofs (see *Critique*, P.W. van der Horst and J. Mansfeld 1974, 86ff). Thus, whilst the philosophical traditions of antiquity indicated that truths concerning the workings of the universe masqueraded beneath myth, which could be 'rescued' according to the way in which those myths were read, the Manichaeans' emphasis on the literal apprehension of their cosmogony enabled their opponents to argue that the Manichaean myth lacked credibility as a foundation narrative, since it contained nothing of any 'scientific' value. Struggles for supremacy between opposing divine forces, and the intimate union of ruling archons and emanatory powers from which a series of creative acts were said to have followed, are some of the characteristic features of Mani's mythology. Descriptions of this kind were not unfamiliar to the cosmogonies of ancient philosophy, although the cultural consensus of the time looked down upon such details as absurdities, a judgement that spawned the consequent consensus which regarded them as interpretive catalysts within the heart of mythological narratives, clues intended to prompt audiences to go beyond a literal reading in order to access something of philosophical value.[9] The Manichaeans' insistence that the absurdities in their account should stand provided a gift to the opponents of the religion. The very prominent place accorded to Mani's myth in almost all anti-Manichaean works is a clear indication that polemicists appreciated the opportunity given to them as a result of the Manichaeans' literalness.

However, as Alexander makes clear, not all Manichaeans upheld this apparent orthodox approach to the presentation of Mani's myth.

> The more cultivated among [the Manichaeans] call to our memory parts of our own [Greek] tradition. They quote the mysteries, comparing the dismemberment of Dionysius by the Titans to the dividing up, in their own teachings, of the divine power over matter. They also refer to the battle of the giants as told in our poetry, which to their mind proves that the poets were not ignorant of the insurrection of matter against God (*Critique of the Doctrines of Manichaeus* (ed. Brinkmann (1895), 8.5–13); trans. P.W. van der Horst and J. Mansfeld 1974, 57).

The Egyptian-based Manichaeans mentioned by Alexander, who used a comparative approach to translate culturally the principal features of their myth, may nevertheless have been the exception to the rule. Evidently, Alexander was aware that the vast majority of the myth had not been accommodated to the philosophical tradition in which he had been reared, and his assessment of the Manichaean myth was representative of the reception which Manichaean teachers received as they offered up Mani's ideas and writings for scrutiny in the towns and cities of the Roman empire, a reception exemplified in the retorts of Augustine.

---

[9]   See Siniossoglou 2008, 147–88.

Offering his opinion of Mani's cosmogony as part of his response (ca. 400) to the teachings of Faustus, an influential Manichaean bishop and teacher active in North Africa during the mid-to-late fourth century, Augustine remarked: 'That myth of yours is long and foolish, a child's plaything, a woman's joke, a hag's raving, containing a truncated beginning, a rotten middle, and a ruinous end.'[10] Sounding rather like a supercilious literary critic rubbishing the plot structure of a dubious 'airport novel', Augustine's assessment in his *Answer to Faustus* echoes the infamous characterisation of the religion in his *Confessions* (4.7.13: 'a monstrous story and a long lie'), although the target of his censure was the heart of Mani's understanding of the beginnings of the cosmos, its historical duration and its eventual obliteration (see below). Augustine's use of the Latin word *fabula* to describe Mani's cosmogony equates approximately with one of the dominant contemporary definitions of the word 'myth' – itself a highly contentious term to define[11] – as a fable or story, although for Augustine the pejorative sense of *fabula* as a story replete with ludicrous and unbelievable details was also strongly implied. However, this description of Mani's cosmogony as myth was carefully chosen: like Alexander, Augustine, as a member of the late Roman cultural elite, shared in an attitude towards myth that was typical of those who had received training in philosophy through the educational curricula of antiquity.

In this regard, myth, as a narrative of fabulous tales, was 'stigmatised' – in the words of Helen Morales[12] – and its cultural value was reassessed so that myth's continued importance was seen to reside, not in its stories, but in what it could offer to the allegorist. As an intellectual prejudice that was determined by an evolutionist ideology, 'a *myth* about myth',[13] the maligning of fable as a form of valid religious expression formed not only an important part of Christian anti-Manichaean polemic, but also an aspect of pagan reactions to Manichaeism, indeed, as it also did of pagan anti-Christian polemic.

Thus, how the pluralistic world of Late Antiquity viewed Mani's contribution to religious knowledge was largely dependent on where the person (or persons) making such an assessment was situated, i.e., on which side of the cultural frontier separating Roman Christianity from Mesopotamian Christianity he or she stood. As a case in point, Augustine is an excellent example of a Roman Manichaean who spent most of his time in the religion anticipating that the rational and substantive truths of Manichaeism would become accessible once the Manichaean teachers known to him were ready to demythologise Mani's myth. However, nothing of the sort happened, or indeed was ever likely to happen, since no demythologised version of Mani's mythological narrative existed (at least, not in the minds of most late-antique Manichaeans).[14] In the mind of Mani and his followers, Mani's narrative of the universe's beginnings *was* rational and substantive according to the cultural language and religious traditions of Mesopotamian Christianity. Mani's manner of communicating certain

---

[10] Augustine, *Answer to Faustus* 13. 6; trans. R.J. Teske 2007, 162.
[11] See Csapo 2005, 1–9.
[12] Morales 2007, 58.
[13] Morales 2007, 58.
[14] See BeDuhn 2010, *passim*.

elements of his teachings in mythological form was entirely in keeping with the prevailing religious tendencies of the region and the traditions that co-existed in western Asia during this time.

Thus, whilst the explication of religious truths via mythological narratives was in a sense a cultural convention specific to certain ancient systems of thought throughout the regions of Mesopotamia and Babylonia, the question that still begs to be addressed is that of why myth retained its hold over a diverse range of thinkers. The influence of precedent on Mani's own choice of literary disclosure for his religious message only really answers half the question. Perhaps the appropriateness of myth as an economic way of conveying to believers deep truths of an ontological and ethical nature must also be considered? Addressing this query – why did Mani choose myth as his principal medium of theological expression – will be of concern in the next section. However, the perceptive analysis of Guy Stroumsa, in his book *Another Seed*, offers some insightful comment whilst these questions are at the forefront of our minds. Although he is speaking about gnostic myth in a more general sense, Stroumsa's comments nevertheless appear also to chime with the implicit rationalism of Manichaean mythology:

> ... [the Gnostic achieved] an externalisation of consciousness through myth. For the Gnostic, myth was the only possible way to relate to a world too dreadful to be confronted with the limited intellectual powers of the individual.[15]

The appeal to Mani of a mythological narrative is not, therefore, satisfactorily explained by a 'love for stories' that he may have harboured.[16] Mani's recognition that a mythological narrative would provide the ideal platform for the dissemination of his revelatory understanding of human nature shares something with contemporary cognitive approaches to storytelling, and the acknowledgement that the cultural value of stories may have more to do with an ability to convey 'deep truths' rather than with other concerns such as entertainment or mnemonics; although the two aspects may not have been as mutually exclusive as commentators sometimes make out. As Brian Boyd has noted:

> We desire deeper explanations. We see cause in terms of agency, and recognize the special characteristics of psychological or 'spiritual' rather than physical causation. We recognise other creatures' different powers. We readily invent, recall, and retell stories involving agents that violate expectations. Across humankind we have therefore repeatedly offered (1) deep causal explanations in terms of (2) beings with powers different from ours, (3) understood in terms of mind or spirit, moved like us by beliefs, desires, and intentions but (4) somehow violating our expectations of things or kinds, especially by transgressing normal physical limits – perhaps by being

---

[15] Stroumsa 1984, 3.
[16] Cf. Stroumsa 1984, 165.

invisible, or existing in more than one place at a time, or being able to change shape or pass through solid obstacles or live forever.[17]

Rather than viewing Mani as the creator of a fable, Manichaeans were inclined to regard their apostle as a revealer of profound truths – a 'scientific' account of the universe – which made him the mediator of literally life-saving knowledge hitherto undisclosed (or at least, of knowledge undisclosed in an uncorrupted form for many generations). The Manichaean homily in Coptic on Mani's imprisonment and death (entitled 'The Section of the Narrative of the Crucifixion') recalls Mani as 'The preacher of life. The interpreter of the land of the great Babylon. Like an arrow from a bow he pierced this world …'.[18] Evidently Mani had something affirming to say about humanity, offering through his myth, in the somewhat unpromising description suggested by Stroumsa, an *etiology*.[19] Nevertheless, etiology is a term well-chosen, referring as it does to the process of diagnosis – a procedure undertaken in order to discover the cause of something – as conceived in the study of modern medicine. A desire to answer life's 'Big Questions', e.g., how the universe, the world, nature and humankind were formed and why, and the reasons for the presence of corruption, sickness, decay and death throughout the created order, were fundamental issues that pre-occupied the majority of ancient thinkers. An important aspect of Mani's own apparent self-designation, along with recollections of the apostle's identity among later generations of his followers, concerned Mani's role as a physician. In the *CMC* (122. 6–7), Mani refers to himself as a physician (Gk *iatros*), which, as John Kevin Coyle suggests, preserves 'an original tradition' about the apostle as healer that may then have entered into a number of biographical writings (e.g. M566; M47; M3[20]) from Turfan.[21] To what extent, though, were the roles of apostle and physician compatible? The modern tendency in conventional medicine to isolate the treatment of bodily ailments from the health and well-being of the mind, has also impacted on the way in which modern commentators undermine ancient understandings of the relationship between the health of the soul and the integrity of the body. Jason BeDuhn has demonstrated that Manichaean approaches to the nature and the condition of the soul and its relationship with the human body stand squarely within a tradition of later Greek (Hellenistic) medical thought, in which there was 'discursive permeability between the spheres of philosophy, medicine, and religion, between the professions of sophist, scientist, physician and prophet.'[22] Such an awareness should in fact mean a reconsideration of the way in which we think about Mani and the Manichaeans' ideas as being genuinely scientific – *etiological* – within the context of ancient thought, rather than them being

---

[17] Boyd 2009, 200–1.
[18] *Manichaean Homilies* 61.16–18; trans. N.A. Pedersen 2006, 61.
[19] Stroumsa 1984, 153.
[20] M566, trans. H.-J. Klimkeit 1993, 208; M47, trans. H.-J. Klimkeit 1993, 211–12; M3, trans. H.-J. Klimkeit 1993, 213–14,
[21] Coyle 2009c, 121.
[22] BeDuhn 1992, 116.

viewed simply as matters pertaining to 'religion' which have been, and continue to be, handled with the safety net of figurative language suspended beneath them.[23] It is this 'medical' approach to understanding the nature of all things, and the desire to seek remedies for individual and collective suffering, that appear to have driven Mani to formulate his great account of the universe: in a sense, therefore, Mani's was a pathologist's quest for answers to the condition of the world which he disseminated in third-century Mesopotamia.

3. The Problem of Evil

Narrative models that offered mythological explanations for life's 'Big Questions' lay all around Mani during this time. A resurgent Zoroastrian religion in the Sasanian period under the imperial guidance of Ardashir I[24] offered an archaic although not wholly unchanged myth about the universe's origins in terms of a comprehensive theogony (a genealogy of the gods and divine powers) and theodicy (i.e., an explanation for the origin and operation of evil in the world), posited along dualistic lines, which can be found in a number of Avestan scriptural texts including the *Bundahishn* (= Creation), a Pahlavi work dating from the ninth century AD, which nevertheless preserves mythological traditions from earlier lost Avestan writings. However, as Werner Sundermann has noted, the 'Zoroastrian influence on Manichaean doctrine has always been, and still is, one of the most controversial topics of Manichaean studies'.[25] The basis for the controversy of which Sundermann speaks derives from a number of concerns, all of which relate to the complex web of phenomenological influence and derivation inherent in the study of Manichaeism as highlighted in Chapter 1. Thus there is difficulty in identifying the type of Zoroastrian dualism that Mani would have been familiar with during the third century, a difficulty arising from the relatively late date of many Zoroastrian scriptural sources, which raises the possibility that, in the area of myth at least, Manichaeism may have been of an influence on Zoroastrianism rather than the other way round; an issue also coupled with the spectre of the politics of syncretism implicit in theses positing the 'Iranian' derivation of Mani's ideas. Nevertheless, Mani's familiarity with not only the names of the gods in the Zoroastrian pantheon but also the dualistic template of Zoroastrian mythology – dualism supplying the building blocks for Mani's myth – is evident throughout his *Šābuhragān*, and also in later Manichaean sources. In answer to the question posed in the title of the article 'How Zoroastrian is Mani's Dualism?', from 1997, Sundermann answered with caution that 'Manichaean dualism is not a simple adoption or imitation of the Zoroastrian',[26] and appended a nuanced list detailing ten points of strong convergences with minor divergences between Zoroastrian and Manichaean dualism, and four additional points of strong divergences between the two traditions. At

---

[23] See BeDuhn 1992, and 2002, *passim*.
[24] See Duchesne-Guillemin 1983, 874–7.
[25] Sundermann 1997, 343.
[26] Sundermann 1997, 350.

the more pessimistic end of the spectrum, Timothy Pettipiece has noted that '[m]ere terminological similarities say nothing about origins and derivations [of the Manichaean myth], especially at a time when Zoroastrian traditions were themselves in such a state of flux'.[27] Furthermore, expositions of dualism existed across Iranian, Greek (Platonic), Jewish-Christian, Gnostic and Christian traditions, and even within those individual traditions enormous contrasts existed in the formulation of dualistic ideas. Just as likely as a Zoroastrian influence on Mani's dualism was the influence that would have arisen from Mani's own readings of Christian writings – foremost being the gospels (apocryphal and canonical) and the writings of Paul – which were reinforced by the glosses of theologians such as Marcion and Bardaisan.[28]

The *Šābuhragān* presents a case in point during discussions of the influence of the prevailing mythological environment of Mesopotamia on Mani. As Manfred Hutter has noted, the *Šābuhragān* may indeed have been consciously inspired by Zoroastrian traditions, but the tendency on Mani's part to present his ideas in imagery drawn from Jewish-Christian traditions, e.g., from biblical texts including the apocryphal Enochic literature, remains visible in spite of their skilful integration by Mani into the myth and eschatology of the work.[29] The embedded presence of themes and motifs drawn from Enochic literature in the *Šābuhragān* and in his other writings, provides some clues as to the types of issues that Mani wanted to address in his myth, foremost among them being an attempt to account for hardship and suffering in the world, which Mani rationalised as deriving from the corrupting influence of evil.

In the classical account of the rebellious angels ('the watchers') from 1 Enoch 6–16, the idea of evil as something which humankind is forced to endure against both its own predisposed nature, and correlatively its better judgement, is introduced into the realm of the earth through corrupt, external agents. Giants, the offspring of the watchers arising from their illicit sexual unions with the 'daughters of earth', rampage through the world, murdering men, stealing resources and destroying all living creatures and the natural world (1 Enoch 7.3–6). Their fathers, the watchers, also teach men about the destructive arts (1 Enoch 8.1–3), e.g., warfare, consumerism, magic, sophistry, all of which increase suffering, sin and impiety. Relief for humankind only comes after the petitions of men are heard by four loyal angels (Michael, Sariel, Raphael and Gabriel), who prompt God to act against the watchers.

As a theologian aware of the need to preserve the integrity of the supreme deity, Mani undoubtedly related to the narrative of the watchers and the giants in terms of where it assigned blame for the presence of evil in the world. According to this Jewish tradition, evil was ultimately caused by primordial beings rebelling against God, whose nefarious habits were transferred almost in a genetic sense to the giants, and on to the spirits which arose from their bodies, i.e., the Nephilim (1 Enoch 15.11; 16.1). Furthermore, Enochic traditions make it clear that humankind was also *prepared* to be led astray (cf. 1 Enoch 8.2), its

[27] Pettipiece 2009, 28.
[28] See de Blois 2000.
[29] See Hutter 1992, 135–9.

collective will enticed by the 'eternal mysteries prepared in heaven' (1 Enoch 9.6) revealed to them by the watchers. Thus, culpability for suffering on earth should not be placed at God's door.

We know that Mani took over the saga of the rebellion of the watchers by incorporating it in a specific sense into his cosmogony as a description of the watchers' (= demons') rebellion against the King of Honour, one of the sons of the Living Spirit, the demiurgical figure of Manichaean myth.[30] However, the lore of the Enochic tradition was likely to have been of an even greater influence on the construction of Mani's ideas concerning the goodness of God, the origin of evil and the nature of sin (i.e., the theodicean elements of Manichaean theology). As Stroumsa has noted, in the extrapolation and integration of mythological elements from other traditions Mani displayed a tendency for 'shifting myths back to earlier stages in the *Vorzeit* [i.e., primordial times] and to higher levels of reality'.[31] For Mani, evil existed independently of the good within its own realm, although it was co-eternal with it: like the good it was a nature (sometimes also called a principle) which ruled over a territory populated with companion worlds. Unlike the good, however, its temperament was marred by an insurgent desire to own the very essence of the good, which was its light, which stood as a direct contrast to the darkness that was the essence of evil. In one of his discourses addressed to Hypatius, Ephraim described how Manichaean writings had indicated that the darkness 'passionately lusted for light', because its nature '… is desirable and beautiful to darkness',[32] which suggests that, like the comeliness of the 'daughters of earth' in 1 Enoch 1–2, the impetus for evil to act, like the rebelliousness of the watchers, was supplied by the apprehension of something that brought aesthetic pleasure to the beholder.[33] However, unlike the watchers who descended to earth in order to satiate their lust, the Manichaean myth describes evil as ascending from its own world to begin its assault on the realm of light.

4. Approaching the Manichaean Myth

As we saw in Chapter 3, Mani set out the details of the myth in a number of his writings. Judging from the evidence offered by sources like *The Chapters*, all of Mani's works mentioned in the Western formulation of the Manichaean scriptural canon were understood in some way to make reference to the myth, which Manichaeans, possibly following the lead of Mani himself, referred as the 'three lessons' or the 'three times' as a way of denoting the periodisation of the mythological narrative's beginning, middle and end (see below), the elements of the Manichaean 'fable' criticised by Augustine and other anti-Manichaean writers.[34] The periods formed an essential element in the soteriological narrative

---

[30] E.g., *The Chapters* 38.92.27–31; trans. I. Gardner 1995, 97. See Henning 1943, 53; also Stroumsa 1984, 153–4.

[31] Stroumsa 1984, 153.

[32] Trans. J.C. Reeves 1997, 227.

[33] See Coyle 2009b, 51–64.

[34] *The Chapters* 5.21–33; trans. I. Gardner 1995, 145.

of Manichaeism, reflecting the extent of the engagement between the two natures, from the point of their isolation from each other, to their 'mixing' – which implied the appropriation of light by the darkness, and concluding with the reestablishment of their separate spheres of influence. Geo Widengren offers the following terse description of the three times:

> The First Epoch embraced the state of the universe prior to the blending of light and darkness; the Second Epoch was concerned with the period of that blending; the Third Epoch signified the sundering of the blended elements. This doctrine of the Three Epochs is together with the Two Principles Manichaeism's main dogma.[35]

The *Šābuhragān*, once thought of as a work concerned wholly with Mani's ideas about the end of days, is now understood to have offered a systematic treatment of the beginnings and operation of the universe. Furthermore, whilst the legendary content of Mani's *Pragmateia* is not fully assured, it was almost certainly concerned with cosmogonic/cosmological material. Befitting his authorial personality as a writer of letters, Mani also sought to clear up the confusions which arose with the cultural translation of his myth as undertaken by his followers who were spread far and wide in the world. Patticius (Patig), one of Mani's closest disciples and his father's namesake, was active in the Roman empire,[36] specifically in Egypt towards the latter half of the third century, when he received a letter (*The Foundation*) in which Mani provided a compact account of his myth demonstrating an especial concern to expand on the seemingly salacious details of the generation of Adam and Eve.[37]

Mani's *Book of Giants* also clearly related details of a cosmological nature, as did the *Living Gospel* and the *Treasury*. However, the nature and purpose of each individual work necessarily determined the reason for the inclusion of the myth, the details given, and the way in which the myth was imparted. It appears rare for Mani to narrate the myth simply for the sake of 'telling the story'. Indeed, it was more usual for the myth to be applied to other areas of Manichaean thought, in the sense of offering the basic data for meditations on anthropogony (the origins of humankind), ontology (the nature of existence), and anthropology. On occasions, the myth also seems to have been employed in order to provide a cosmic 'mytho-historical' identity for his community – thereby indicating the antiquity of his teachings – by fixing it centrally within the soteriological scheme of the universe, as in the case of the eschatological scenes from the *Šābuhragān* (see Chapter 1), along with reinforcing specific cultic and ritualised roles for members of his church.

---

[35] Widengren 1965, 68. See also Heuser 1998, 18–24.
[36] See I. Gardner and S.N.C. Lieu 2004, 111.
[37] Portions of *The Foundation* are preserved in a number of Latin Patristic writings, including substantially in Augustine's response to the letter; see Stein 2002 for a recent edition of *The Foundation*'s fragments; an English translation of the fragments has been assembled by I. Gardner and S.N.C. Lieu 2004, 168–72 (see frg. 4a in Gardner and Lieu for references to Adam and Eve). For a study of the work see esp. Scopello 2001.

Works composed by Manichaeans, likely patterned on the teachings and writings of Mani, also include references to the myth, including the valuable insights regarding the doctrinal adaptation of Mani's mythology by his followers offered throughout *The Chapters*,[38] together with liturgical and devotional renderings of Mani's theogony and mythology in the *Psalm-Book* and the *Homilies* (some of which have been collected and translated in Gardner and Lieu 2004, 176–230). Along with the fragments which are now assigned to the *Šābuhragān*, many Middle Persian and Parthian fragments from Turfan also contain material of a mythological orientation.[39] The myth was therefore susceptible to extrapolation, reformulation, expansion and contraction, depending on the demands of the cultural environment and audience for which it was being recounted: indeed, this adaptability appears to have been one of its main 'selling points'. It is, therefore, important to take on board the following observation made by Jason BeDuhn concerning the manner of narrative representations of the Manichaean myth across this diverse range of literature:

> That which is presented as an orderly, synthetic cosmogonic narrative in most twentieth-century scholarship on Manichaeism stands in the various [Manichaean and anti-Manichaean] sources as a tangled collection of conflicting accounts, in need of careful literary-historical analysis.[40]

Precisely because the myth presented such great opportunities for opponents of Manichaeism to deride so fantastic an account of the universe, attacks on the myth became the stock-in-trade for writers hostile to the religion. Notable anti-Manichaean sources from Late Antiquity that provide tendentious, although still valuable, accounts of the myth include: the *Critique* of Alexander of Lycopolis; the *Acts of Archelaus* (esp. 7.1–13.4, trans. M. Vermes 2001, 44-58, with a superb set of notes by S. Lieu); Augustine's *Answer to the Letter of Mani known as the Foundation*, and his *Answer to Faustus* (esp. 15.5–6 and 20.2); Ephraim's *Prose Refutations* (conveniently collected by J.C. Reeves with a commentary 1997, 224–8); the 123rd homily of Severus of Antioch (trans. J.C. Reeves 1992, 167–70); and the summary of Mani's 'abominable teaching' in the *Scholia* of Theodore bar Koni (trans. J.C. Reeves 1992, 189–93).

Of all of these accounts, Theodore bar Koni's so-called résumé of the myth is considered by many commentators to be the most prized: dating from the eighth century, Theodore wrote his work in Syriac, for which reason it is believed that he preserved 'terminology traceable to Mani himself'.[41] It is likely that Theodore was working from copies of Mani's own writings, which he excerpted directly and introduced with the words 'He (i.e., Mani) says' as a way of reporting direct speech.[42] However, whilst acknowledging the evident value of Theodore's résumé, it is also important to recognise the artificial nature of it, being the

[38] On this, see esp. Pettipiece 2009, *passim*.
[39] See Sundermann 1993.
[40] BeDuhn 2002, 75–6.
[41] Reeves 1992, 188–9.
[42] See Burkitt 1925, 14–15; cf. Tardieu 2008, 75–6.

work of a heresiologist, whose ambition was to highlight what he considered to be the absurd details of Mani's teachings, which he achieved first and foremost by decontextualising the myth from whichever work(s) he had taken it from,[43] decontextualisation and reductionism being the principal weapons in the armoury of the heresy-hunter.

Of the Islamic sources, the *Fihrist*'s detailed account of the myth from the tenth century (Dodge 1970, II.777–88) remains of great value, having been scrutinised by Carsten Colpe in 1954,[44] and more recently by François de Blois (2005).

5. The Myth

The Cosmic Conflict and the Sacrifice of Light

Mindful of the fact, therefore, that Manichaeans themselves probably did not apprehend their myth 'as an orderly, synthetic account' of the universe, it is nevertheless appropriate to ask what account of existence did the myth narrate? Following the names and terms from Theodore bar Koni's summary (trans. J.C. Reeves 1992, 189–93), the beginning period witnessed the good nature, also called the Father of Greatness (i.e., God), residing in the Realm of Light with his five dwellings (or members),[45] mind, knowledge, intellect, thought and reflection. These five dwellings, denoting the presence of the Father, sensed that the corresponding principle of the good nature, the evil nature, or the King of Darkness, who with his five worlds ('aeons') of smoke, fire, wind, water and darkness, had been casting envious glimpses towards his realm. The separateness of these two co-eternal natures was thus undermined with evil's 'contemplation of ascent' (cf. J.C. Reeves 1992, 190), an act which triggered the dramatic events of the middle period, in which the world would eventually be established.

The dwellings of the Father became unnerved by the attentions of their southern neighbour. Reluctant to send the good nature's five attributes to counter the challenge from below, the five who had been 'created … for tranquillity and peace' (Theodore bar Koni; trans. J.C. Reeves 1992, 190), the evil nature was engaged by the Father himself. However, the Father could only do so through the act of 'calling forth' from his own essence an emanation, the Mother of Life; the speech-act of calling thus leaving the Father's immaculate divinity unsullied by masking any suggestion that the emergence of the emanation came about through reproduction, which in Mani's mind had no place in his theogony, belonging properly to his demonology. The Mother of Life then called forth the First Man (also termed the Primal Man), who called forth his Five Sons, the elemental air, wind, water, light and fire. Wearing his Sons like a suit of armour, the First Man sacrificed himself and his Sons to the five Sons of Darkness, who

[43] See Hunter 2005.
[44] *Der Manichäismus in der arabischen Überlieferung* (Göttingen: 1954): *Non vidi*.
[45] See Williams Jackson 1932, 223, nt. 6.

consumed them, infecting their powers of reason, and sending them into a deadly torpor.

It is important to note the extent to which the account of the loss of the Sons to the darkness and their eventual recovery lay at the very heart of the myth, and also the extent to which this episode from the myth determined the essence of Manichaean anthropology and soteriology. The Sons of the First Man were understood by Manichaeans to be 'the stuff of souls',[46] not in any transferred sense, but as a genealogical statement of fact: each individual human soul derived from, and in its essence was, the armour of the First Man, i.e., the Living Soul (sometimes referred to as the Living Self). Thus the soul, whether constrained in the natural world, in foodstuffs, or in the human body, being composed of the five primary elements, was of a material, elemental quality, although of a different type of substance than that which constituted its antithetical rival (commonly referred to in modern accounts by the Greek word *hyle* – Matter; for an ancient precedent, see Faustus in Augustine, *Answer to Faustus* 20.3).

As a result of the ubiquity of light/soul in the material world, Manichaeans understood it to be constantly at risk of being damaged, even during seemingly mundane tasks such as harvesting crops and the production and consumption of foodstuffs. The latter formed an especially emotive concern for Manichaeans, since the organisational and ritual dimensions of the religion existed largely to facilitate the purification of light in the daily, ritual meal consumed by the Elect, the only members of the Manichaean church who were fit to consume food in the 'right way', i.e., in a way that would lead to the liberation of light contained within it, their fitness determined by their commitment to a carefully prescribed series of ascetic and ethical commandments (see below). The meal itself was a ritual occurrence which, in its central concern with the purification of the divine in the material world, appears to have shared some of the rationales evident in the liturgies of Zoroastrianism (e.g., *yasna*) – certainly at least sharing fewer with the Christian Eucharist; however, Manichaeism's emphasis on the realisation of the ritual through the acts of eating and meditation performed by the Elect alone meant that the ritual apparatuses necessary for the performance of the meal were very different from those in Zoroastrianism.[47]

Furthermore, in line with other late-antique religious approaches to ritualised meals,[48] the vegetarian Elect did not consume sacralised animal meat, on account of the Manichaean belief that cooked animal flesh carried a preponderance of matter, containing very little in the way of light.[49] However, a concern with the conceptual role and language of sacrifice was transposed by Manichaeism into the realm of its mythology – primarily in the sacrifice of the First Man, as a representation of an archetypal act of violent suffering, an offering-up of life for protection rather than propitiation. The purposeful 'sacrificial' injury to something divine was further transposed into the realm of ritual, where the food brought as alms by Hearers to the Elect was seen to undergo both harm

---

[46] BeDuhn 2005, 12.

[47] For what appears here, see BeDuhn 2000.

[48] See esp. Stroumsa 2009 and Petropoulou 2008.

[49] See Augustine, *On Heresies* 46.11; trans. I. Gardner and S.N.C. Lieu 2004, 189.

– in being harvested – but also redemption, as the living substance of the ritual meal.[50]

The sacrifice of the First Man and his Sons tended to be intentionally misrepresented in the responses of heresiologists to the myth, who instead sought to characterise the act not as a sacrifice but as a tumultuous defeat for the good nature. The thinking behind their intention was to suggest that Mani's conception of God was inherently flawed, since the First Man's 'defeat' indicated that God was not impervious, but was capable of being attacked and corrupted by the contrary nature. For instance, the *Acts of Archelaus* describes the descent of the First Man in the following manner:

> Equipped with these [his Five Sons], as if in readiness for war, he came down to fight against the Darkness. However, the Prince of Darkness fought back and devoured part of his armoury, namely the soul. Then the First Original Man was severely beaten down by the Darkness (*Acts of Archelaus* 7.3–4; trans. M. Vermes 2001, 47).

However, as Jason BeDuhn has noted, the sacrifice of the First Man and his Sons, 'the collective soul', was an 'act of good will'[51] on the part of these figures, since through their voluntary 'leap' into the realm of evil they were endeavouring not only to distract but also to placate the colonial desire for territorial expansion on the part of the evil nature who had already moved uncomfortably close to the Realm of Light. The sacrifice achieved its aim of stopping this advance, 'throwing a spanner into the works' of the ambitions of the evil nature. The biblical origin of this idea of divine self-sacrifice was revealed by Fortunatus, a Manichaean from North Africa challenged by Augustine at the end of the fourth century, who quoted Paul from Philippians 2.5–8 as a way of comparing the willingness of the soul to humble itself for the cause of defeating the sin of the evil nature, with the readiness of Jesus to 'empty himself' (Gk *kenoō*; hence, Kenotic Christology) in order to overcome death.[52]

As BeDuhn notes, the significance of this aspect of the myth has continued to escape many commentators who have perhaps followed patristic characterisations of the narrative a little too closely. Indeed, the significance of this aspect may indeed have informed other areas of Manichaean theology, such as Christology. It is a widely held view among commentators that the Manichaeans regarded the historical Jesus (i.e., Jesus the Apostle) as only appearing to become incarnate and to experience bodily suffering during the Passion, because he remained fundamentally a spiritual being – an idea that arose primarily from the Manichaeans' association of the human form with matter, as something not befitting a divine being. This has given rise to the common assumption that Manichaean Christology concerning Jesus the Apostle was docetic (from Gk *dokeō*, 'appearing to be something'), meaning that the appearance of Jesus as

---

[50] See BeDuhn 2002, 165–208.
[51] BeDuhn 2005, 12.
[52] Augustine, *A Debate with Fortunatus* 7; trans. R.J. Teske 2006, 147. See BeDuhn 2005, 13–14.

having a real, physical body was in fact illusory. Whilst this assumption about what the Manichaeans may have thought about the historical Jesus has been challenged of late,[53] there may have been no need for Mani and his followers to insist on Jesus having endured real suffering during the Passion, precisely because there was already an archetypal figure belonging to their narrative tradition – the First Man – who not only suffered tremendous hardship at the hands of the evil nature, but who also did so willingly.

The Demiurge Fights Back

The second call from the Father of Greatness implemented the processes by which the First Man and his Sons were recovered from the realm of darkness through the evocation of the demiurgical deities. Upon hearing the First Man's prayers for assistance, the Father called forth the Beloved of Lights, who in turn called forth the Great Builder, who in turn called forth the Living Spirit, who in turned called forth his Five Sons: the Ornament of Splendour, the Great King of Magnificence, the Adamas of Light, the King of Glory, and the Porter (cf. Pettitpiece 2009, 225). The Living Spirit, together with a hypostasised Call and Response evoked through their dialogue with the imprisoned First Man, joined with the Mother of Life and descended to the realm below to begin the liberation of the First Man and his Sons. Although not disclosed in Theodore bar Koni's account, certain sources – notably the cosmogonic portions in *The Chapters* – indicate that the Sons were left behind in the realm of darkness. As Manfred Heuser notes, 'With the release of the Primal Man, his five sons who comprise his soul remain behind in the Darkness. In this way, the fate of the Primal Man is separated from that of his sons. In memory of her origin in the land of Life, the soul is frequently called "Living Soul". The Living Soul is mixed with elements of Darkness and cut into pieces in numerous forms and figures.'[54]

The demiurgical deities of the second call are thus charged with effecting the rescue of the Sons as the Living Soul from the world of darkness through the creation of a cosmic structure – the universe – situated above it; the demiurge of the Manichaean pantheon is therefore aligned with the good nature, and creation is associated with salvific activity.[55] The universe serves as an astral machine geared towards the purification of the Living Soul as light, and is frequently referred to in modern analyses of the myth as the *macrocosm*. The Living Spirit, together with the Mother of Life, began their creative work by subduing the evil powers, defeating and flaying the bodies of the sons (archons) of darkness, from which the demiurgical deities made ten or eleven heavens (see Reeves 1992, 203, nt. 38), and eight earths, which emerge from the bodies of the archons cast down into the world of darkness. The earths themselves are used to constrain the sons of darkness, acting as a series of prisons. The five sons

---

[53] See esp. Franzmann 2003, 51–87.

[54] Heuser 1998, 36.

[55] Cf. Williams 1999, 98–100.

of the Living Spirit shoulder the burden of maintaining the integrity of these structures, with each being given a specific realm of authority.

In order to obtain from the sons of darkness a concentrated portion of the very essence of the Five Sons, which is divine light itself, the female Living Spirit[56] exposed herself to the sons of darkness. The first of two seminal incidents in the myth, this particular release permitted the Living Spirit to construct the Sun and the Moon, together with three elemental wheels of wind, water and fire, all of which formed a mechanism for facilitating the release of the light. Just as a water-wheel scoops liquid from the bottom to the top of its arc, the elemental wheel moves light across the 'extended spatial structure'[57] of the universe towards the Sun and the Moon in order to be separated from matter which originated in the evil world – from whence the purified light sets out on its journey home, ascending to its place alongside the Father of Greatness.

Casting an eye over the cosmogonic fragments M98 and M99 from the *Šābuhragān* (trans. H.-J. Klimkeit 1993, 225–7), we gain a clear impression for Mani's appreciation of detail in narrating the industry of the demiurgical powers, especially the Living Spirit (appearing there as Mihr Yazd [i.e., Mithra-yazata]). His description of the demiurge's intricate construction of the eight earths, laid on top of one another with 'our own earth's surface contiguous to the bordering area of the celestial light',[58] all surrounded by defensive ditches and walls, reflects not only the mind of an author with a painter's imagination and eye for detail,[59] but also the circumstances surrounding the composition of that particular work. The emphasis on architectural detail, the palatial sense of the worlds' construction, would certainly have found favour with the *Šābuhragān*'s audience, the Sasanian royal elites who, with the continuation of Ardashir's endeavours by his son Shapur, had initiated a palatial and civic building programme of a highly ambitious nature.[60]

The astral mechanism was thus set in motion by the Third Messenger, the principal deity of the third call. However, before the Messenger could do this, he had to obtain a further ejaculation of divine essence. Together with the Twelve Virgins, the Messenger exploited the lustfulness that was an inherent attribute of the sons of darkness, by exposing himself, 'who was beautiful in his forms', to them (Theodore bar Koni, trans. J.C. Reeves 1992, 192). This led to a further release of captured light, although the sin which had been mixed with the light nevertheless tried to remain bound to the light, a ruse spotted by the Messenger, who cast the sin back down onto the sons of darkness. The archons rejected it, and it fell again, some onto dry land where it produced five trees, some into the sea where it 'became an odious beast in the likeness of the King of Darkness, and the Adamas of Light was set against her' (Theodore bar Koni, trans. J.C. Reeves 1992, 192), defeating it in battle.[61]

---

[56] See Pettitpiece 2009, 227, nt. 29.
[57] Heuser 1998, 38.
[58] Williams Jackson 1932, 25.
[59] See Tardieu 2008, 88.
[60] See Huff 2008.
[61] See esp. Stroumsa 1984, 156, nt. 61.

The Appearance of the Protoplasts, Adam and Eve

The perpetuity of lust present within the natures of the sons of darkness meant that the female archons had been pregnant before their lascivious exchange with the Third Messenger. These archons, upon seeing the form of the Messenger, released their abortions, which also fell to the earth and devoured the buds of the trees. The abortions, closely aligned with the offspring (the Nephilim) of the rebellious Watchers in the Enochic tradition,[62] lusted for the form of the Third Messenger: 'Where is the form(s) that we saw?' (Theodore bar Koni, trans. J.C. Reeves 1992, 192). Ashqalun, the lead archon, the son of the King of Darkness, promised to recreate the form of the Messenger for the abortions, on the condition that the abortions brought their children to him and his female companion Namrael, to be consumed by them. After having eaten the children of the abortions, Ashqalun and Namrael copulated, and Namrael produced first Adam, followed by Eve, both of whom were patterned according to the form of the Third Messenger.

Thus, anthropogony followed cosmogony in such a way as to bring humanity into the heart of the mythological narrative. Since a proportion of Adam and Eve, specifically their souls, was composed of whatever residue of divine essence (i.e., the light of the Living Soul) remained on the earth, whilst their bodies were nevertheless constituted of matter, the protoplasts (i.e., the first human beings) represented in archetypal form the paradoxical nature of human existence. The overwhelming density of matter meant that their bodies ultimately subdued their souls in a way not dissimilar to the manner in which primordial matter had suppressed the rational faculties of the First Man and his Sons during their internment in the world of darkness. Nevertheless, light remained in Adam and Eve; therefore it had to be rescued, a task which fell to the divine bearer of self-awareness, the most celebrated of the 'Jesus figures' in the religion, Jesus the Splendour (cf. Pettitpiece 2009, 228), who

> ... roused [Adam] and shook him and awakened him, and chased away the deceptive demon, and bound apart from him the great (female) archon. Then Adam examined himself and recognised who he was, and (Jesus) showed him the Fathers on high, and (revealed to him) regarding his own self all that which he had fallen into – into the teeth of leopards and the teeth of elephants, swallowed by voracious ones and absorbed by gulping ones, consumed by dogs, mixed and imprisoned in all that exists, bound in the stench of Darkness (Theodore bar Koni, trans. J.C. Reeves 1992, 193).

Adam began to see his real self – his soul – as light cast down into the midst of a body and an earth that was hostile to him, a realisation which evoked the response: 'Woe, woe to the one who formed my body, and to the one who bound my soul, and to the rebels who have enslaved me' (Theodore bar Koni, trans. J.C. Reeves 1992, 193). Nevertheless, that Jesus the Splendour introduced Adam to

---

[62] Stroumsa 1984, 158–67.

his real self meant that the first man became the primary *microcosm*, reflecting in miniature the purpose of the cosmos as the macrocosm, as a further way in which light was to be recovered. Adam and Eve had, after all, been modelled on the image of the Third Messenger, which meant that even though they were formed by the archons, they nevertheless retained a sense of the Messenger's desire to achieve the release of the Living Soul.

Jesus the Splendour was certainly one of the most important deities in the entire Manichaean pantheon, since he not only brings self-knowledge to the protoplasts at the beginning of creation, but also remains a principal figure during those important times when apostles of light are awoken and commissioned to teach humankind about the nature of reality, and at the end of days in his role as judge during the eschaton.[63] His roles thus intersect the prominent soteriological, eschatological and prophetological lines within Manichaeism.

The Eschaton

The interim point between the rousing of Adam and the final appearance of Jesus the Splendour is the period covered by humankind and its industry, a time for the liberation of the remaining light in the world, but also a time when human activity leads to a tightening of the bonds around the Living Soul, on account of the lustful inclinations of humankind comprising arrogance, greed and excess in eating, drinking and reproduction – motivations and actions which emerge from the forces of evil present within both the macrocosm (the universe) and the microcosm (the body), and which mirror the temperament of the evil nature. Moving away from Theodore bar Koni's eighth-century résumé to consider the eschatological fragments from Mani's *Šābuhragān* (see H.-J. Klimkeit 1993, 242–7), Jesus the Splendour returns to earth in order to make a final judgement on sinners, which the *Šābuhragān* characterises as those who abuse 'the righteous ones', namely the Manichaean Elect: they are enemies of the light and the gods since they have harmed the Elect who have been working towards the light's liberation. Those who have also assisted the Elect, namely the Hearers, will also gain the New Paradise as a reward. As the universe, the earths and the heavens begin to collapse, the Living Spirit descends on a chariot and calls all the gods and the righteous heavenward. Archons, demons and sinners will then be engulfed by a fire lasting 1,486 years, during which time the final particles of light will be cleansed and sent heavenwards towards the Father of Greatness.[64] All unredeemable beings and entities (i.e., all matter) will then be incarcerated in 'the eternal prison' (*Šābuhragān*, trans. H.J. Klimkeit 1993, 247).

In this regard, a close reading of the *Šābuhragān* overturns yet another patristic characterisation of Manichaeism, namely allegations of its inherent determinism. The notion of determinism holds that the individual human being has little control over her own sense of self-determination, especially in the arena of ethical choice: dualistic theologies were particularly susceptible to accusations

---

[63] See esp. Franzmann 2003, 27–49.

[64] Alternative Manichaean ideas about the end-times are discussed in Heuser 1998, 82–9.

of being deterministic, since the influence of the adverse nature on an individual, as a result of the body's demonic derivation, was considered to overwhelm the operation of the will. In this regard, Augustine of Hippo offered the classical characterisation of the Manichaean will, acting under the weight of the evil nature. Speaking of his time as a Hearer, Augustine wrote in his *Confessions*:

> I still thought that it is not we who sin, but some alien nature which sins in us. It flattered my pride to be free of blame and, when I had done something wrong, not to make myself confess to you [i.e., to God] that you might heal my soul; for it was sinning against you. I liked to excuse myself and to accuse some unidentifiable power which was with me and yet not I (*Confessions* 5.10.18; trans. H. Chadwick 1998, 84).[65]

The apportioning of blame features prominently in Mani's depiction for Shapur of the last judgement; however, the blame falls squarely on those who have failed to choose the course of life which the 'righteous ones' (i.e., Manichaeans) have practised and propagated. As the 'evildoers', writhing in the torment of the great conflagration, plead their case to be saved, the 'righteous ones' proclaim:

> Do not prate, you evildoers, [for] we remember that in the [world] you were greedy and lustful and oppressive ... And you [did not] consider the soul, and [to us you have been] hostile. You have pursued and persecuted us from land to land, and you did not believe [that] we are the ones who fulfil the wishes of the gods. And you did not consider (this), 'Misfortune may befall us [and] hold us ...'. But if you had [accepted] the wisdom and knowledge of the gods from us, and had been soul-loving and had gone on the path of the gods and had been (our) travelling companions and helpers, then your bodies would not have [brought forth] Āz (greed) and Lust ... Then you soul would not have come [to eternal] misfortune (*Šābuhragān*, M470a V+M505a R, 'On the Souls of the Evildoers'; trans. H-J. Klimkeit 1993, 246).

Thus, whilst many opportunities may have been presented to them, the 'evildoers' repeatedly chose not to attend to the care of the soul. Mani's eschatology thus presupposes a concern with choosing good from evil through an unfettered exercise of the will.[66] It is clear that determinism had no place in Manichaean myth, and instead the theology of the religion should be thought of as comprising 'the combination of an embattled free will with a concept of grace'.[67] Within Manichaeism, therefore, Matter may have been regarded as being capable of swaying an individual's inclinations and actions towards the negative, largely through the influence of the zodiacal signs,[68] but not so comprehensively as to prevent that individual from choosing the morally sound course of action

---

[65] See Brown 2000, 35–49.
[66] See the important discussion by BeDuhn 2005.
[67] BeDuhn 2005, 17.
[68] See Jones 1997.

over the immoral one. Mani may even perhaps be considered to be an early proponent of the idea of compatibilism, a philosophical position which holds that determinism and free will can exist alongside one another. Furthermore, the role of something akin to the idea of grace – i.e., the intervention of divine assistance in the realisation of salvation – also existed in Manichaeism, and was represented by the figure of the Light-Nous (Nous: Gk for Mind; see below), who works within individuals to free souls from the corrupting influences of the evil nature.

The influence of Mani's teaching as glimpsed in the *Šābuhragān* on the ideas of his followers can be seen clearly in the following excerpt from a letter, addressed to Augustine at the beginning of the fifth century by the mysterious Secundinus, a Latin-speaking Manichaean. Speaking about Paul and Mani's teachings on the soul's role in overcoming the desires of the body, Secundinus notes that

> ... [i]n their midst is placed a soul, to which from the beginning its own nature has given the victory. If this soul acted in unity with the spirit of virtues, with that spirit it shall have eternal life and possess that kingdom to which our lord invites us; if on the other hand it begins to be led astray by the spirit of vices and gives its consent, and then after its consent shows repentance, it will obtain a source of pardon for these disgraces. For it is seduced by being mixed with flesh, not by its own volition; but if having learnt to know itself it consents to evil and does not arm itself against the enemy, it has sinned by its own volition (*Letter to Augustine* 2; trans. I. Gardner and S.N.C. Lieu 2004, 137).[69]

In conclusion, this discussion has indicated that Mani's revelation was based on a materialistic view of the entire universe, including souls, and on a dualism represented by a constant battle between good and evil. As a consequence, it centred around the notion of universal suffering: all human souls share a common divine origin; however, as a result of a supra-temporal conflict between the ruling supra-temporal elites, souls have become imprisoned in a hostile material world. The imprisonment and abuse of the Living Soul in a world of matter inimical to it – its tearing apart 'in the teeth of leopards and elephants' – made for a highly visceral sense of reality. Thus, whilst light may have spiritual qualities, it nevertheless endures a material existence of suffering, restraint and disfigurement.

6. The Myth and the Manichaean Body

Whilst many scholarly treatments of Manichaeism suggest (justifiably) that Mani's myth was principally concerned with offering an answer to the age-old question, 'Where does evil come from?' (Lat *Unde malum?*), little consideration is given in such accounts to the other central purpose which the myth served, namely to provide reasons for the existence and activities of the Manichaean

---

[69] Concerning Secundinus, see van Oort 2001b

community, particularly in relation to its ascetic and ritual practices. Many modern summary accounts of Manichaeism move from presenting the details of the myth in one chapter to descriptions of the structural organisation of the community in the next, without providing any sense in which the two could be linked to one another: yet, precisely how the narrative impacted on the bicameral structure of the Manichaean church, on the lives of the senior Manichaeans, the Elect, and the lay Manichaeans, the Hearers, is surely a fundamental question in appreciating the nature of this late-antique religion.

Manichaeans themselves recognised clearly the relationship which existed between the universe, as depicted in their myth, and the 'realities' of their daily lives. Late-antique followers of Mani responsible for the editing of *The Chapters* included two accounts (nos 38 and 70; trans. I. Gardner 1995, 93–105 and 179–84 respectively), both ascribed to Mani, that considered the ways in which the environment and behaviour of the microcosm of the body replicated those same concerns in the macrocosm of the universe, and *vice versa*.[70] For instance, the discord and rebellious actions of the evil nature in the universe during the imprisonment of the archons by the five sons of the Living Spirit – the rebellions of the watchers against the King of Honour (38.92.24–31), and the abortions against the Adamas of Light (38.92.32–93.2 and 70.171.19–21) – reverberate through the body of the individual as a result of the equivalence existing between the spheres of governance of the sons of the Living Spirit in the universe, and the spheres of governance of the Light-Nous in the human body:

> Like these five watch-stations, which exist in this great … these five camps, which I have recounted to you. This is also the case with this body the elect wear. There are another five camps there, and the Light Mind is watching over them, and the new man is with them (*The Chapters* 70.171.28–172.4; trans. I. Gardner 1995, 181).

Thus, as it is with the universe, 'so also is this body!' (38.94.17; trans. I. Gardner 1995, 99). The importance of demonstrating the connectedness between the rebellions of the evil nature in the universe with the rebellions occurring throughout the individual lay in highlighting the fragile condition of the new man, the 'child of righteousness' (38.96.26–7), which the Light-Nous assists in establishing in individuals (the Elect), as he frees the intellectual operations (mind, thought, insight, counsel and consideration; patterned on the Five Sons of the Father) from their enslavement in the body: '… he shall release the members of the soul, and make them free from the five members of sin … he shall set right the members of the soul; form and purify them, and construct a new man of them, a child of righteousness' (38.96.22–7; trans. I. Gardner 1995, 101). Rebellion within the individual is therefore linked, as it was within the universe, to the role of sin, which in Manichaeism became 'an active power'[71] constantly threatening to disturb the on-going endeavour to purify the light. With the assistance of the Light-Nous, the old man of sin is replaced by the new

---

[70] See esp. Pettipiece 2009, 36–42.
[71] Colditz 2009, 79.

man of righteousness: a further indication of Mani and the Manichaeans' indebtedness to the terminology of Paul (cf. Romans 6.5).[72] However, just as rebellions continue to break out against the rule of the sons of the Living Spirit, so also the Light-Nous experiences the occasional weakening of the individual in abiding by its guidance, and also in abiding by the precepts of religion.

Exceptions to the conventional types of analysis concerning the associations between myth and cultic practice in Manichaeism nevertheless do exist, and one in particular has been highly influential in transforming modern, academic discussions of Manichaeism. *The Manichaean Body* by Jason BeDuhn, published in 2000 (and republished in 2002), provides a clear-eyed yet detailed assessment of the carefully defined cultic associations which existed between the mythology of the religion, and the ritual and ascetic components of Manichaeism. Central to BeDuhn's study is the notion that the narrative traditions of the religion supplied the *rationales* for both the way in which Manichaeans behaved towards themselves, the natural world, and their 'gods', i.e., their *disciplinary rationales*, but also for supplying their *alimentary rationales*, i.e., what they ate and how they ate it, which were geared towards the realisation of the principal ritual act of the religion, namely the consumption of a daily meal by the Elect, the purpose of which was to liberate the Living Soul.[73] As BeDuhn notes:

> … [t]he significance of the Manichaean universe – in the sense of why it is there in the first place or what its function is for those who describe it – lies in relation to the practices that presuppose it. Any given ritual requires for its effectiveness a specific configuration of the universe. Likewise, the codes that guide participation for ritual performance rely on a particular structure in nature in order to accomplish their task. Such a universe must really exist; it must be there literally.[74]

BeDuhn's analysis is remarkable for very many reasons, but arguably its most important achievement lies in the re-establishment of Manichaeism as a ritual faith, a characterisation which had been lost to history under the influence of the ancient heresiological refusal to take seriously Manichaean practice, a correlative to the concern with highlighting the inconsistency of Manichaean beliefs. Even with the recent emergence of ancient Manichaean sources, consideration of the ritual face of the religion, especially the role of the Elect in the primary task of freeing the enslaved light, remained a distant concern for scholars during the best part of the previous century. F.C. Burkitt's apparent disinterest in this regard was therefore typical: 'Exactly *how* the fully qualified Manichee [i.e., the Elect] separates the Light that is mixed in the substances with which he is concerned our documents do not inform us. I doubt very much whether Mani himself had a really consistent theory about it.'[75] The fact was, however, the documents *could* inform us about this process, and indeed have subsequently done so, although

---

[72] See Klimkeit 1998.
[73] See BeDuhn 2002, 144–60.
[74] BeDuhn 2002, 70.
[75] Burkitt 1925, 47.

it was necessary to concentrate the conceptual horizons of research on a much more immediate concern, namely with the role taken by the physical body of the Elect in realising the original soteriological ambitions of Mani. BeDuhn achieved this act of ritual restoration by reconstructing the religion's explanations for human psychology and physiology, which were most readily associated with the efficacious consumption of food by the Manichaean Elect, as the principal way of freeing light from the constraints of matter. Reading *The Manichaean Body*, it becomes apparent that, for the individual Manichaean, the *gnosis* of self-awareness – understood in archetypal terms as the awakening of Adam by Jesus the Splendour – was in itself insufficient for achieving the wider salvation of the soul as light in the universe. Rather, the heart of Manichaean soteriology resided in the way that the Elect Manichaean in particular exerted his will over his own body, in such a way as to transform its metabolic, psychic and intellectual functions from being something that was harmful to light into something that was helpful.

The disciplinary conditioning of the bodies of the Elect was achieved through their commitment to the ascetic ordinances of the religion, the 'commandments' of Manichaeism (see below). The ascetic practices followed by the Elect – e.g., celibacy, fasting, vegetarianism and a life of non-violence – were all intended to foster in senior Manichaeans a duty of care towards the light trapped in the material world. However, the specific purpose of the commandments was to transform the bodies of the Elect into highly efficient 'systems' capable of purifying light present in foodstuffs, through the consumption of the daily ritual meal; a conditioning which was achieved by the abstention on the part of the Elect from particular behaviours and activities – e.g., from harmful emotions, violence, sexual intercourse – all of which not only had a negative impact on the Living Soul present in the world, but were also likely to corrupt the saintly temperament required of the Elect.

BeDuhn's argument concerning the alignment of the religion's soteriology with the training of the human body owes indeed much to the earlier, insightful work of Jorunn Jacobsen Buckley who, in a series of articles that focused on the *CMC* and Mani's break from Elchasaite practices including daily baptism and his repositioning of ritual practice within the matrix of the body, made the important observation that 'soteriological gnosis ... involves speculation *and* down-to-earth, ritual "know-how"',[76] thereby overturning another, patristic-inspired characterisation of ancient Gnosticism as being pre-occupied with the internalisation of 'metaphysical, conceptual aspects'.[77]

Whilst the body itself as matter was therefore considered irredeemable, it could nevertheless be put to work as a 'tool of conviviality' (adapting the famous phrase of Ivan Illich) – as something which facilitated the divine ambition to free light. However, in order for this to be realised, the effect of the evil nature on the way the Elect thought and acted had to be minimised. As a result of the complex interplay between psychology and physiology, Manichaeans recognised the need to suppress those emotions and feelings that were endemic to the evil

---

[76] Buckley 1986, 399.

[77] Buckley 1986, 399. Also see Buckley 1983.

nature, which exerted their influence on their day-to-day lives, and which, if not controlled, could affect the efficacy of an adherent's engagement with the primary tasks of the religion. In this, Manichaeans were guided by a range of precepts for governing conduct in line with the principal ideological idioms of the religion, and which determined in the wider sense their engagement with the world at large.

7. The Ordinances and Activities of the Manichaean *Ecclesia*

The demarcation of specific codes of conduct determined the separation of the Elect the and Hearers, the principal organisational division within Manichaeism. As Iris Colditz has noted, 'Religious commandments regulate the ethical conditions of [an adherent's] life and call upon him to perform religious services'.[78] However, religious commandments do much more than this: for instance, they create and reinforce structural hierarchies within an institution, not only by determining membership of a community in terms of the willing internalisation of a community's code of conduct by individuals, but also by defining the institutional status of individuals within a hierarchy in relation to the extent of their internalisation and performance of (in other words, their commitment to) those commandments. The structural role of religious commandments in determining the 'shape' of the Manichaean community is neatly expressed in a passage from the *Fihrist*. Writing in the tenth century, al-Nadim offered the following report, credited to Mani himself, summarising the distinctions between the Hearers and the Elect:

> He [Mani] said: 'He who would enter the cult [i.e., Manichaean religion] must examine his soul. If he finds that he can subdue lust and covetousness, refrain from eating meats, drinking wine, as well as from marriage, and if he can also avoid (causing) injury to water, fire, trees, and living things, then let him enter the cult. But if he is unable to do all of these things, he shall not enter the cult. If, however, he loves the cult, but is unable to subdue lust and craving, let him seize upon guarding the cult and the Elect, that there may be an offsetting of his unworthy actions, and times in which he devotes himself to work and righteousness, night-time prayer, intercession, and pious humility (supplication). That will defend him during his transitory life and at his appointed time, so that his status will be the second status in the life to come' (*Fihrist*, trans. B. Dodge 1970, II.788).

Whilst the passage does not explicitly name the Hearer as the person/class responsible for 'guarding the cult and the Elect', it is nevertheless apparent that a division is being drawn between Hearers and Elect on the basis of an

[78] Colditz 2009, 73.

individual's willingness or ability to commit to a lifestyle of significant austerity and non-violence: a third distinction is also raised briefly, although its purpose is to define 'non-membership', in terms of a failure to commit to the religion's code of behaviour. The enumeration of the religion's disciplinary requirements – prohibition of specified foods and of marriage, and the avoidance of injuring all 'living things' (due to the presence of the Living Soul throughout the created order) – is in agreement with other witnesses to the commandments of the Elect, as also are the religious commitments of the Hearers.

Whilst differences in the formulation and presentation of Manichaeism's religious commandments for both grades is to be expected in the relevant sources, given the geographical, cultural, linguistic and chronological spread of the religion, broad agreement is nevertheless evident in what the Manichaean religion through history expected from its adherents. It should be noted that descriptions of commandments drawn up by Manichaeans themselves, for both Hearers and Elect, are to be found largely in those sources which had explicit roles as liturgical and confessional texts: the communal setting for the performance of liturgical and confessional formulae during particular weekly events (e.g., confession occurring for both Elect and Hearers every Monday; see *Xwāstwānīft* 13.1; trans. H.-J. Klimkeit 1993, 304) and annual festivals (notably, the Bema, commemorating Mani's martyrdom and accession to the Realm of Light) meant that when confirmation of an individual's commitment to the religion's precepts was required in the context of a performative act, an adherent's attitude to the religion's precepts became a matter for collective scrutiny, and not just of individual conscience.[79]

For Hearers, the starting point for their performative act of commitment was (ironically) a weekly acknowledgement of their failure to live up to the demands of the religion. Unlike the Elect, Hearers were presented with a greater number of opportunities for infringing the demands placed upon them by the precepts of the religion, for the simple reason that Hearers conducted a portion of their lives beyond the watchful eye of their religious brethren, by living and working in the secular world.[80] The extant confessional formulas for Manichaeism appear to have made allowances for the situation of Hearers, who 'stood in permanent conflict between the religious and the secular sphere',[81] in relation to the comprehensiveness of those sins which the Hearer was required to expiate. The most detailed example of a confessional formulary is the Turfan *Xwāstwānīft*, a Manichaean confessional prayer in Uighur (Old Turkish) which also exists partially in Sogdian:[82] 'The text was probably spoken by a *qoštar*, a "Master" or "Superior", that is, a Manichaean priest of high rank. The laymen would respond together, reciting the same portion the Master had spoken in Turkish, or at least the request for forgiveness, which is in Parthian, possibly the original language of the text.'[83]

---

[79] Cf. BeDuhn 2002, 42.

[80] See Colditz 2009.

[81] Colditz 2009, 84.

[82] On the role of confession in Manichaeism, see esp. Asmussen 1965.

[83] Klimkeit 1993, 299–300.

The Uighur confessional text enumerates a detailed list of 'anti-doctrinal conduct and moral lapses'[84] committed by Hearers: the specific belief or practice that a Hearer had failed to observe is narrated prior to the setting out of the expiation formula. Thus, in relation to the central cosmological teaching concerning the presence of the Five Sons (the Living Soul) in the world – 'the ten-storied heaven above and the eight-layered earth below exist only for the sake of the Fivefold God' (*Xwāstwānīft* 3.2; trans. H.-J. Klimkeit 1993, 301) – the following statement of expiation was provided for Hearers who had failed to maintain the integrity of 'the Fivefold God':

> My God, if we should ever, involuntarily, on account of evil and wickedness, have broken or injured the Fivefold God, if we have inflicted on Him the fourteen wounds, if we should in any way have tortured and pained the Living Soul, (namely) the God (the divine element) in food and drink, with (our) ten serpentheaded fingers and (our) thirty-two teeth, and if we should in any way have sinned against the dry and wet earth, against the five kinds of living beings, against the five kinds of plants, then my God, I now pray to be delivered from sin. [Parthian]: Forgive my sin! (*Xwāstwānīft* 3.3; trans. H.-J. Klimkeit 1993, 301).

This particular portion of the confession was especially relevant for Hearers, since the sin of damaging the Living Soul would have been regularly committed by them during their efforts in gathering food as alms for presenting to the Elect. Like the Elect, Hearers were required to avoid harming the Living Soul; however, as the *Xwāstwānīft* demonstrates with its distinction of involuntariness in the Hearers' treatment of the Five Sons, they were nevertheless required at times to engage in practices – mainly of an agricultural kind such as harvesting (the sin 'against the dry and wet earth') – which would harm the light. Nevertheless, such practices received an institutional sanction since they enabled the Elect to live the religious lives prescribed for them by Mani. Turning back towards the fifth century, Augustine offers a partly tendentious explanation for the way in which the religion dealt on an institutional level with the fundamental Manichaean idea concerning the omnipotence of light throughout the natural world:

> For [the Elect] are convinced that plants and trees possess sentient life and can feel pain when injured, and therefore that no one can pull or pluck them without torturing them. Therefore, they consider it wrong to clear a field even of thorns. Hence, in their madness they make agriculture, the most innocent of occupations, guilty of multiple murder. On the other hand, they believe that these crimes are forgiven their hearers because the latter offer food of this sort to the elect in order that the divine substance, on being purged in their stomachs, may obtain pardon for those through whose offering it is given to be purged. And so the elect themselves perform no labours in the field, pluck no fruit, pick not even a leaf, but expect all these things to be brought for their use by their hearers, living

---

[84] Widengren 1965, 83.

all the while, according to their own foolish thinking, on innumerable and horrible murders committed by others. They caution their same hearers, furthermore, when they eat meat, not to kill the animals, to avoid offending the princes of darkness who are bound to the celestials. From them, they claim, all flesh has its origin (Augustine, *On Heresies* 46.12; trans. I. Gardner and S.N.C. Lieu 2004, 189–90).

The sin which accrued to the Hearer in his donation of food to the Elect was therefore a necessary evil, which the Elect in a sense 'cancelled out' through their good work – the release of the Living Soul – performed by them during their ritualised daily meal. Since the salvation of light itself rested on the performance of this ritual, both grades of the *ecclesia* showed some anxiety (and probably not a little confusion) about what the effect of the provision of food by Hearers, and its consumption by the Elect, was likely to be on their own salvation. By way of clearing up confusion with regard to understanding this particular demand, *The Chapters* offered an entire discourse on the matter, in which a Hearer addressed Mani with the question:

> 'Perhaps the good I perform will not repay the sin I am doing to the living soul?', to which Mani replied: 'Do not be frightened of the sin you will commit that day to the alms! For all that you do [to] this alms on that day you do to [cause it] to be healed. You are bringing this alms-offering that you have made to life and rest' (93.236.19–27; trans. I. Gardner 1995, 243).

Through the psychological and physiological operations of the Elect, through prayer, through the exercise of a pure conscience, but also through the spiritual-metabolic processes of their own bodies, the portion of the Living Soul present in the donation of food provided by the Hearer was freed. However, food was just one type of alms provided by Hearers for the Elect: 'Now, that [Hearer], the Mind that is in the holy church ... at every moment, and its gifts and its ... and its honours and graces that benefit his life. It steers them to the holy church ...' (*The Chapters* 91.229.28–230.1; trans. I. Gardner 1995, 237). Hearers, under guidance from the Light-Nous, supplied all the material gifts which they could muster for the benefit of the Elect who, because of the demands for simplicity placed on them by their own precepts, were prevented from owning, or laying a claim to owning, anything of worldly artifice. The relationship between the two grades involved a balanced, reciprocal transaction, a 'spiritual exchange',[85] whereby the Elect received nourishment, shelter and clothing, which enabled them to commit themselves to their religious duties without a care for the mundane, and in so doing the Elect subsidised the Hearers' salvation by helping them store up credits of a spiritual kind: the promise of salvation, perhaps not now, but certainly later, was the reward for the attentive Hearer, who in a future life would find their soul (as part of the larger Living Soul) incarnated in the body of a future Elect: 'Whereas the Elect receive the reward of ascent into

[85] See Brown 2008, 148.

heaven upon their death, the less-rigorous lifestyle of the Auditor leads to further reincarnation, but in an improved state corresponding to the merit earned in previous life-times of supporting the religion.'[86]

It is almost certainly correct to think that the religion's codes of conduct derived originally from Mani himself. In his list of Mani's writings, al-Nadim notes two(?) otherwise unattested works, entitled 'Ordinances of the Hearers' and 'Ordinances of the Elect' (*Fihrist*; trans. B. Dodge 1970, II.798). In *The Chapters* (91.230; see Chapter 3), Mani indicates that he had set out in his *Treasury* the ways in which Hearers were to achieve salvation in this life, 'each one of them in accordance with the deeds and his contribution to the church' (91.230.22–3; trans. I. Gardner 1995, 238).

Both Manichaean and anti-Manichaean sources also maintain this differentiation between the two grades in their articulation of the religion's commandments.[87] With regard to the Elect, five commandments are noted across the range of Manichaean writings. For instance, the Coptic Psalm-Book (no. 235) indicates, in a psalm sung over the course of the Bema festival, the commitment of the Elect to, (i) Truth ('that we lie not'), (ii) Non-violence ('that we kill not'), (iii) Vegetarianism/Veganism[88] ('that we eat no flesh'), (iv) Chastity ('that we make ourselves pure'), and (v) 'Blessed Poverty'.[89] Extended presentations of these fundamentals are also to be found in a number of sources. In a Sogdian confessional work for the Elect from Turfan, M801 (*Book of Prayer and Confession*), which also appears to have had some place in the liturgical proceedings of the Bema, the five commandments for the Elect are laid out in great detail. Whilst the text is fragmentary, with only the second and third commandments preserved in a near-complete state, it is apparent that the intention of the confession was to locate the authority for each precept in the teachings of Mani as found in his writings (2.A: '... as He (Mani) teaches in the Scripture'; trans. H.-J. Klimkeit 1993, 139). Confessional formulae follow the statement of authority, within which are included an anticipated range of activities that would likely lead an Elect to violate the commandments.[90]

Alongside the duties which the religion required Hearers to undertake – e.g., daily prayer, weekly and annual fasting, weekly public confession of their sins,[91] encouraging others to join the ranks of the *ecclesia* (cf. *The Chapters* 81.193.9–10: 'a gift for righteousness'; trans. I. Gardner 1995, 202), and perhaps most importantly within an institutional context, the provision of alms for the Elect – Hearers were also expected to uphold a number of ordinances. Following Manichaean traditions which indicate the ten commandments of Hearers, al-Nadim notes the following:

---

[86] BeDuhn 2002, 103.

[87] On the commandments for Hearers and Elect, see Sims-Williams 1985; also BeDuhn 2002, 40–65.

[88] For Augustine's comments concerning the attitude of the Elect to the consumption of milk and eggs, see his *On Heresies* 46.11; trans. I. Gardner and S.N.C. Lieu 2004, 189.

[89] *Psalms of the Bema* 235.18–23; trans. C.R.C. Allberry 1938, 33.

[90] Trans. H.-J. Klimkeit 1993, 139–43.

[91] See Tardieu 2008, 69–71.

Renouncing the worship of idols; renouncing the telling of lies; renouncing avarice; renouncing killing; renouncing adultery; renouncing stealing; the teaching of defects; magic; the upholding of two opinions, which is about the faith; neglect and lassitude in action (*Fihrist*; trans. B. Dodge 1970, II.789).

The confessionary *Xwāstwānīft* notes 'ten kinds of sins', which partially reflect the commandments for Hearers in so far as they enumerate instances of deviation from those precepts:[92]

If we should have been false in any way or have committed perjury in any way; if we should have acted in any way as a witness for a dishonest person; if we should have prosecuted an innocent person in any way; or if we, by spreading rumours and by gossip, should have instigated a person in any way and (thus) have corrupted his heart and mind; if we should have practiced black magic in any way; if we should have killed many living beings in any way; or if we should have cheated and deceived (others) in any way; if we should in any way have used another person's goods (entrusted to our care); if we should in any way have done a deed of which the God of the Sun and the Moon would not approve; if we should have sinned and erred in any way with the 'first self' and with 'this self', after having been reborn as men; if we should have inflicted destruction and ruin somehow on many living beings; then, my God, we now pray to be delivered from the ten kinds of sins. [Parthian]: Forgive my sins! (*Xwāstwānīft* 6.2; trans. H.-J. Klimkeit 1993, 302).

Alongside the rubric of the commandments, Manichaeans also expressed their commitment to a religious life through their use of the short-hand formula known as the 'Three Seals'. Variously attested in the range of Manichaean and anti-Manichaean sources, the act of sealing in Manichaean terms represented the way in which adherents, both Elect and Hearers, disclosed their intention to refrain from certain fundamental human activities, which Manichaeism regarded as being incompatible with its fundamental religious duties. The act of sealing, Augustine notes, is intended to make the Manichaeans 'pure and blameless in word, deed and thought',[93] and pertain to the mouth (denoting purity of thought and speech), hand (denoting purity of action), and breast (denoting sexual continence). Whilst the Three Seals were probably not meant to serve as a direct match with the commandments, certain associations between the two codes are apparent. The seal of the breast in particular related to the religion's attitude to sexual activity, which for the Elect meant absolute chastity, and for Hearers involved a continent marriage, with the avoidance of 'adultery', which probably implied intercourse that led to the production of children. As Jason

[92] See BeDuhn 2002, 54–5.
[93] Augustine, *On the Morals of the Manichaeans* 10.19; 18.65; trans. I. Gardner and S.N.C. Lieu 2004, 237, credited to S. Llewelyn. Concerning Augustine's response to Manichaean asceticism, see Coyle 1978, 193–240.

BeDuhn indicates, Manichaeans tended towards a *traducian* view of the soul, which meant that the Living Soul (or parts of it at least) was passed on to future generations through the act of reproduction as a constituent part of semen, which itself derived from the consumption of food as one of the products of digestion.[94] BeDuhn notes what Augustine – who paid great attention to the 'philosophy' underpinning Manichaean ritual and ascetic practices – had to say in this regard; note especially Augustine's location of this belief in the mythological narrative of the religion:

> And if they make use of marriage, they should, however, avoid conception and birth to prevent the divine substance, which has entered into them through food, from being bound in the chains of flesh in their offspring. For this is the way, indeed, they believe that souls come into all flesh, that is, through food and drink. Hence, without doubt, they condemn marriage and forbid it as much as is in their power, since they forbid the propagation of offspring, the reason for marriage. They assert that Adam and Eve had as their parents princes of smoke, since their father, whose name was Saclas [i.e., Ashqalun], had devoured the children of all his associates, and in lying with his wife had, as if with the strongest of chains, bound in the flesh of his offspring whatever he had received mixed with the divine substance.[95]

8. The Communal Dimension of the Manichaean *Ecclesia*

The Manichaean *ecclesia* was a community of living saints, i.e., a church of the Elect, which existed primarily in order to play its part in the great struggle for the liberation of the Living Soul. Its very organisation indeed appears to have reflected the structure of the universal macrocosm, in terms of the calendrical workings of the universe that were in operation during the process of liberation.[96] Adopting a pyramidical form, the church was overseen at the top by Mani, and after his death by his successors (Gk sing. *archēgos* = leader), below whom were arrayed 12 Teachers (sometimes called Masters or Apostles), followed by 72 Bishops, and then by 360 Presbyters.[97] In the liturgical sections of the Turfan text M801 (*Book of Prayer and Confession*), further divisions are introduced into this hierarchy, including '… prayer leaders, wise preachers, valiant scribes, singers of melodious hymns…' (M801.6.1; trans. H.-J. Klimkeit 1993, 136). The belief that the normative Christian model of ecclesiastical organisation was the main influence on the numerical values stressed in the Manichaean hierarchy, which was first emphasised by Augustine himself (*On Heresies* 46.16; trans. I. Gardner

---

[94] BeDuhn 2002, 171–2.
[95] Augustine, *On Heresies* 46.13–14; trans. I. Gardner and S.N.C. Lieu 2004, 190, credited to S. Llewelyn.
[96] See esp. Leurini 2009.
[97] See Tardieu 2008, 57–62.

and S.N.C. Lieu 2004, 190), has waned in recent times. Whilst the mediation of this influence through the Christian traditions of the Elchasaites of Mesopotamia may have determined the offices and also perhaps the final numbers of senior positions within Mani's community,[98] it also seems plausible that the hierarchy's numerology, its 12 Teachers, 72 Bishops and 360 Presbyters, reflected in some way Mani's own understanding of the organisation of the cosmos. Whilst Michel Tardieu had already seen a calendrical precedent in the number 360 for the quota of elders, Claudia Leurini has taken the argument one stage further and proposed a holistic explanation to account for the numbers of senior figures in the *ecclesia*: 'Under the Chief of the Church stood twelve Teachers, one for every month, and underneath them stood seventy-two Bishops, one for each solar cycle during one year, and below them three hundred and sixty Presbyters, one for each day of the year.'[99]

These senior positions were filled by individuals who were chosen from amongst the pool of the Elect: the pool itself was composed of both men and women, although it is uncertain as to whether or not female Elect (Lat. sing. *electa*) graduated to senior roles within the church.[100] At the base of the pyramid, as its foundation, lay the catechumenate, i.e., the class of Hearers, also composed of both men and women, who made the church a living, salvific and economic reality. However, whilst we know more about the history, beliefs and practices of the Manichaean church than we have ever done, we continue none the less to know very little about the communal, daily lives of Manichaeans, in terms of where and how they lived.

For late-antique Manichaeism, evidence for the organisation of the Manichaean *ecclesia* is a patchy affair. Prior to the appearance of genuine Manichaean writings during the previous century, the impression was largely based on what patristic authors were prepared to disclose about the organisational structures of the Manichaean church, and it goes without saying that the heresiologists largely focused on the organisational failures of Manichaeism. In his work *On the Morals of the Manichaeans* (AD 387), Augustine relates an account of a Manichaean community in Rome, which operated within the house (Lat. *domus*) of a wealthy Hearer. As described by Augustine, the community was composed principally of Elect who, under the supervision of a Bishop, followed a rule of conduct taken from a letter written by Mani himself.[101] In spite of the best efforts of the well-meaning Hearer, whom Augustine later reveals to have been named Constantius (see Augustine, *Answer to Faustus* 5.5), the Elect failed to apply themselves to the rigours of the rule, and, after an additional scandal broke concerning the conduct of the Bishop, the community dissolved.

In opening up his own residence to Rome's senior Manichaeans, Constantius was behaving like a model Hearer, placing all his worldly possessions at the disposal of the Elect. Late-antique sources indicate that the houses of Hearers

---

[98] See Jones 2004.

[99] Leurini 2009, 177.

[100] See Coyle 2009d, 141–54.

[101] Augustine, *On the Morals of the Manichaeans* 20.74; trans. I. Gardner and S.N.C. Lieu 2004, 134–6.

evidently played a central role in the daily workings of the religion, Hearers being encouraged to cultivate, as part of their alms commitment to the Elect, an attitude of equal regard for both the church and their own houses.[102] An additional, although somewhat vague, injunction from *The Chapters* (80.193.12–14; trans. I. Gardner 1995, 202) also stresses the expectation that Hearers 'will build a dwelling or construct some place', possibly as a place of rest and worship for Elect Manichaeans. Hearers' residences likely served as way-stations for the Elect who, under the guidance of their ordinances, became rootless wanderers, moving between different locations in the performance of their duties.[103]

The relationship between Hearers and Elect during the fourth century has been greatly illuminated by the appearance of personal correspondence written by Manichaeans based in Roman Kellis, in the Dakhleh Oasis. The letters exchanged between Manichaeans within one discrete group, headed by Makarios (across letters numbered 19–29, and also 52), portray a family of Hearers with close ties to the Egyptian Elect, most significantly with a figure called the Teacher, whom Iain Gardner rightly assumes to be 'the foremost Manichaean leader in Egypt at the time' (i.e., as one the twelve universal Teachers).[104] This figure, who is only ever referred to by his ecclesiastical title, led an itinerant life, performing his religious duties throughout the Nile valley.[105] The support given by Makarios and his sons – who were also based in the valley, whilst his wife Maria remained in Kellis – included the provision of an occasional residence for the Teacher and other Elect.[106] Furthermore, in P.Kell.Copt. 20,[107] Makarios writes to Maria informing her that their son Piene is travelling with the Teacher, during which time he is also learning Latin, possibly in order to realise missionary ambitions further west. In P.Kell.Copt. 29 Piene himself writes to his mother Maria, and tells her that 'I am following the Teacher and will go to Alexandria'.[108] Thus, in keeping with the injunction expressed in *The Chapters* (80.193.4–6; trans. I. Gardner 1995, 202), the family had 'given' their child to the community, who was evidently being trained to join the ranks of the Elect.

There also appears to have been a monastery sited within the immediate vicinity of Kellis, which provided further support for the Elect of the region.[109] However, no uniform impression of the monastic and ecclesiastical establishments of Manichaeism can be drawn from the late-antique period, arising perhaps from a less than uniform interpretation of certain doctrinal regulations across the church, or more likely as a result of uncompromising external pressures, such as pagan and Christian persecutions of the religion guided by the Roman state, the direct consequence of which was that Manichaean

---

[102] See *The Chapters* 91.229.7–9; trans. I. Gardner 1995, 235.

[103] See Coyle 2009d, 144.

[104] I. Gardner, Alcock and Funk 1999, 75.

[105] See Gardner, Alcock and Funk 1999, 53.

[106] P. Kell.Copt. 24; ed. and trans. I. Gardner, A. Alcock and W.-P. Funk 1999, 182–6.

[107] Ed. and trans. I. Gardner, A. Alcock and W.-P. Funk 1999, 166–72.

[108] Ed. and trans. I. Gardner, A. Alcock and W.-P. Funk 1999, 202–4 (quote from 203).

[109] See Gardner 2000.

communal life in Late Antiquity remained a rather private affair.[110] Whilst later historiographical texts (e.g., the Middle Persian fragment M2; trans. I. Gardner and S.N.C. Lieu 2004, 111) from Turfan indicate that monasteries had been established during the religion's early wave of missionary fervour in the Roman world, the situation in Late Antiquity nevertheless contrasts markedly with the detailed and complex monastic foundations of the religion in Central Asia, especially during the period of its implantation in the Uighur capital of Chotcho (also Kocho and Qočo). As Sam Lieu remarks, '[f]ree from persecution and enjoying royal patronage, Manichaeism manifested itself in fully developed cenobitism'.[111]

According to the *Chinese Compendium*, a work originally written in Parthian and translated into Chinese by imperial commission for the ruling T'ang government in 731,[112] Manichaean monasteries appear as well-organised although rather austere institutions. The simple style of the monastic life as laid out in the *Compendium*, which appears to revolve around the institutional realisation of the religion's ordinances for both Elect and Hearers, is presumably an account of an ideal monastery, 'a blueprint' in Lieu's description.[113] It stands in contrast to a later description of an operational Manichaean monastery in Chotcho, preserved in an Uighur royal charter (inv. no. Zong 8782 T.82) dating from the tenth or eleventh century.[114] The charter describes a monastic institution that owned lands governed by a number of officials, and which drew rent – in the form of essential commodities – from its tenants.[115] Of particular interest are the descriptions of the monastery's management of agricultural land (including vineyards), along with the presence of animals in the monastery and surrounding lands – e.g., horses as transportation for the Teacher and Bishop – practices which stand in obvious contravention of the religion's normative ordinances, which were intended to preserve the Living Soul from harm.[116] However, rather than regarding the document as evidence of the religion's 'relaxation of the rules of Manichaean monasticism' (S.N.C. Lieu 1998a, 93), the charter demonstrates more precisely the transformation of the religion's fortunes as a result of its alignment with the Uighur empire, in terms of Manichaean monasteries' integration into the economic concerns of an imperial power.

Drawing this chapter to a close, it is worth remarking that, whilst material evidence for Manichaean ecclesiastical foundations (i.e., churches and monasteries) is largely absent from the historical record,[117] the self-identity of Manichaeans as an exceptional *ecclesia* lay in the collective expression of its commitment to the teachings of Mani, and to the sanctification of his memory.

---

[110] See Bowes 2008, 192–8.

[111] S.N.C. Lieu 1998a, 83.

[112] S.N.C. Lieu 1998a, 83–4; also see S.N.C. Lieu 1992, 244.

[113] S.N.C. Lieu 1998a, 85, supplies an English translation of the *Compendium*'s Fifth Article, 'On the Buildings of the Monastery'.

[114] Klimkeit 1993, 352.

[115] Trans. H.-J. Klimkeit 1993, 353–6; see also Zieme 1975, and Geng 1991.

[116] Klimkeit 1993, 353–4; see S.N.C. Lieu 1998a, 92–4.

[117] Cf. Gardner 2000, 256.

In this regard, the festival of the Bema represented the church's central act of remembrance for Mani, for the entire Manichaean community – living and dead – and also for the gods of the Manichaean pantheon. It commemorated in particular Mani's eternal governance of the *ecclesia*. Michel Tardieu has presented a remarkable reconstruction of the place of the festival in the Manichaean calendar, the preparation for which began in late autumn (November) with one 48-hour fast, repeated twice more in the month of January, and followed by 'a discontinuous fast' of 30 days from February to March, the end of which marked the opening of the festival.[118] The day prior to the Bema festival and meal was filled with the singing of hymns, whilst the day proper was conducted through the celebration of a detailed liturgy, which has been partially preserved in the text M801. Throughout the entire festival, the attentions of all grades and classes remained fixed on the Bema, the seat that was centrally located in the church, which was regarded as being synonymous with Mani, whose absence it was taken to represent. Indeed, the liturgy illustrates clearly that the community's sense of 'selfhood' was drawn from its own narrative about Mani, his personal history, his theology, and his real and imagined achievements, as demonstrated by the following hymn from M801 (7.1; trans. H.-J. Klimkeit 1993, 137):

> We bend our knees in deep veneration, we worship and praise the mighty God, the praised King and Lord of the Worlds of Light, worthy of honor, according to whose wish and will you (Mani), our exalted God, did come to us.

> We worship Jesus, the Lord, the Son of Greatness, who has sent you, blessed one, to us.

> We worship the exalted Maiden (of Light), the bright Twin, who was your comrade and companion in every battle.

> We worship the great Vahman [i.e. the Light-Nous] whom you have planted in the hearts of the pious.

> We worship your great Glory, our Father, Apostle of Light, oh Mani, oh Lord!

> We worship this wonderful Bema and the bright seat on which you did seat yourself.

> We worship the shining diadem that you did place upon your head.

> We worship this wondrous appearance and this beautiful image.

> We worship the gods and messengers that came with you.

---

[118] Tardieu 2008, 71–4.

We honor the whole community of elect and your blessed representative, oh Lord.

We honor the great teachers.

We honor the mighty bishops.

We honor the wise presbyters.

We honor the virtuous scribes.

We honor the singers of the melodious hymns.

We honor the pure righteous ones (the Elect).

We honor the holy virgins.

We honor and praise the whole Flock of Light which you yourself chose in the spirit of Truth.

Of your Glory, oh Lord, and of the glory of all of these, I would request, as a grace for all my (soul's) limbs, that remembrance may come into my heart, thought into my mind, consciousness in my nous ...

Conclusion

From the long view accorded to a writer of the eleventh century, Mani's apostolic and missionary success could be explained solely by the sponsorship that he had secured for himself and his disciples from the Persian ruling elite and its vassals throughout *Iranshahr*. The reasons for the worldly success of the Manichaeans as provided by al-Biruni's assessment of Mani's religion in his *Chronology of Ancient Nations*, where, under the protection of Ardashir I, Shapur I and Hormizd I, 'Manichaeism increased by degrees',[1] appear to be corroborated in the historiographical traditions of Manichaeism. In the later historicising sources from Central Asia, relationships leading to imperial protection proceeded directly from the teaching and healing abilities of Mani in the courts of the Sasanian empire.[2] The conversion of Shapur's brother, Mihr-Shah, the ruler of Mesene in southern Babylonia, from devout sceptic to awed follower, after Mani had shown him the gardens of the 'Paradise of Light', represents the type of visionary experience associated with Mani's speculative teachings that was so prized by the followers of the apostle.[3] Furthermore, in Turfan text M566 I, which may preserve a tradition recounting Mani's first audience with Shapur I, Mani announces before a monarch 'I am a physician from Babylon', followed by his healing of an unnamed female, presumably of royal lineage, who declares, 'From where are you, my God and my redeemer?'[4]

For al-Biruni, so long as Mani could maintain good relations with kings and princes, both he and his disciples were protected and at liberty to teach and attract followers. However, Mani's fortunes changed with the accession of Vahram I, the brother of Hormizd, to the Sasanian throne in 273. Al-Biruni saw two issues as responsible for the termination of imperial support, both appearing to be reversals of the very things that had won Mani support in the first place, i.e., his role as restorer of physical wellbeing, and his teachings. In the first instance, al-Biruni recalls the comments made by the Christian author Jibra'il b. Nuh in his anti-Manichaean work written as a response to the ninth-century treatise of the Manichaean leader during the Abbasid period, Abu Ali Raja ibn Yazdanbakht (cf. al-Nadim, *Fihrist*; B. Dodge 1970, II.805), that Mani was arrested and thrown into prison by Vahram because he had failed to free a relative of the king from possession by the devil.[5] That Mani appears to have offended Vahram as a result of the inefficacy of his healing is also indicated in a portion of a biographical work (M3) recounting Mani's final audience

---

[1] *The Chronology of Ancient Nations* 208; trans. C.E. Sachau 1879, 191.
[2] *The Chronology of Ancient Nations* 208; trans. C.E. Sachau 1879, 191.
[3] M47; trans. H.-J. Klimkeit 1993, 211–12.
[4] Trans. H.-J. Klimkeit 1993, 208; see Ort 1967, 215.
[5] *The Chronology of Ancient Nations* 208; trans. C.E. Sachau 1879, 191.

before Vahram at the royal palace in Belapat in Khuzistan in 276. 'You are not welcome', was the terse insult addressed by Vahram to Mani as he stood waiting for his royal audience at the doors of the palace. Vahram continued: 'Eh, what are you good for since you go neither fighting nor hunting? But perhaps you are needed for this doctoring and this physicking? And you don't do even that!'[6]

The second 'failing' noted by al-Biruni constitutes, on the surface at least, a clash of ideologies, with Vahram quoted as saying of Mani: 'This man has come forward calling people to destroy the world. It will be necessary to begin by destroying him, before anything of his plans should be realised.'[7] Vahram's words explaining his antipathy to Mani echo demonstrably the eschatological 'impulse' within Manichaeism, as evidenced, for example, in the *Šābuhragān* or the Coptic Homilies, and is reminiscent of Jesus's saying in Luke's gospel 12.49: 'I have come to set fire to the earth, and how I wish it were already kindled!' The suggestion that Manichaeism represented a threat to the established social order may also be found in the infamous rescript issued in 302 by the Roman emperor Diocletian and his partners in imperial rule – known collectively as the *Tetrarchy* (i.e., the Four Rulers). The Tetrarchs pronounced that the Manichaeans' influence on Roman society should be severely checked, if necessary through the application of the death penalty, because of their habitual tendency to commit 'many evil deeds, disturbing the tranquillity of the peoples and causing the gravest injuries to the civic communities [of the Roman empire].'[8] Both complaints almost certainly convey the reaction of the ruling authorities to the impact of Mani's theological radicalism on the religious landscapes of Persian and Roman society, although both are also clear expressions of Mani's and Manichaeans' inability to argue convincingly at different times for protected status from the ruling powers of Rome and Persia.

Other factors, some within Mani's control and some outside, also led to a loss of authoritative support for the religion during the third century. Vahram's anxiety about Mani winning away a local client king, Baat, from the Mazdean religious law of the Sasanian court[9] was coupled with the rise of the ambitious Zoroastrian, Karder, chief of the magi, who was given a central role in mediating the insinuations levelled against Mani before Vahram, as portrayed in the narrative of Mani's final days from the Coptic homilies of Medinet Madi.[10] In the case of the Tetrarchs' reaction to those Manichaeans appearing in Roman territory late in the third century, their hostility was conditioned as much by their own ambitions for a renewal of Roman religious and imperial identity as it was by their hostility to Persia and the assumed Persian origins of the Manichaeans. In both cases, acting against the Manichaeans provided the perfect excuse for the intensification of power by those already in a position of privilege greater than that enjoyed by the Manichaeans themselves. However, whilst the

---

[6] M3, ed. and trans. W.B. Henning 1942, 951; reproduced in Gardner and Lieu 2004, 84–5.
[7] *The Chronology of Ancient Nations* 208; trans. C.E. Sachau 1879, 191.
[8] Trans. I. Gardner and S.N.C. Lieu (2004), 116–18. For commentary, see Dignas and Winter 2007, 216–18.
[9] E.g., *Manichaean Homilies* 44.22; trans. N.A. Pedersen 2006, 44.
[10] *Manichaean Homilies* 45.14–20; trans. N.A. Pedersen 2006, 45.

Manichaeans' career as 'the Other' may have begun in the pagan- and Mazdean-influenced courts of Late Antiquity, it was their Christian brethren who did the most to refine the identity of the Manichaeans as religious deviants. Patristic writers left to posterity the portrait of the Manichaeans as insane heretics, their madness deemed to derive not from their teachings alone but also from the 'mania' of Mani himself, a characterisation deriving from the similarity of Mani's name to the Greek participle *maneis* meaning 'raving': an appropriate etymological description, so thought his opponents, for the madness of the apostle and for the insane beliefs and practices of his church.[11]

During its long history and across the breadth of its geographical diffusion, the Manichaean church perpetually rubbed up against the authority of the state. Nevertheless, exclusiveness and collective suffering provided the Manichaeans with important components of their own identity, which they located in the cosmic template of the loss of the Five Sons and their troubled existence in the world as the persecuted Living Soul, and also in the historical template of Mani's own persecution under Vahram I. The last days of Mani's life, as revealed by al-Biruni's sources and the Parthian and Middle Persian historical fragments M6033 I, M6031 II and M3,[12] likely all emerged from the homiletic tradition of Manichaeism's 'lamentation literature', exemplified by the contents of the Coptic homilies recently edited and translated anew by Nils Arne Pedersen (2006). Mani's fall from favour, his imprisonment and death, were soon memorialised by his followers as a 'Narrative about the Crucifixion', in imitation of Jesus the Apostle's passion and death. In the narrative from the codex, Mani's passion is analogised alongside that of Jesus, and in a manner which portrays the persecutions of the early Sasanian Manichaean church, beginning during the reign of Vahram I and intensified under Vahram II, as a continuation of the bodily suffering of Mani as he lay weighed down by the chains and shackles of his gaolers (*Manichaean Homilies* 48.19–22).

In spite of the persecution of Manichaeans at various times by Sasanian, Roman and Byzantine authorities, the followers of Mani survived and indeed flourished for many centuries, not least in the Uighur empire under the rule of Bügü Khan during the eighth century.[13] The longevity of eastern Manichaeism stood in stark contrast to the fate of the Manichaeans at the hands of the Byzantine inheritors of Roman rule where, at some unspecified point in the sixth century, they are considered to have been eradicated following an especially fierce round of anti-Manichaean laws and activities instituted by the emperor Justinian I (ruling 527–65).[14] However, in the Christian theological tradition, 'Manichaean' lived on as a term of abuse: the defining features of the term as a heresiological identifier – dualism, docetism, diet, rejection of the Old Testament and repudiation of marriage – derive almost entirely from the anti-Manichaean writings of Late Antiquity, which were put to the service

[11] See Tubach and Zakeri 2001.
[12] Collected and trans. in H.-J. Klimkeit 1993, 212–14; see also Henning 1942.
[13] See esp. Clark 2000.
[14] See S.N.C Lieu 1992, 207–18; see Gardner and Lieu 2004, 149–50, for the relevant Justinianic laws.

of providing an imposed, heretical identity for those Christian traditions appearing to exhibit one or more of these 'Manichaean' characteristics. In the Byzantine empire from the eighth century onwards, 'Manichaean' was applied to those Christian parties who were viewed as standing in the tradition of a dualistic theology, foremost among them being the so-called Paulicians and Bogomils.[15] In the medieval West of the eleventh century, the charge of being 'Manichaean' was widely cast onto various dissenting groups,[16] and most notoriously towards the Cathars during the twelfth century. It is highly problematical to suggest that a genealogical association existed between the Manichaeans of Late Antiquity and the 'Manichaeans' of Byzantine and medieval times, as some commentators have nevertheless tried to do, for the principal reason that the identities of the latter-day 'heretics' were drawn primarily from the long-standing catalogue of Manichaean traits supplied by writers such as Augustine.[17] Nevertheless, the development of the label 'Manichaean' in the medieval period shared a fundamental similarity with its emergence in Late Antiquity. During the fourth century and beyond, the term played a central role in the 'heresiological name-game'[18] by assisting in the criminal prosecution of religious parties and individuals who, whether through real or invented connections with genuine Manichaeans, faced a range of disabling civil actions under the anti-heresy laws introduced by Theodosius I during the final three decades of the 300s.[19] Similarly, during the medieval period of Europe's 'great heresies', the prosecution and punishment of heretics proceeded from the identification of those 'Manichaean' traits displayed in the beliefs and practices of dissenting individuals or parties.[20]

There was a predictable continuation of the use of 'Manichaean' in the accusatory exchanges between Catholic and Protestant parties during the European Reformation of the sixteenth and seventeenth centuries, with patristic characterisations of Manichaean teaching as deterministic and damaging to the free employment of the will featuring prominently in the debates of the period.[21] However, it was Mani's idea that the presence and operation of evil in the world is attributable to the contrary substance, the very thing which Augustine claimed had failed to convince him of Mani's teachings, which rescued Manichaeism from being eternally condemned as *the* substantialist heresy of the early church. In Pierre Bayle's *Historical and Critical Dictionary* (published 1697), a work of enormous influence on the European Enlightenment, Manichaeism remained a substantialist heresy that was nevertheless to be preferred to Catholicism in that, according to Bayle's entry on the Manichaeans, it offered a rationally defensible account of God's goodness in its ascribing of the origins of physical suffering to

---

[15] See esp. Loos 1974, *passim*.

[16] See Lambert 2002, 25ff.

[17] See Baker-Brian *forthcoming*.

[18] Humfress 2007, 248.

[19] For details, see Beskow 1988; selections of the so-called 'Theodosian laws' against the Manichaeans are collected in Gardner and Lieu 2004, 145–9.

[20] See Harrison 1991.

[21] For a detailed analysis, see Ries 1988, 17–57.

a separate principle co-eternal with God.[22] It is in the Enlightenment adoption of the ancient Manichaeans as the deistic alternative to Catholicism's supposedly irrational defence of God, evil and creation, that the roots of the historical study of Manichaean theology are to be found. The Huguenot scholar Isaac de Beausobre developed Bayle's defence of Manichaeism in his *Critical History*, a two-volume study published between 1734 and 1739, producing 'a precise and careful account of the history of Manichaeism'.[23] For Beausobre, the *critical* approach of his work concerned a detailed handling of the patristic sources for Mani and Manichaeism from Late Antiquity, very many of which had become available for the first time in new, critical editions which Beausobre made very good use of: he was largely reluctant to conclude that the Greek and Latin sources about Manichaeism contained anything other than lies and distortions of Mani's life and teachings.

Whilst Reformation and Enlightenment interest in the religion of Mani was influenced by the concerns of apologetics and polemics, these have since made way during the twentieth century for 'the task of legitimation and recovery',[24] in the industry of scholars working on the 'cultural products', i.e., the ideas, texts and art of Manichaeism. As Richard Lim has noted, a move beyond the work of legitimation and recovery is surely on the cards, perhaps indeed in a direction beyond the seemingly solid edifice of 'Manichaean' and 'Manichaeism', as the principal way of discussing and compartmentalising the products of those followers who recognised the spiritual worth of Mani's teachings: 'By insisting on the identification and recovery of Manichaeans across the centuries and the continents as one of their chief goals, scholars in the field are unwittingly joining forces with the likes of Augustine to create and sustain *a master discourse* about who and what the Manichaeans were.'[25]

Finally, whilst those studying Manichaeism catch brief glimpses of the appeal that Mani held for his followers during Late Antiquity and beyond, it is perhaps fair to say that the full spectrum of reasons for the flourishing of the religion will continue to elude us. Mani's ancient Christian opponents certainly witnessed at first hand the appeal of Mani, although the central rationale of their writings was to convey a reversal of the religious value of Mani's teachings. The historical investigation of sources, therefore, will continue to leave numerous gaps in our appreciation of Mani and the Manichaeans, some of which may nevertheless be filled via other forms of imaginative expression. Alongside the great, scholarly monuments of Manichaean studies, it is perhaps worth concluding with a brief mention of arguably the most thoughtful and ingenious treatment of Mani's life and times from the last century, Amin Maalouf's 'historical novel', *The Gardens of Light*. Academic research and historical fiction differ primarily, I would argue, in the way that fiction conveys the concerns and prejudices of its author in the characterisation of its subject; these interests are experienced more acutely and

---

[22] For an abridged English translation of Bayle's entry on the Manichaeans, see Popkin 1965, 144–53.

[23] Popkin 1967, 41.

[24] Lim 2008, 165.

[25] Lim 2008, 166–7. My emphasis.

certainly acknowledged more openly by the novelist than by the scholar, for the very reason that the characters created by the novelist often serve as mediums for the expression of some intensely personal influences and experiences. In the novel's epilogue, Maalouf addresses a question which will have crossed the minds of all those who have thought about and studied Mani and Manichaeism over the years:

> Nothing remains of [Mani's] books, of his works of art and of his fervour, nothing of his generous faith, his passionate quest, his message of harmony between men, nature and the deity. Of his religion of beauty, of his subtle religion of Darkness and Light, we have retained only the words 'Manichaean', 'Manichaeism', which have become insults on our lips. Because all the inquisitors of Rome and Persia conspired together to disfigure Mani and wipe out his name and memory. In what way was he so dangerous that it was necessary to even drive him out of our memories?[26]

Few scholars would be willing to address this question, let alone provide a concrete answer. By contrast, different parameters operate in the world of the novel, and the curious combination of radicalism and toleration in the actions and teachings of Maalouf's Mani provide a partial answer to the question as he walks through a very modern-sounding landscape of religious and civil conflict. This Mani is portrayed as offering a consistent challenge to the established voices of authority: the religious order of the 'White-clad brethren' in which he was raised, the conventions of his own social class and the caste system of Persian society, and the majesty of the Sasanian kings and princes, are all 'turned upside down' by Mani's personality and message. In line with the ancient Manichaean sources, Mani falls from Vahram's favour because he has failed to show his worth to the ruling dynasty, and because his teachings pay little regard to the dogmatic pretensions of the chief magus, Karder. Maalouf has imagined a character that inhabits fully the historical landscape of third-century Persia by prompting seismic shifts in its religious and social order as a result of Mani disclosing to the world the revelations made known to him by his divine Twin. This appears to be one of many impressions of Mani that students obtain from studying Manichaeism, particularly in its late-antique context, and it will almost certainly continue to be the case that, whether through fiction or academic investigation, Mani and Manichaeism will have an impact on all those who encounter this most fascinating ancient religion.

---

[26] Maalouf 1997, 247.

Bibliography

Editions, Translations and Source Collections

A. Adam (trans.) (1969), *Texte zum Manichäismus* (Berlin: Walter de Gruyter).

C.R.C. Allberry (ed. and trans.) (1938), *A Manichaean Psalm-Book Part II*, with a contribution by H. Ibscher (Stuttgart: Kohlhammer).

J.P. Asmussen (trans.) (1975), *Manichaean Literature: representative texts chiefly from Middle Persian and Parthian writings* (New York: Scholars' Facsimiles & Reprints).

Augustine, *Confessions*, trans. H. Chadwick (Oxford: Oxford University Press, repr. 1998).

—— *Answer to Adimantus, a Disciple of Mani,* trans. R.J. Teske in *The Manichean Debate* (Hyde Park, New York: New City Press, 2006), 176–223

—— *A Debate with Fortunatus, a Manichean,* trans. R.J. Teske in *The Manichean Debate* (Hyde Park, New York: New City Press, 2006), 145–162.

—— *Answer to Felix, a Manichean,* trans. R.J. Teske in *The Manichean Debate* (Hyde Park, New York: New City Press, 2006), 280–316.

—— *Answer to the Letter of Mani known as The Foundation,* trans. R.J. Teske in *The Manichean Debate* (Hyde Park, New York: New City Press, 2006), 234–67.

—— *Answer to Secundinus, a Manichean,* trans. R.J. Teske in *The Manichean Debate* (Hyde Park, New York: New City Press, 2006), 363–90.

—— *Answer to Faustus, a Manichean,* trans. R.J. Teske (Hyde Park, New York: New City Press, 2007).

M. Black (1985), *The Book of Enoch or 1 Enoch: A New English Edition with Commentary and Textual Notes*, in consultation with James C. VanderKam (Leiden: Brill).

A. Böhlig (ed. and trans.) (1966), *Kephalaia I. Zweite Hälfte, Lieferung 11/12* (Seite 244–91) (Stuttgart: W. Kohlhammer).

—— (ed. and trans.) (1995), *Die Gnosis III: Der Manichäismus* (Zürich: Artemis & Winkler).

M. Boyce (1975), *A Reader in Manichaean Middle Persian and Parthian: Texts with Notes* (Leiden: Brill).

—— (trans.) (1984), *Textual Sources for the Study of Zoroastrianism* (Manchester: Manchester University Press).

A. Brinkmann (ed.) (1895) *Alexandri Lycopolitani contra Manichaei opiniones disputatio* (Leipzig: Teubner).

B. Dignas and E. Winter (trans.) (2007), *Rome and Persia in Late Antiquity: Neighbours and Rivals* (Cambridge: Cambridge University Press).

B. Dodge (ed. and trans.) (1970), *The Fihrist of al-Nadim: A Tenth-Century Survey of Muslim Culture* vol. 2 (New York: Columbia University Press).

Epiphanius (*Medicine Chest*), *The Panarion of St. Epiphanius, Bishop of Salamis: Selected Passages* trans. P. Amidon (New York; Oxford: Oxford University Press, 1990).

W.-P. Funk (ed.) (1999), *Kephalaia (I): Zweite Hälfte (Lieferung 13–14)* (Stuttgart: Kohlhammer).

—— (ed.) (2000), *Kephalaia (I): Zweite Hälfte (Lieferung 15–16)* (Stuttgart: Kohlhammer).

I. Gardner (1995), *The Kephalaia of the Teacher.* The Edited Coptic Manichaean Texts in Translation with Commentary (Leiden: Brill).

—— (ed. and trans.) (1996), *Kellis Literary Texts*, vol. 1, with contributions by S. Clackson, M. Franzmann and K.A. Worp (Oxford: Oxbow Books).

—— (ed. and trans.) (2007a), *Kellis Literary Texts*, vol. 2, with contributions by M. Choat, M. Franzmann, W.-P. Funk and K.A. Worp (Oxford: Oxbow Books).

I. Gardner, A. Alcock and W.-P. Funk (1999) (eds and trans.), *Coptic Documentary Texts from Kellis*, vol. 1 (Oxford: Oxbow Books).

I. Gardner and S.N.C. Lieu (2004) (eds and trans.), *Manichaean Texts from the Roman Empire* (Cambridge: Cambridge University Press).

S. Geng (ed. and trans.) (1991), 'Notes on an Ancient Uighur Official Decree Issued to a Manichaean Monastery', *Central Asiatic Journal* 35, 209–30.

Hegemonius, *Acta Archelai* (*The Acts of Archelaus*), trans. M. Vermes, with introduction and commentary by S.N.C. Lieu, with the assistance of K. Kaatz. Manichaean Studies IV (Louvain: Brepols, 2001).

A. Henrichs and L. Koenen (1975), 'Der Kölner Mani-Codex (P.Colon. inv. nr. 4780): Edition der Seiten 1–72', *Zeitschrift für Papyrologie und Epigraphik* 19, 1–85.

—— (1978), 'Der Kölner Mani-Codex (P.Colon. inv. nr. 4780): Edition der Seiten 72,8–99,9', *Zeitschrift für Papyrologie und Epigraphik* 32, 87–199.

—— (1981), 'Der Kölner Mani-Codex (P.Colon. inv. nr. 4780): Edition der Seiten 99,100–20', *Zeitschrift für Papyrologie und Epigraphik* 44, 201–318.

—— (1982), 'Der Kölner Mani-Codex (P.Colon. inv. nr. 4780): Edition der Seiten 121–92', *Zeitschrift für Papyrologie und Epigraphik* 48, 1–59.

P.W. van der Horst and J. Mansfeld (trans.) (1974), *An Alexandrian Platonist against Dualism: Alexander of Lycopolis' 'Critique of the Doctrines of Manichaeus'* (Leiden: Brill).

M. Hutter (ed. and trans.) (1992), *Manis kosmogonische Šābuhragān-Texte. Edition, Kommentar und literaturgeschichtliche Einordnung der manichäisch-mittelpersischen Handschriften M98/99 I und M7980–7984* (Wiesbaden: Otto Harrassowitz).

H.-J. Klimkeit (trans.) (1993), *Gnosis on the Silk Road: Gnostic Texts from Central Asia* (San Francisco: Harper Collins).

L. Koenen and C. Römer (eds. and trans.) (1988), *Der Kölner Mani-Kodex (Über das Werden seines Leibes). Kritische Edition aufgrund der A. Henrichs und L. Koenen besorgten Erstedition* (Opladen: Westdeutscher Verlag).

D.N. MacKenzie (ed. and trans.) (1979), 'Mani's *Šābuhragān*', *Bulletin of the School of Oriental and African Studies* 42(3), 500–34.

—— (1980), 'Mani's *Šābuhragān*', *Bulletin of the School of Oriental and African Studies* 43(2), 288–310.

J.T. Milik (1976), *The Books of Enoch: Aramaic Fragments of Qumran Cave 4*, with the collaboration of Matthew Black (Oxford: Oxford University Press).

N.A. Pedersen (ed. and trans.) (2006), *Manichaean Homilies: With a number of hitherto unpublished fragments* (Turnhout: Brepols).

H.J. Polotsky and A. Böhlig (eds and trans.) (1940), *Kephalaia I. 1.* Hälfte (Lieferung 1–10) (Stuttgart: W. Kohlhammer).

R.H. Popkin (trans.) (1965), *Pierre Bayle: Historical and Critical Dictionary. Selections.* With the assistance of C. Brush (New York: Bobbs-Merrill).

J.C. Reeves (1997), 'Manichaean Citations from the *Prose Refutations* of Ephrem', in P. Mirecki and J. BeDuhn (eds), *Emerging from Darkness: Studies in the Recovery of Manichaean Sources* (Leiden: Brill), 217–88.

S.G. Richter (ed. and trans.) (1998), *Psalm Book Part II, Fasc. 2: Die Herakleides-Psalmen* (Turnhout: Brepols)

J.M. Robinson (ed. and trans.) (1990), *The Nag Hammadi Library: The Definitive Translation of the Gnostic Scriptures Complete in One Volume* (New York: Harper Collins).

C.E. Sachau (trans.) (1879), *The Chronology of Ancient Nations: An English Version of the Arabic Text of the Athar-ul-Bakiya of Albiruni or 'Vestiges of the Past'* (London: W.H. Allen & Co.)

—— (trans.) (1910), *Alberuni's India: An Account of the Religion, Philosophy, Literature, Geography, Chronology, Astronomy, Customs, Laws and Astrology of India about AD 1030* (London: Kegan Paul, Trench and Trubner).

M. Stein (ed. and trans.) (1998), *Epistula ad Menoch. Manichaica Latina 1* (Opladen: Westdeutscher Verlag).

—— (ed. and trans.) (2002), *Manichaei epistula fundamenti. Manichaica Latina 2* (Paderborn: Ferdinand Schöningh).

—— (ed. and trans.) (2004), *Codex Thevestinus. Manichaica Latina 3.1* (Paderborn: Ferdinand Schöningh).

A. Villey (trans.) (1985), *Alexandre de Lycopolis. Contre la doctrine de Mani* (Paris: Cerf).

G. Wurst (ed. and trans.) (1996), *Psalm Book Part II. Fasc. 1: Die Bema-Psalmen* (Turnhout: Brepols)

P. Zieme (ed. and trans.) (1975), 'Ein uigurischer Text über die Wirtschaft manichäischer Klöster im uirgurischen Reich', in L. Ligeti (ed.), *Researches in Altaic Languages* (Budapest: Akadémiai Kiadó), 331–8.

Secondary Literature

A. Abel (1961–2), 'Les sources arabes sur le manichéisme', *Annuaire de l'institut de philologie et d'histoire orientales et slaves* 16, 31–73.

P. Alfaric (1918–19), *Les écritures manichéennes*, 2 vols (Paris: Nourry).

J.P. Asmussen (1965), *Xuāstvānīft. Studies in Manichaeism*, trans. N. Haislund (Copenhagen: Munksgaard).

—— (1983), 'Christians in Iran', in E. Yarshater (ed.), *The Cambridge History of Iran* vol. 3 (2). *The Seleucid, Parthian and Sasanian Periods* (Cambridge: Cambridge University Press), 924–48.

J. Assmann (2006), *Religion and Cultural Memory: Ten Studies*; trans. R. Livingstone (Stanford: Stanford University Press).

N. Baker-Brian (2007), 'Modern Augustinian Biographies: Revisions and Counter-Memories', *Zeitschrift für Antike und Christentum* 11 (1), 151–67.

—— (2009), *Manichaeism in the Later Roman Empire: A Study of Augustine's Contra Adimantum* (Lewiston, NY; Queenston; Lampeter: The Edwin Mellen Press).

—— (forthcoming), 'Manichaeism', in K. Pollmann and W. Otten (eds), *The Oxford Guide to the Historical Reception of Augustine* (Oxford: Oxford University Press).

W. Bauer (1972), *Orthodoxy and Heresy in Earliest Christianity*, trans. R.A. Kraft and G. Krodel (London: SCM Press).

I. de Beausobre (1734–9), *Histoire critique de Manichée et du Manicheisme* vols. I–II. Original imprint, Amsterdam: J.F. Bernard (Vol. II posthumously edited by J.H.S. Formey); repr. Leipzig: Zentralantiquariat der DDR, 1970).

J.D. BeDuhn (1992), 'A Regimen for Salvation: Medical Models in Manichaean Asceticism', *Semeia* 58, 109–34.

—— (2000), 'Eucharist or Yasna? Antecedents of Manichaean Food Ritual', in R.E. Emmerick, W. Sundermann and P. Zieme (eds), *Studia Manichaica. IV. International Congress zum Manichäismus* (Berlin: Akademie Verlag), 14–36.

—— (2002), *The Manichaean Body in Discipline and Ritual* (Baltimore: The Johns Hopkins University Press).

—— (2005), 'The Leap of the Soul in Manichaeism', in A. van Tongerloo and L. Cirillo (eds), *Il Manicheismo: Nuove Prospettive Della Ricerca* (Louvain: Brepols), 9–26.

—— (ed.) (2009), *New Light on Manichaeism* (Leiden: Brill).

—— (2010), *Augustine's Manichaean Dilemma, I: Conversion and Apostasy, 373–388 c.e.* (Philadelphia: University of Pennsylvania Press).

J. BeDuhn and P. Mirecki (eds) (2007a), *Frontiers of Faith: The Christian Encounter with Manichaeism in the Acts of Archelaus* (Leiden: Brill).

—— (2007b), 'Placing the *Acts of Archelaus*', in J. BeDuhn and P. Mirecki (eds), *Frontiers of Faith: The Christian Encounter with Manichaeism in the Acts of Archelaus* (Leiden: Brill), 1–22.

P. Beskow (1988), 'The Theodosian Laws against Manichaeism', in P. Bryder (ed.), *Manichaean Studies. Proceedings of the First International Conference on Manichaeism* (Lund: Plus Ultra), 1–11.

F. De Blois (2000), 'Dualism in Iranian and Christian Traditions', *Journal of the Royal Asiatic Society* 3rd series 10 (1), 1–19.

—— (2005), 'New Light on the Sources of the Manichaean Chapter in the *Fihrist*', in A. van Tongerloo and L. Cirillo (eds), *Il Manicheismo: Nuove Prospettive Della Ricerca* (Louvain: Brepols), 37–45.

A. Böhlig (1983), 'The New Testament and the Concept of the Manichaean Myth', in A.H.B. Logan and J.M. Wedderburn (eds), *The New Testament and Gnosis: Essays in Honour of Robert McL. Wilson* (Edinburgh: T&T Clark), 90–104.

K. Bowes (2008), *Private Worship, Public Values, and Religious Changes in Late Antiquity* (Cambridge: Cambridge University Press).

M. Boyce (1983), 'The Manichaean Middle Persian Writings', in E. Yarshater (ed.) *The Cambridge History of Iran* vol. 3 (2). *The Seleucid, Parthian and Sasanian Periods* (Cambridge: Cambridge University Press), 1196–204.

—— (1987), *Zoroastrians: Their Religious Beliefs and Practices* (London and New York: Routledge & Kegan Paul).

B. Boyd (2009), *On the Origin of Stories: Evolution, Cognition, and Fiction* (Cambridge, MA: The Belknap Press of Harvard University Press).

M. Browder (1988), 'Al-Biruni's Manichaean Sources', in P. Bryder (ed.) *Manichaean Studies. Proceedings of the First International Conference on Manichaeism* (Lund: Plus Ultra), 19–28

—— (1992), 'The Formulation of Manichaeism in Late Umayyad Islam', in G. Wiessner and H.-J. Klimkeit (eds), *Studia Manichaica II. Internationaler Kongress zum Manichäismus, 6–10. August, 1989* (Wiesbaden: Otto Harrassowitz), 328–33.

P. Brown (1969), 'The Diffusion of Manichaeism in the Roman Empire', *Journal of Roman Studies* 59, 92–103.

—— (2000), *Augustine of Hippo: A Biography* (London: Faber & Faber).

—— (2008), 'Alms and the Afterlife: A Manichaean View of an Early Christian Practice', in T.C. Brennan and H.I. Flower (eds) *East and West: Papers in Ancient History presented to Glen W. Bowersock* (Cambridge, MA, and London: Harvard University Press), 145–58.

P. Bryder (ed.) (1988), *Manichaean Studies. Proceedings of the First International Conference on Manichaeism* (Lund: Plus Ultra).

J.J. Buckley (1983), 'Mani's opposition to the Elchasaites: A Question of Ritual', in P. Slater and D. Wiebe (eds), *Traditions in Contact and Change* (Waterloo, Ontario: Wilfrid Laurier University Press), 323–36.

—— (1986), 'Tools and Tasks: Elchasaite and Manichaean Purification Rituals', *Journal of Religion* 66, 399–411.

—— (2002), *The Mandaeans: Ancient Texts and Modern People* (Oxford: Oxford University Press).

F.C. Burkitt (1925), *The Religion of the Manichees: Donnellan Lectures for 1924* (Cambridge: repr. AMS, 1978).

R.A. Burridge (2006), 'Reading the Gospels as Biography', in B. McGing and J. Mossman (eds), *The Limits of Ancient Biography* (Swansea: The Classical Press of Wales), 31–49.

H. Chadwick (2009), *Augustine of Hippo: A Life* (Oxford: Oxford University Press).

L. Cirillo and A. Roselli (eds) (1986), *Codex Manichaicus Coloniensis: Atti del Simposio (Rende-Amantea 3–7 settembre 1984)*, (Cosenza: Marra Editione).

L. Cirillo and A. van Tongerloo (1997) (eds), *Atti del Terzo Congresso Internazionale di Studi 'Manicheismo e Oriente Cristiano Antico'*, (Leuven: Brepols).

L. Clark (2000), 'The Conversion of Bügü Khan to Manichaeism', in R.E. Emmerick, W. Sundermann and P. Zieme (eds), *Studia Manichaica. IV. International Congress zum Manichäismus* (Berlin: Akademie Verlag), 83–123.

I. Colditz (2009), 'Manichaean Time-Management: Laymen between Religious and Secular duties', in J. BeDuhn (ed.), *New Light on Manichaeism* (Leiden: Brill), 73–99.

C. Colpe (1983), 'Development of Religious Thought' in E. Yarshater (ed.), *The Cambridge History of Iran* vol. 3 (2). *The Seleucid, Parthian and Sasanian Periods* (Cambridge: Cambridge University Press), 819–65.

J.K. Coyle (1978), *Augustine's 'De Moribus Ecclesiae Catholicae': A Study of the Work, its Composition and its Sources* (The University Press: Fribourg).

—— (2009a), *Manichaeism and Its Legacy* (Leiden: Brill).

—— (2009b), 'The Idea of the "Good" in Manichaeism', in J.K. Coyle, *Manichaeism and Its Legacy* (Leiden: Brill), 51–64.

—— (2009c), 'Healing and the "Physician" in Manichaeism', in J.K. Coyle, *Manichaeism and Its Legacy* (Leiden: Brill), 101–21.

—— (2009d), 'Prolegomena to a Study of Women in Manichaeism', in J.K. Coyle, *Manichaeism and Its Legacy* (Leiden: Brill),141–54.

E. Csapo (2005), *Theories of Mythology* (Malden, MA: Blackwell Publishing).

V.S. Curtis and S. Stewart (eds.) (2008), *The Sasanian Era: The Idea of Iran, Vol. III* (London: I.B. Tauris).

T. Daryaee (2009), *Sasanian Persia: The Rise and Fall of an Empire* (London and New York: I.B. Tauris).

F. Decret (1974), *Mani et la tradition manichéenne* (Paris: Seuil).

—— (1978), *L'Afrique manichéenne (IVe–Ve siècles). Étude historique et doctrinale* 2 vols (Paris: Études augustiniennes).

M. Deeg and I. Gardner (2009), 'Indian Influence on Mani Reconsidered: The Case of Jainism', *International Journal of Jaina Studies* 5 (2), 1–30: available online at www.soas.ac.uk/research/publications/journals/ijjs/

J. Dillon (2006), 'Holy and not so holy: on the interpretation of late antique biography', in B. McGing and J. Mossman (eds), *The Limits of Ancient Biography* (Swansea: The Classical Press of Wales), 155–67.

M.H. Dodgeon and S.N.C. Lieu (1991), *The Roman Eastern Frontier and the Persian Wars (AD 226–363): A Documentary History* (London and New York: Routledge).

H.J.W. Drijvers (1966), *Bardaisan of Edessa* (Assen: Van Gorcum & Comp.).

J. Duchesne-Guillemin (1983), 'Zoroastrian Religion', in E. Yarshater (ed.), *The Cambridge History of Iran* vol. 3 (2). *The Seleucid, Parthian and Sasanian Periods* (Cambridge: Cambridge University Press), 866–908.

R.E. Emmerick, W. Sundermann and P. Zieme (eds) (2000), *Studia Manichaica. IV. International Congress zum Manichäismus* (Berlin: Akademie Verlag).

M. Franzmann (2003), *Jesus in the Manichaean Writings* (London & New York: T&T Clark: A Continuum Imprint).

W.P. Funk (2009), 'Mani's Account of Other Religions According to the Coptic Synaxeis Codex', in J.D. BeDuhn (ed.), *New Light on Manichaeism* (Leiden: Brill), 115–27.

I. Gardner (1997), 'Personal Letters from the Manichaean Community at Kellis', in L. Cirillo and A. van Tongerloo (eds), *Atti del Terzo Congresso Internazionale di Studi 'Manicheismo e Oriente Cristiano Antico'*, (Leuven: Brepols), 77–94.

—— (2000), 'He has gone to the monastery …' in R.E. Emmerick, W. Sundermann and P. Zieme (eds), *Studia Manichaica. IV. International Congress zum Manichäismus* (Berlin: Akademie Verlag), 247–57.

—— (2001) 'The Reconstruction of Mani's *Epistles* from Three Coptic Codices (Ismant El-Kharab and Medinet Madi)', in P. Mirecki and J. BeDuhn (eds), *The Light and the Darkness: Studies in Manichaeism and its World* (Leiden: Brill), 93–104.

—— (2007b), 'Mani's Letter to Marcellus: Fact and Fiction in the *Acta Archelai* Revisited', in J. BeDuhn and P. Mirecki (eds), *Frontiers of Faith: The Christian Encounter with Manichaeism in the Acts of Archelaus* (Leiden: Brill), 33–48.

I.M.F. Gardner and S.N.C. Lieu (1996), 'From Narmouthis (Medinet Madi) to Kellis (Ismant El-Kharab): Manichaean Documents from Roman Egypt', *Journal of Roman Studies* 86, 146–69.

J.E. Goehring (2000), 'Libertine or Liberated: Women in the So-called Libertine Gnostic Communities', in K. King (ed.), *Images of the Feminine in Gnosticism* (Harrisburg, PA: Trinity Press International), 329–34.

I. Gruenweld (1983), 'Manichaiesm and Judaism in the Light of the Cologne Mani Codex', *Zeitschrift für Papyrologie und Epigraphik*, 50, 29–45.

Z. Gulácsi (2005), *Mediaeval Manichaean Book Art: A Codicological Study of Iranian and Turkic Illuminated Book Fragments from 8th–11th Century East Central Asia* (Leiden: Brill).

A. von Harnack (1990), *Marcion: The Gospel of the Alien God*: trans. J.E. Steely and L.D. Bierma (Durham, NC: The Labyrinth Press).

G. Harrison and J. BeDuhn (2001), 'The Authenticity and Doctrine of (Ps.?) Mani's *Letter to Menoch*', in P. Mirecki and J. BeDuhn (eds), *The Light and the Darkness: Studies in Manichaeism and its World* (Leiden: Brill), 128–72.

R. Harrison (1991), 'Eckbert of Schönau and Catharism: A Reevaluation', *Comitatus* 22 (3), 41–54.

R. Hays (1989), *Echoes of Scripture in the Letters of Paul* (New Haven: Yale University Press).

L.R. Helyer (2002), *Exploring Jewish Literature of the Second Temple Period: A Guide for New Testament Students* (Downers Grove, IL: Intervarsity Press).

W.B. Henning (1942), 'Mani's Last Journey', *Bulletin of the School of Oriental and African Studies* 10, 941–53.

—— (1943), 'The Book of the Giants', *Bulletin of the School of Oriental and African Studies* 11, 52–74.

A. Henrichs (1979), 'The Cologne Mani Code Reconsidered', *Harvard Studies in Classical Philology* 83, 339–67.

A. Henrichs and L. Koenen (1970), 'Ein griechischer Mani-Codex (P.Colon. inv. nr. 4780), *Zeitschrift für Papyrologie und Epigraphik* 5, 97–216.

M. Heuser (1998), 'The Manichaean Myth According to the Coptic Sources', in M. Heuser and H.-J. Klimkeit, *Studies in Manichaean Literature and Art* (Leiden: Brill), 3–108.

M. Heuser and H.-J. Klimkeit (1998), *Studies in Manichaean Literature and Art* (Leiden: Brill).

D. Huff (2008), 'Formation and Ideology of the Sasanian State in the Context of Archaeological Evidence', in V.S. Curtis and S. Stewart (eds), *The Sasanian Era* (London: I.B. Tauris), 31–59.

C. Humfress (2007), *Orthodoxy and the Courts in Late Antiquity* (Oxford: Oxford University Press).

E.C.D. Hunter (2005), 'Theodore bar Koni and the Manichaeans', in A. van Tongerloo and L. Cirillo, *Il Manicheismo: Nuove Prospettive Della Ricerca* (Louvain: Brepols), 167–78.

H. Jonas (1992), *The Gnostic Religion: The Message of the Alien God and the Beginnings of Christianity* (London: Routledge).

F.S. Jones (1997), 'The Astrological Trajectory in Ancient Syriac-Speaking Christianity (Elchasai, Bardaisan, and Mani)', in L. Cirillo and A. van Tongerloo (eds), *Atti del Terzo Congresso Internazionale di Studi 'Manicheismo e Oriente Cristiano Antico'* (Leuven: Brepols), 183–200.

—— (2004), 'The *Book of Elchasai* in its Relevance for Manichaean Institutions with a Supplement: The *Book of Elchasai* Reconstructed and Translated', *ARAM* 16, 179–215.

K. Kessler (1889), *Mani: Forschungen über die manichäische Religion. Ein Beitrag zur vergleichenden Religionsgeschichte des Orients*, I: Voruntersuchungen und Quellen (Berlin: G. Reimer).

K. King (1992), 'A Progress Report on the Editing of the Manichaean *Synaxeis* Codex', in M. Rassart-Debergh and J. Ries (eds), *Actes du IVe Congrès copte* vol. 2 (Louvain-la-Neuve), 281–8.

—— (ed.) (2000), *Images of the Feminine in Gnosticism* (Harrisburg, PA: Trinity Press International).

—— (2005) *What is Gnosticism?* (Cambridge, MA and London: The Belknap Press of Harvard University Press).

A.F.J. Klijn and G.J. Reinink (1973), *Patristic Evidence for Jewish-Christian Sects* (Leiden: Brill).

O. Klima (1962), *Manis Zeit und Leben* (Prague: Verlag der Tschechoslowakischen Akademie der Wissenschaften).

H.-J. Klimkeit (1998), 'The Manichaean Doctrine of the Old and the New Man', in M. Heuser and H.-J. Klimkeit, *Studies in Manichaean Literature and Art*, (Leiden: Brill), 123–41.

J.W. Knust (2006), *Abandoned to Lust: Sexual Slander and Ancient Christianity* (New York: Columbia University Press).

L. Koenen (1978), 'Augustine and Manichaeism in Light of the Cologne Mani Codex', *Illinois Classical Studies* 3, 154–95.

—— (1986), 'Manichaean Apocalypticism at the Crossroads of Iranian, Egyptian, Jewish and Christian Thought', in L. Cirillo and A. Roselli (eds), *Codex Manichaicus Coloniensis: Atti del Simposio Internazionale (Rende-Amantea 3–7 settembre 1984)*, (Cosenza: Marra Editore), 285–332.

H. Koester (1990), *Ancient Christian Gospels: Their History and Development* (London: SCM).

A.-M. Kotzé (2004), *Augustine's Confessions. Communicative Purpose and Audience* (Leiden: Brill).

M. Lambert (2002), *Medieval Heresy: Popular Movements from the Gregorian Reform to the Reformation*, 3rd edition (Oxford: Blackwell Publishing).

P. Lampe (2003), *From Paul to Valentinus: Christians at Rome in the First Two Centuries*: trans. M. Steinhauser, ed. M.D. Johnson (London: Continuum, T & T Clark).

R. Lane-Fox (1988), *Pagans and Christians in the Mediterranean world from the second century AD to the conversion of Constantine* (Harmondsworth: Penguin).

A. Le Boulluec (1985), *La notion d'hérésie dans la littérature grecque IIe–IIIe siècles Vol. 1, De Justin à Irénée* (Paris: Études augustiniennes).

C. Leurini (2009), 'The Manichaean Church between Earth and Paradise', in J.D. BeDuhn (ed.) *New Light on Manichaeism* (Leiden: Brill), 169–179.

J.M. Lieu (2004), *Christian Identity in the Jewish and Graeco-Roman World* (Oxford: Oxford University Press).

S.N.C. Lieu (1992), *Manichaeism in the Later Roman Empire and Medieval China,* 2nd edition, revised and expanded. (Tübingen: J.C.B. Mohr).

—— (1994), *Manichaeism in Mesopotamia and the Roman East* (Leiden: Brill).

—— (1998a), *Manichaeism in Central Asia and China* (Leiden: Brill).

—— (1998b), 'The Self-Identity of the Manichaeans in the Roman East', *Mediterranean Archaeology* 11, 205–27.

—— (2001), 'Introduction', in M. Vermes, S.N.C. Lieu and K. Kaatz, *Hegemonius: Acta Archelai (The Acts of Archelaus)* (Louvain: Brepols), 1–34.

—— (2005), 'Manichaean *Technici Termini* in the *Liber Scholiorum* of *Theodore Bar Koni*', in A. van Tongerloo and L. Cirillo, *Il Manicheismo: Nuove Prospettive Della Ricerca* (Louvain: Brepols), 245–54.

R. Lim (2008), 'The *Nomen Manichaeorum* and Its Uses in Late Antiquity', in E. Iricinschi and H. M. Zellentin (eds), *Heresy and Identity in Late Antiquity* (Tübingen: Mohr Siebeck), 143–67.

L.J. van der Lof (1974), 'Mani as the Danger from Persia in the Roman Empire', *Augustiniana* 24, 75–84.

A.H.B. Logan (2004), *Gnostic Truth and Christian Heresy: A Study in the History of Gnosticism* (London: T&T Clark; Continuum).

J.M. Lössl (2001), *Julian von Aeclanum. Studien zu seinem Leben, seinem Werk, seiner Lehre und ihrer Überlieferung* (Leiden: Brill).

M. Loos (1974), *Dualist Heresy in the Middle Ages*; trans. I. Lewitová (Prague: Akademia).

G.P. Luttikhuizen (1985), *The Revelation of Elchasai: Investigations into the Evidence for a Mesopotamian Jewish Apocalypse of the Second Century and its Reception by Judeo-Christian Propagandists* (Tübingen: J.C.B. Mohr).

A. Maalouf (1997), *The Gardens of Light*, trans. D.S. Blair (London: Abacus).

C. Markschies (2003), *Gnosis: An Introduction*, trans. J. Bowden (London and New York: T&T Clark; Continuum).

R. Merkelbach (1986), *Mani und sein Religionssystem* (Opladen: Westdeutscher Verlag).

G.B. Mikkelsen (1997), *Bibliographia Manichaica: A Comprehensive Bibliography of Manichaeism through 1996* (Turnhout: Brepols).

F. Millar (1994), *The Roman Near East 31 BC–AD 337* (Cambridge, MA: Harvard University Press).

P. Mirecki (2007), '*Acta Archelai* 63.5–6 and *PGM* I. 42–195: A Rooftop Ritual for Acquiring an Aerial Spirit Assistant', in J. BeDuhn and P. Mirecki (eds), *Frontiers of Faith: The Christian Encounter with Manichaeism in the Acts of Archelaus* (Leiden: Brill), 149–55.

P. Mirecki and J. BeDuhn (eds) (1997), *Emerging from Darkness: Studies in the Recovery of Manichaean Sources* (Leiden: Brill).

P. Mirecki and J.D. BeDuhn (eds) (2001): *The Light and the Darkness: Studies in Manichaeism and its World* (Leiden: Brill).

A.A. Moon (1955), *The De Natura Boni of Saint Augustine: A Translation with an Introduction and Commentary* (Washington, DC: Catholic University of America Press).

H. Morales (2007), *Classical Mythology: A Very Short Introduction* (Oxford: Oxford University Press).

H.S. Nyberg (1935), 'Forschungen über den Manichäismus', originally published in *Zeitschrift für die neutestamentliche Wissenschaft und die Kunde der älteren Kirche* 34 (1935), 70–91; repr. in G. Widengren (1977) (ed.), *Der Manichäismus* (Darmstadt: Wissenschaftliche Buchgesellschaft), 3–28.

J.J. O'Donnell (2005), *Augustine, Sinner & Saint: A New Biography* (London: Profile Books).

J. van Oort (1997), 'Manichaeism and Anti-Manichaeism in Augustine's *Confessiones*', in L. Cirillo and A. van Tongerloo (eds), *Atti del Terzo Congresso Internazionale di Studi 'Manicheismo e oriente Cristiano antico'* (Louvain: Brepols), 235–47.

—— (2001a), *Mani, Manichaeism & Augustine: The Rediscovery of Manichaeism & Its Influence on Western Christianity* (Tbilisi: Georgian Academy of Sciences).

—— (2001b), '*Secundini Manichaei Epistula*: Roman Manichaean "Biblical" Argument in the Age of Augustine', in J. van Oort, O. Wermelinger and G. Wurst (eds) *Augustine and Manichaeism in the Latin West*. Proceedings of the Fribourg-Utrecht Symposium of the International Association of Manichaean Studies (Leiden: Brill), 161–73.

—— (2004), 'The Emergence of Gnostic-Manichaean Christianity as a Case of Religious Identity in the Making', in J. Frishman, W. Otten and G. Rouwhorst (eds), *Religious Identity and the Problem of Historical Foundation: The Foundational Character of Authoritative Sources in the History of Christianity and Judaism* (Leiden: Brill), 275–85.

J. van Oort, O. Wermelinger and G. Wurst (eds) (2001), *Augustine and Manichaeism in the Latin West*. Proceedings of the Fribourg-Utrecht Symposium of the International Association of Manichaean Studies (Leiden: Brill).

L.J.R. Ort (1967), *Mani: A Religio-Historical Description of his Personality* (Leiden: Brill).

E. Pagels (1990), *The Gnostic Gospels* (London: Penguin).

B.A. Pearson (2007), *Ancient Gnosticism: Traditions and Literature* (Minneapolis: Fortress Press).

N.A. Pedersen (1996), *Studies in The Sermon on the Great War: Investigations of a Manichaean-Coptic Text from the Fourth Century* (Aarhus: Aarhus University Press).

—— (2004), *Demonstrative Proof in Defence of God: A Study of Titus of Bostra's* Contra Manichaeos: *The Work's Sources, Aims and Relation to its Contemporary Theology* (Leiden: Brill).

L. Pernot (2005), *Rhetoric in Antiquity*, trans. W.E. Higgins (Washington, DC: The Catholic University of America Press).

W.L. Petersen (1994), *Tatian's Diatessaron: Its Creation, Dissemination, Significance, and History in Scholarship* (Leiden: Brill).

M.-Z. Petropoulou (2008), *Animal Sacrifice in Ancient Greek Religion, Judaism, and Christianity, 100 BC to AD 200* (Oxford: Oxford University Press).

T. Pettipiece (2009), *Pentadic Redaction in the Manichaean* Kephalaia (Leiden: Brill).

R.H. Popkin (1967), 'Manichaenism in the Enlightenment', in K.H. Wolff and B. Moore Jnr. (eds), *The Critical Spirit: Essays in Honor of Herbert Marcusse* (Boston: Beacon Press), 31–54.

P. Pourshariati (2008), *Decline and Fall of the Sasanian Empire: The Sasanian–Parthian Confederacy and the Arab Conquest of Iran* (London: I.B. Tauris).

H.-C. Puech (1949), *Le manichéisme: son fondateur, sa doctrine* (Paris: Musée Guimet).

—— (1991), 'Other Gnostic Gospels and Related Literature', rev. by B. Blatz, in W. Schneemelcher, *New Testament Apocrypha* I Gospels and Related Writings, trans. R.McL.Wilson (Cambridge: James Clark & Co.; Louisville: Westminster/John Knox Press), 354–413.

A. Quiroga (2007), 'From *Sophistopolis* to *Episcopolis*: The Case for a Third Sophistic', *Journal for Late Antique Religion and Culture* 1, 31–42. Available online at www.cardiff.ac.uk/clarc/jlarc/

C. Reck (2009), 'A Sogdian Version of Mani's *Letter of the Seal*', in J.D. BeDuhn (ed.), *New Light on Manichaeism* (Leiden: Brill), 225–39.

—— (2010) '*Šābuhragān*', *Encyclopaedia Iranica*. Available online at www.iranica.com/

J.C. Reeves (1992), *Jewish Lore in Manichaean Cosmogony: Studies in the Book of Giants Traditions* (Cincinnati, OH: Hebrew Union College Press).

—— (1996), *Heralds of that Good Realm: Syro-Mesopotamian Gnosis and Jewish Traditions* (Leiden: Brill).

—— (1999), '*Manichaica Aramaica*? Adam and the Magical Deliverance of Seth', *Journal of the American Oriental Society* 11 (3), 432–9.

J. Ries (1988), *Les études manichéennes. Des controverses de la réforme aux découvertes du XXe siècle* (Louvain-la-Neuve : Centre d'histoire des religions).

J.M. Robinson (1992), 'The Fate of the Manichaean Codices of Medinet Madi 1929–1989', in G. Wiessner and H.-J. Klimkeit (eds), *Studia Manichaica II. Internationaler Kongress zum Manichäismus, 6–10. August, 1989* (Wiesbaden: Otto Harrassowitz), 19–62.

C. Römer (1994), *Manis frühe Missionreisen nach der Kölner Manibiographie. Textkritischer Kommentar und Erläuterungen zu p.121–p.192 des Kölner Mani-Kodex* (Opladen: Westdeutscher Verlag).

K. Rudolph (1987), *Gnosis: The Nature and History of Gnosticism* (New York: Harper Collins).

H.H. Schaeder (1927), 'Urform und Fortbildungen der manichäischen Systems', in F. Saxl (ed.), *Vorträge der Bibliothek Warburg* (Leipzig: Teubner), 65–157.

H.M. Schenke (1997), 'Marginal Notes on Manichaeism from an Outsider', in P. Mirecki and J. BeDuhn (eds), *Emerging from Darkness: Studies in the Recovery of Manichaean Sources* (Leiden: Brill), 289–94.

M. Scopello (1995), 'Vérités et contre-vérités: la vie de Mani selon les *Acta Archelai*', *Apocrypha* 6 (1995), 203–34.

—— (2001), 'L'*Epistula Fundamenti* à la lumière des sources manichéennes de Fayoum', in J. van Oort, O. Wermelinger and G. Wurst (eds), *Augustine and Manichaeism in the Latin West*. Proceedings of the Fribourg-Utrecht Symposium of the International Association of Manichaean Studies (Leiden: Brill), 205–29.

—— (2005), *Femme, Gnose et Manichéisme: De l'espace mythique au territoire du réel* (Leiden: Brill).

N. Sims-Williams (1985), 'The Manichaean Commandments: A Survey of the Sources', in A.D.H. Bivar (ed.), *Papers in Honour of Professor Mary Boyce* (Leiden: Brill), 573–82.

P. Singer (2004), *The President of Good and Evil: Taking George W. Bush Seriously* (London: Granta).

N. Siniossoglou (2008), *Plato and Theodoret: The Christian Appropriation of Platonic Philosophy and the Hellenic Intellectual Resistance* (Cambridge: Cambridge University Press).

P.O. Skjærvø (1997), 'Counter-Manichaean Elements in Kerdir's Inscriptions. Irano-Manichaica II', in L. Cirillo and A. van Tongerloo (eds), *Atti del Terzo Congresso Internazionale di Studi 'Manicheismo e Oriente Cristiano Antico'* (Louvain: Brepols), 313–42.

E. Spät (2004), 'The "Teachers" of Mani in the *Acta Archelai* and Simon Magus', *Vigiliae Christianae* 58, 1–23.

C. Stewart and R. Shaw (eds) (1994), *Syncretism/Anti-Syncretism: The Politics of Religious Synthesis* (London and New York: Routledge).

G.A.G. Stroumsa (1984), *Another Seed: Studies in Gnostic Mythology* (Leiden: Brill).

—— (1985), 'Gnostics and Manichaeans in Byzantine Palestine', in E.A. Livingstone (ed.), *Studia Patristica* XVIII (Kalamazoo), 273–8.

—— (1986), '"Seal of the Prophets": The Nature of a Manichaean Metaphor', *Jerusalem Studies in Arabic and Islam* 7, 61–74.

—— (2000), 'The Birth of Manichaean Studies: Isaac de Beausobre Revisited,' in R.E. Emmerick, W. Sundermann and P. Zieme (eds), *Studia Manichaica IV* (Berlin: AkademieVerlag), 601–612.

—— (2008), 'The Scriptural Movement of Late Antiquity and Christian Monasticism', *Journal of Early Christian Studies* 16, 61–76.

—— (2009), *The End of Sacrifice: Religious Transformations in Late Antiquity*: trans. S. Emanuel (Chicago and London: The University of Chicago Press).

W. Sundermann (1986), 'Mani, India and the Manichaean Religion', *South Asian Studies* 2, 11–19.

—— (1986–7), 'Studien zur kirchengeschichtlichen Literatur der iranischen Manichäer': I *Altorientalische Forschungen* 13/1 (1986), 40–92; II *Altorientalische Forschungen* 13/2 (1986), 239–317; *Altorientalische Forschungen* 14/1 (1987), 47–107.

—— (1993), 'Cosmogony and Cosmology III: In Manicheism', *Encyclopaedia Iranica* 6, 310–15; also available online at www.iranica.com/

—— (1994), 'Mani's "Book of the Giants" and the Jewish Books of Enoch. A Case of Terminological Difference and What it Implies', *Irano-Judaica* 3, 40–8.

—— (1997), 'How Zoroastrian is Mani's Dualism?', in L. Cirillo and A. van Tongerloo (eds), *Atti del Terzo Congresso Internazionale di Studi 'Manicheismo e Oriente Cristiano Antico'*, (Leuven: Brepols), 342–60.

—— (2005), 'Was the *Ārdhang* Mani's Picture Book?', in A. van Tongerloo and L. Cirillo, *Il Manicheismo: Nuove Prospettive Della Ricerca* (Louvain: Brepols), 374–84.

—— (2009a), 'Mani', *Encyclopaedia Iranica*. Available online at www.iranica.com/

—— (2009b), 'A Manichaean Collection of Letters and a List of Mani's Letters in Middle Persian', in J.D. BeDuhn (ed.), *New Light on Manichaeism: Papers from the Sixth International Congress on Manichaeism* (Leiden: Brill), 259–77.

M. Tardieu (2008), *Manichaeism*, with an introduction by P. Mirecki: trans. by M.B. DeBevoise (Urbana and Chicago: University of Illinois Press).

A. van Tongerloo and L. Cirillo (eds) (2005), *Il Manicheismo: Nuove Prospettive Della Ricerca* (Louvain: Brepols).

X. Tremblay (2001), *Pour une histoire de la Sérinde: Le manichéisme parmi les peuples et religions d'Asie Centrale d'après les sources primaires* (Vienna: Österreichische Akademie der Wissenschaften).

F.R. Trombley (2001), *Hellenic Religion and Christianization* c. 370–529, vol. 1 (Leiden: Brill).

J. Tubach and M. Zakeri (2001), 'Mani's Name', in J. van Oort, O. Wermelinger and G. Wurst (eds), *Augustine and Manichaeism in the Latin West*. Proceedings of the Fribourg-Utrecht Symposium of the International Association of Manichaean Studies (Leiden: Brill), 272–86.

C.R. Whittaker (1997), *Frontiers of the Roman Empire: A Social and Economic Study* (Baltimore and London: The Johns Hopkins University Press).

G. Widengren (1965), *Mani and Manichaeism*: trans. by C. Kessler (London: Weidenfeld and Nicolson).

—— (1983), 'Manichaeism and its Iranian Background' in E. Yarshater (ed.), *The Cambridge History of Iran* vol. 3 (2). *The Seleucid, Parthian and Sasanian Periods* (Cambridge: Cambridge University Press), 965–90.

J. Wiesehöfer (2007), *Ancient Persia from 550 BC to 650 AD*. trans. by A. Azodi (London and New York: I.B. Tauris).

G. Wiessner and H.-J. Klimkeit (eds) (1992), *Studia Manichaica II. Internationaler Kongress zum Manichäismus, 6–10. August, 1989* (Wiesbaden: Otto Harrassowitz).

M.A. Williams (1999), *Rethinking Gnosticism: An Argument for Dismantling a Dubious Category* (Princeton, NJ: Princeton University Press).

A.V. Williams Jackson (1932), *Researches in Manichaeism with Special Reference to the Turfan Fragments* (New York: Columbia University Press).

—— (1938), 'The Personality of Mani, the Founder of Manichaeism', *Journal of the American Oriental Society* 58 (2), 235–40.

E. Yarshater (ed.) (1983) *The Cambridge History of Iran* vol. 3 (2). *The Seleucid, Parthian and Sasanian Periods* (Cambridge: Cambridge University Press).

Index